AUSTRALIA'S BEST
National Parks

A Visitor's Guide

Lee Atkinson

To Bill

Thank you for sharing my love of the bush and the outback
and for introducing me to the delights of swagging under the stars;
thank you for coming with me.

Contents

Kings Canyon

Kakadu wetlands

Australia's National Parks

Australia is a wild-at-heart continent with one of the largest and most comprehensive national park networks in the world, protecting and conserving a staggering 67 million hectares of beautiful and wild country. There are more than 7000 designated national parks, nature reserves, conservation areas and marine parks. In addition, Australia has 17 world heritage sites, 15 of which are natural wonders or wilderness areas, as well as one-third of the world's protected marine areas.

But it wasn't always so. When European settlers first arrived in the country, land not cleared of trees and vegetation was considered a waste. Conservation was not a consideration.

Times and values change, however, and the first actual nature reserve to be declared in Australia was the Jenolan Caves Reserve in the New South Wales Blue Mountains, in 1866. Australia's first national park was proclaimed on 26 April 1879. Originally named simply The National Park, it became The Royal National Park when Queen Elizabeth II visited the park in 1955. It is the second oldest national park in the world, second only to Yellowstone National Park in the USA, which was declared in 1872.

Back then, the focus was on leisure and recreation rather than environmental conservation, and the various state and federal government bodies responsible for managing our vast network of national parks and reserves have always had to walk a fine line between conservation and recreation—balancing the needs of tourism and protection.

Some of our parks are pure wilderness, with little or no facilities or even restricted access; but most offer a range of activities from camping and caravanning, bushwalking, picnicking, four-wheel driving, mountain biking and other adventure pursuits. All of them strive to protect significant sections of landscape, delicate ecosystems and precious cultural heritage for future generations.

These days, spending time in a national park is not always about roughing it. Many feature luxury accommodation, mostly in the form of eco-sensitive 'wilderness retreats' or permanent safari tents like those found in the private game parks of Africa. This has opened up sensitive areas of the environment to a whole new group of people who would sooner dig their own grave than dig a hole to bury their own waste or go without a hot shower for more than 24 hours.

From red sandy deserts to wild, windswept beaches, snow-covered mountain peaks and lush green rainforests, Australia's collection of national parks encompasses the best of our national landscape, a landscape so varied and diverse that you could spend years exploring it and still discover something new.

A book this size could never hope to cover all of our parks and reserves, so we've chosen to highlight 150 that are special not just for their inherent natural and cultural values, beauty and biodiversity, but because they are easily accessible and have a range of visitor facilities. It's a traveller's guide to the best 150 parks around the country, if you like. Choosing which ones to leave out was an often agonising decision and there are hundreds of parks beyond these 150 that worth visiting and exploring in depth. What are you waiting for?

MAP KEY:

	State Boundary
	National Park, Conservation Park, State Forest Area
❶	Key No.: National Park, Conservation Park, State Forest Area
○	City, Town
▫	Feature, Cave, Gorge, Waterfall
▪	Roadhouse, Settlement
	Highway, Road
	Walking Track, 4WD Track
ABNER RANGE	Mountain Range, Hills
+	Mountain
	River, Stream, Creek
	Lake, Pond

Symbols used in this book

 4WD

 Aboriginal sites

 bird watching

 boating

 bushwalking

 camping

 canoeing/sea kayaking

 caravans

 caves

 cycling/mountain biking

 dogs allowed

 fees apply

 fishing

 fossicking

 fuel stove only

 heritage sites

 horse riding

 lookouts

 picnics

 rockclimbing/abseiling

 sailing

 scenic drives

 scenic flights

 skiing and snow boarding

 snorkelling/diving

 surfing

 swimming

 whale watching

 whitewater rafting

 wildflowers

 wildlife

 windsurfing and kitesurfing

 World Heritage Site

Australia's World Heritage Treasures

The United Nations Educational, Scientific and Cultural Organization (UNESCO) seeks to encourage the identification, protection and preservation of cultural and natural heritage around the world considered to be of outstanding value to humanity. UNESCO explains that 'what makes the concept of World Heritage exceptional is its universal application. World Heritage sites belong to all the peoples of the world, irrespective of the territory on which they are located'.

Australia has 17 world heritage sites, and apart from the Sydney Opera House and Melbourne's Royal Exhibition Building, all the rest are natural or wilderness areas and protected by national parks. This outstanding collection of natural beauty and wilderness puts us near the top of the list of countries with the most world heritage sites. All of Australia's heritage sites them, except for the subantarctic islands, are covered in this guide.

Australian Fossil Mammal Sites (Riversleigh/ Naracoorte): these two fossil sites, in western Queensland's Lawn Hill National Park (page 18) and South Australia's Naracoorte Caves National Park (page 255), are among the world's 10 greatest fossil sites. According to UNESCO, 'they are a superb illustration of the key stages of evolution of Australia's unique fauna'.

Fraser Island: is the largest sand island in the world; 'the combination of shifting sand dunes, tropical rainforests and lakes makes it an exceptional site', says UNESCO. (see page 110)

Gondwana Rainforest of Australia: This outstanding area of natural beauty consists of 41 national parks and reserves straddling the Great Dividing Range in New South Wales and Queensland on Australia's east coast. 'The outstanding geological features displayed around shield volcanic craters and the high number of rare and threatened rainforest species are of international significance for science and conservation' says UNESCO. Gondwana rainforests featured in this guide include Nightcap National Park (page 88), Washpool National Park (page 80), Gibraltar Ranger National Park (page 38), Iluka Nature Reserve (page 30), New England National Park (page 88), Oxley Wild Rivers National Park (page 70), (Dorrigo National Park (page 34), Werrikimbe and Willi Willi National

Wallaman Falls, Queensland's wet tropics. Image courtesy Tourism Queensland.

Park (page 82), Barrington Tops National Park (page 18), Springbrook National Park (page 126) and Lamington National Park (page 116).

Great Barrier Reef: one of the first sites to be inscribed on the list in 1981, the Great Barrier Reef has the world's largest collection of coral reefs (see page 134).

Greater Blue Mountains Area: these stunning mountains that rise west of Sydney are a favourite wilderness playground on the doorstep of the city. Comprised of eight protected areas, it is 'noted for its representation of the evolutionary adaptation and diversification of the eucalypts in post-Gondwana isolation on the Australian continent', says UNESCO (see page 22).

Heard and McDonald Islands: visits to these remote Southern Ocean islands approximately 1700km from the Antarctic continent and 4100km south-west of Perth are strictly controlled and usually restricted to scientific visits. 'As the only volcanically active subantarctic islands they 'open a window into the earth, thus providing the opportunity to observe ongoing geomorphic processes and glacial dynamics. The distinctive conservation value of Heard and McDonald—one of the world's rare pristine island ecosystems— lies in the complete absence of alien plants and animals, as well as human impact' says UNESCO.

Lord Howe Island Group: one of just four island groups to be inscribed on UNESCO's World Heritage list, approximately 75 per cent of the island's original natural vegetation remains intact and undisturbed. (see page 52)

Macquarie Island: lying 1500km south-east of Tasmania and approximately halfway between Australia and the Antarctic continent, the island is the only place on earth where rocks from the

Three Sisters, Blue Mountains. Image courtesy Tourism NSW.

Purnululu, WA.

earth's mantle (6km below the ocean floor) are being actively exposed above sea-level.

Purnululu National Park: one of Australia's most astonishing natural wonders, the distinctly striped domes of the Bungle Bungle Range in north-western Western Australia is 'by far, the most outstanding example of cone karst in sandstone anywhere in the world' according to UNESCO (see page 204).

Shark Bay: Western Australia's Shark Bay has the largest area of seagrass and the largest number of species ever recorded in one place on the planet. Shark Bay is also home to the Hamelin Pool stromatolites—the oldest and largest living fossils in the world (see page 206).

Wet Tropics of Queensland: this vast area of tropical rainforest stretches along the north-east coast of Australia for some 450km from Cooktown to Townsville, incorporating 19 national parks and several state forests and other reserves. Wet Tropics included in this book are Barron Gorge National Park (page 92), and Daintree National Park (page 104).

Kakadu National Park: inscribed on the World Heritage list for both its cultural and natural values, the area has been inhabited continuously by its Aboriginal traditional owners for more than 50,000 years. 'The cave paintings, rock carvings and archaeological sites record the skills and way of life of the region's inhabitants, from the

South West wilderness, Tasmania. Image courtesy Tourism Tasmania and Ian Riley.

hunter-gatherers of prehistoric times to the Aboriginal people still living there. It is a unique example of a complex of ecosystems, including tidal flats, floodplains, lowlands and plateaux', says UNESCO (see page 262).

Tasmanian Wilderness: one of the last true wilderness regions, the Tasmanian Wilderness area includes Cradle Mountain and Lake St Clair National Park (page 292), Southwest National Park (page 306), Franklin-Gordon Wild Rivers National Park (page 296), Mole Creek Karst National Park (page 312) and the Walls of Jerusalem (page 315). 'In a region that has been subjected to severe glaciation, these parks and reserves, with their steep gorges, covering an area of over one million hectares, constitute one of the last expanses of temperate rainforest in the world' says UNESCO.

Uluru-Kata Tjuta National Park: one of Australia's most iconic outback locations, Uluru (Ayers Rock) and Kata Tjuta, the rock domes located west of Uluru, 'form part of the traditional belief system of one of the oldest human societies in the world' says UNESCO (see page 274).

Willandra Lakes Region: Mungo National Park (page 58) in western New South Wales is at this centre of the region, where fossils of mammals and evidence of human occupation dating from 45–60,000 years ago have been found in the ancient remains of a lake. UNESCO says it 'is a unique landmark in the study of human evolution on the Australian continent'.

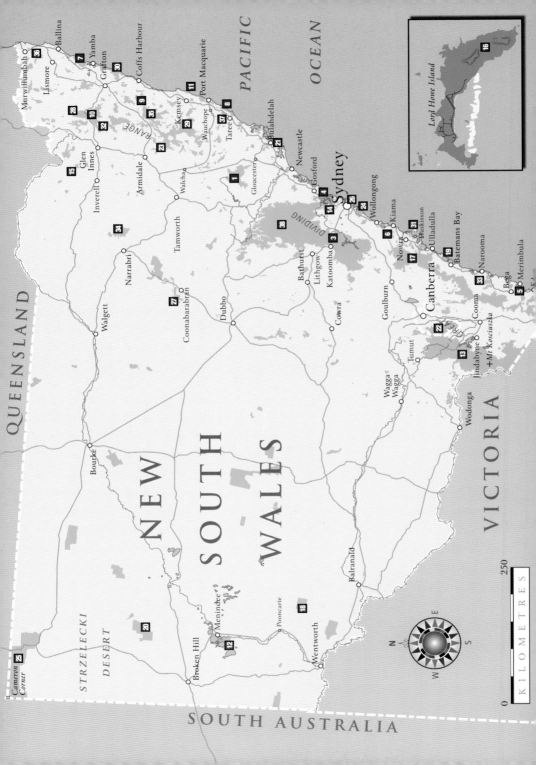

New South Wales and ACT

From snow-clad mountains to parched outback deserts, from densely wooded mountains, rugged gorge country, wild rivers and lush world-heritage rainforests, to offshore islands and deserted beaches, no other Australian state or territory packs so much diversity into a relatively small space. More than seven per cent of the state is protected with 750 national parks or nature reserves, much more than any other Australian state.

Wilderness tracks, wheelchair-accessible boardwalks, historic lighthouses, Aboriginal art, cliff-top picnic sites, bush camps, historic cabins and powered caravan sites are just some of the many highlights of New South Wales' parks and reserves. While some parks are wilderness areas with little or no facilities, others provide opportunities for horseriding, mountain biking, rock climbing and four-wheel-driving. Many offer ranger-guided tours during school holiday periods.

Fewer than 50 of the 750 parks charge vehicle entry fees, although many do charge a small fee for camping. There are four different annual park passes to choose from: a single park pass (for any one designated park in country New South Wales except Kosciuszko National Park); a country parks pass (covers all country parks except Kosciuszko); a multi-park pass (all New South Wales parks except Kosciuszko); and an all parks pass, which covers every park, including Kosciuszko. Passes do not cover camping fees. You can order a pass over the phone. Tel: (02) 9585 6068 or 1300 361 967 or online at www.environment.nsw.gov.au/annualpass/.

For more information on NSW parks visit www.environment.nsw.gov.au.

Barrington Tops National Park

How to get there

Barrington Tops is approximately 320km north-west of Sydney; 37km from Dungog and 42km from Gloucester. To get to the Barrington Tops Plateau area, use the very scenic Barrington Tops Forest Road between Gloucester and Scone.

When to go

The following temperatures are for Gloucester; expect much cooler temperatures in the mountains—dustings of snow are not uncommon in winter and nights are cold. Weather conditions can change quickly, so always be prepared for the worst. The Barrington Trail is closed each year between 1 June and 30 September.

- January: 16–26°C
- July: 6–13°C

The rugged cliffs and rainforests of the Barrington and Gloucester Tops are part of the Mount Royal Range, which runs north-south and reaches a height of 1577m at Polblue. Full of contrasts, this rugged high-altitude wilderness was carved out of an ancient volcano. The lower valleys contain World-Heritage listed subtropical rainforests with subalpine woodland up on the plateau.

The northern section of the park has numerous trails suitable for mountain bikes and the Barrington Trail is a popular 4WD trail from Barrington Tops Forest Road to Mount Barrington that is open only during the summer months. The park also features some stunning lookouts and almost a dozen beautiful picnic areas.

Top tracks and trails

Thunderbolts Lookout: an easy 20-minute stroll through snow gums and Antarctic beech to a spectacular view on the edge of the escarpment.

Polblue Swamp Track: a one-hour loop around the Polblue Swamp. Good for spotting grey kangaroos and the occasional wombat.

Jerusalem Creek Trail: a one-way downhill walk to Jerusalem Creek Falls. You can return the same way (uphill) or walk 2.5km back along the road to the picnic area.

Antarctic Beech Forest Track: a pleasant 90-minute loop through cool temperate rainforest full of Antarctic beech and tree ferns and beside mossy creeks. You can link this with the Gloucester Falls Track and River Track for a four-hour Gloucester Tops circuit.

Carey Peak Trail: a 7km one-way walk over the plateau to Careys Peak from the end of the 4WD Barrington Trail following the rim of the escarpment.

Corker Trail: if you are after a challenge (for fit walkers only) try the 20km, 10-hour walk from Lagoon Pinch to Careys Peak, a long, steep climb up to the Barrington Tops Plateau and down again.

The Barrington Trail: a 4WD-only track that runs off the Barrington Tops Forest Road. The trail leaves the Barrington Tops Forest Road about 1.7km east of Polblue Swamp.

Best picnic spots

There are some great picnic areas scattered throughout the park, but favourites include Polblue, Gloucester River (free gas barbecues and good swimming) and Gloucester Falls.

Camping, caravanning and accommodation options

Polblue camping area is a roomy campground suitable for cars and caravans; at 1450m above sea level it can get chilly at night. Also suitable for caravans are the Horse Swamp camping area on Tubrabucca Road and Gloucester River campground off the Gloucester Tops Road. Four-wheel-drive accessible camping spots include the Gummi Falls, Junction Pools and Little Murray Swamp. There are also several walk-in campgrounds and you can bush camp anywhere in the park as long as it is at least 200m from any road or track.

Contact information

For more information call the Gloucester park office on (02) 6538-5300 or visit www.environment.nsw.gov.au/NationalParks.

Whitewater canoeing on the Barrington River. Image courtesy Tourism NSW.

How to get there

Ben Boyd National Park is 8km south of Eden.

When to go

Temperatures are moderate most of the year. March is usually the wettest month but water temperatures are usually good for swimming from November through to April. Best time to see whales is between September and November.

- January: 16–23°C
- July: 6–16°C

Split into two stretches of bush-flanked coastline north and south of Eden on Twofold Bay, the national park was named after one of the area's more flamboyant historical figures. A London stockbroker who arrived in Australia in 1842, Ben Boyd had a vision of building a port on the shores of Twofold Bay to rival Sydney and Port Phillip Bay, which would be based on his whaling, shipping, trade and farming empire.

Boyd's tower, a huge square tower built by Boyd in 1846 in the southern section of the park, was part of this vision. It was originally intended to be a lighthouse, but the government would not give permission to use the privately owned structure as a light so it was used as a lookout for whales, the main industry in Eden at the time. By 1849 Boyd's financial empire

had collapsed and he left the colony, his debts unpaid. Rumours abound about his final end, with some saying he chased gold in the Californian goldfields, others that he was eaten by cannibals somewhere in the South Pacific. His name lives on in nearby Boydtown.

Another legacy of the whaling era is Davidson Whaling Station historic site, where you can wander around the remains of the old processing plant. Other highlights include Green Cape Lightstation (built in 1883), the folded red rocks near Leather Jacket Bay and the Pinnacles, white sand cliffs topped by red gravel.

Top tracks and trails

Pinnacles: 30-minute walk to the Pinnacles and Long Beach.

Green Cape to Pulpit Rock: a lovely little short walk from the Lightstation with great scenery.

Saltwater Creek to Bittangabee Bay: the most popular section of the Light to Light coastal track that connects the two main camping areas. It's 9km one-way so allow two to three hours.

Light to Light Coastal Track: a two to three-day, 30km easy walk along the coast from Boyd's Tower to Mowarry Point. Break the walk at Saltwater Creek and Bittangabee Bay.

Best picnic spots

There are picnic tables at Haycock Point,

Barmouth Beach, Severs Beach and Terrace Beach in the north, and Saltwater Creek and Bittangabee Bay in the south of the park. They all have barbecues, but you'll need to bring your own wood.

Camping, caravanning and accommodation options

There are campgrounds at Bittangabee Bay and Saltwater Creek and both are great for swimming, snorkelling and have gas/electric barbecues and rainwater tanks. Neither are suitable for caravans. Both areas get very busy during summer and school holidays and you'll need to book well ahead. You can also stay in the lighthouse keeper's cottages at Green Cape Lightstation. Built in 1880, the two cottages both sleep six and have a fully equipped kitchen. Bring your own food and linen. For bookings, call the NPWS in Merimbula.

Contact information

For more details call the Merimbula park office on (02) 6495-5000 or visit www.environment.nsw.gov.au/NationalParks.

Green Cape Lightstation.

Blue Mountains National Park

How to get there

The Blue Mountains are approximately two hours west of Sydney by car (via the Great Western Highway) or train from Central Station in Sydney.

When to go

The Blue Mountains are great to visit all year. Warmer months are popular with bushwalkers, climbers and abseilers. You can still do these activities in winter, but only if you've got good cold-weather gear.

- January: 13–23°C
- July: 2–9°C

Gaze at the spectacular views from the many lookouts, or walk, cycle or drive the cliff-top paths. Part of the Greater Blue Mountains World Heritage Area, the park's landscapes range from exposed, windswept plateaus and ridges to cool, damp canyons and deep gorges. Highlights include Leura Cascades, intriguing formations such as Mount Solitary, the Ruined Castle, Katoomba Falls and Cascades, and of course the much-photographed Three Sisters at Echo Point in Katoomba.

With more than 140km of walking tracks ranging from easy wheelchair accessible paths to challenging wilderness hikes and plenty of 4WD tracks and cycle trails in the park, it's a popular place with bushwalkers as well as

Leura Cascades. Image courtesy Tourism NSW.

mountain bike riders, horseriders, abseilers and canyoners.

Top tracks and trails

The Giant Stairway: one of the most popular short walks in the park, the three-hour walk starts at Echo Point and descends (via 900 steps) into the valley and along the base of the cliffs. If you don't fancy the hard slog back up, climb aboard the Scenic Railway or take a ride on the scenic skyway or cable car. Allow three hours.

Prince Henry Cliff Walk: follows the line of the cliff edge from Katoomba Cascades in the west to Gordon Falls, near Leura. If you like lookouts, you'll love this 9km walk.

National Pass trail: a difficult four-hour walk that winds its way along a ledge halfway up the sheer cliffs around Wentworth Falls, but well worth doing.

Overlooking the Jamison Valley. Image courtesy Tourism NSW.

Glenbrook Gorge Track: a three-hour walk that involves wading and boulder-hopping your way down the beautiful Glenbrook Gorge.

Grand Canyon Track: this 5km walk takes you deep into the Grand Canyon and is a good introduction to canyoning and great in summer when you can enjoy the shade and cool waterfalls.

The Six Foot Track: following the 44km route of the original 1884 bridle track from Katoomba to Jenolan Caves, the Six Foot Track (named for its width, not its length) is a long but beautiful walk through the heart of the park. The walk is strenuous, you'll need to carry your own water and arrange transport from Jenolan Caves back to Katoomba at the end. Allow three days and spare a thought for those that enter the annual Six Foot Marathon who manage to run the entire course in less than four hours!

Best picnic spots

Pack yourself a picnic and head to any one of dozens of perfect picnic spots: Wentworth Falls Lake; Gordon Falls Reserve in Leura; and Evans Lookout, Govetts Leap and Bridal Veil Falls in Blackheath top the list. They have access to lookouts or bushwalking trails.

Camping, caravanning and accommodation options

The most popular spot is Euroka at Glenbrook Gorge. Other good camp spots are at Murphys Glen south of Woodford and Perrys Lookdown north of Blackheath.

Contact information

Contact: for more information call the park office Blackheath on (02) 4787-8877 or visit www.environment.nsw.gov.au/NationalParks.

How to get there

Bouddi National Park is 20km south-east of Gosford, not far from the village of Kincumber.

When to go

Temperatures are mild most of the year. Late summer and early autumn can be stormy.

- January: 17–28°C
- July: 5–17°C

Maitland Bay.

Stretching north of Broken Bay on the Central Coast, Bouddi National Park is a beautiful pocket of bushland surrounded by urban development, 20km south-east of Gosford. Featuring wonderfully deserted beaches flanked by rainforest and eucalypt forests, steep hills and sandstone cliffs, there are a number of great walking tracks that lead down to the sea, although what goes down must also come up and many of the tracks can be quite steep in places.

A highlight of the park is Maitland Bay, a lovely crescent-shaped beach named after the paddle steamer *Maitland* that was wrecked on the rocks in 1898 with the loss of 26 lives. The rusting remains are still visible at low tide. Maitland Bay is a great swimming spot, as are Putty Beach and Tallow Beach, although the latter often has strong rips and currents and

is best for strong swimmers only. None of the beaches are patrolled.

Around 100 Aboriginal sites have been recorded in the park, including rock engravings of fish and whales, some up to 20m long, as well as axe-grinding grooves and middens.

Fishing is another popular pastime in the park but the section between Gerrin Point and Third Pointone is a 300ha Marine Extension, where all marine life is protected.

Top tracks and trails

Bouddi Spur: a one-hour medium walk from the Mount Bouddi picnic area to Bouddi lookout for panoramic views.

The Maitland Bay Track: the park's most popular, this great half-hour (each way) walk from Maitland Bay information centre winds down to Maitland Bay. It's a bit of a steep return slog.

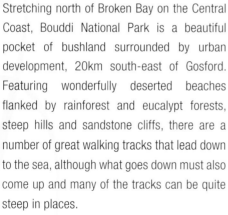

Bouddi has some great swimming beaches. Image courtesy Tourism NSW.

Bouddi Coastal Walk: a four-hour one-way walk with fantastic views along the coast, including the distant Sydney skyline and some great swimming beaches along the way, including beautiful Maitland Bay. It begins at the eastern end of Putty Beach and finishes at MacMasters Beach, so if possible try to arrange a vehicle pick-up at one end.

Best picnic spots

Putty Beach and Little Beach both have gas barbecues. Mount Bouddi (Dingeldei) has picnic tables and drinking water, but bring your own stove.

Camping, caravanning and accommodation options

There are three campgrounds in the park, and all of them are walk-in only. A favourite is Putty Beach where you can set up camp adjacent to the car park. Gas barbecues, water and toilets are provided. You have to carry your camping gear (and your own water) 750m from the car park down to Little Beach, where facilities include gas barbecues and composting toilets. If you really want to get away from it all, the most remote campsite at Bouddi is Tallow Beach, which involves a one-kilometre walk down a fairly steep track.

Contact information

For more information call the Gosford park office on (02) 4320-4200 or visit the Maitland Bay Information Centre on the corner of Maitland Bay Drive and The Scenic Road, Killcare Heights. See also www.environment.nsw.gov.au/NationalParks.

How to get there

Bournda is 16km north of Merimbula, 20km south of Bega.

When to go

Temperatures are moderate most of the year. March is usually the wettest month but water temperatures are usually good for swimming from November through to April.

- January: 16–23°C
- July: 6–16°C

A popular summer holiday spot, spending time at Bournda National Park is all about being either in, on or beside the water, because the park features not just saltwater and freshwater lakes, but also a lagoon, a creek and plenty of beaches.

Encircling the serene expanse of Wallagoot Lake the park is roughly split into two sections, north and south of the lake. Highlights of the northern section include the rugged coastline south of Kianinny Bay, which back in the 1830s was a port that shipped produce and logs from the surrounding farmlands and forests to cities north and south. In the southern section is the lovely freshwater lagoon behind the dunes of Bournda Beach called Bondi Lake and a network of walking trails and the camping area.

Wallagoot Lake is the main focus of most activities, however. The clear tea-tree-stained waters are great for swimming; there are two lovely lakeside beaches and small kids love splashing in the shallows. It's also popular with anglers (as is Bournda Beach), paddlers, sailors and waterskiers.

Eastern grey kangaroos are common in the park (they can be annoying in the campground as they will try and steal your food as soon as your back is turned—we had to shoo one out of our campervan). Birdlife is prolific, particularly waterbirds and sea eagles.

Top tracks and trails

Bournda Lagoon to North Tura Beach via Bournda Headland: a nice 1km stroll with good views of the coast, lagoon and Bournda Island along the way.

Hobart Beach to Bournda Lagoon: this easy 2.5km-long track leads from the campground to Bournda Lagoon, where you can swim or follow the Sandy Creek loop walking track to Bournda Island.

Bournda Track: a reasonably challenging 6km loop takes in the lagoon, Bournda Island and beaches and the upper reaches of the Sandy Creek. Highlights are patches of rainforest, wetlands, beaches and a headland.

Kangarutha Track: the hardest walk in the park, this 9km walk (allow five hours) features rugged coastline with many small sandy or pebbly beaches and spectacular cliffs. The walk can be broken into sections.

Best picnic spots

Kianinny Bay has gas/electric barbecues and a boat ramp, which makes it a great spot to go fishing. There are picnic facilities at Wallagoot Lake Boat Club but you'll need to bring your own wood for the wood barbecues. There are also picnic table and toilets at Turingal Head.

Camping, caravanning and accommodation options

Hobart Beach campground, wedged between the surf beach and beautiful Wallagoot Lake, is the only campground in the park, but it does have space for caravans (no power), hot showers, gas/electric barbecues, and drinking water. As you would expect, however, it gets extremely busy in summer and bookings are essential. Easter bookings open at midnight on 1 February and Christmas bookings open at midnight on 1 August each year.

Contact information

For more information call the Merimbula park office on (02) 6495-5000 or visit www.environment.nsw.gov.au/NationalParks.

Bournda Lagoon.

Budderoo National Park

How to get there

Minnamurra Rainforest Centre is 15km from Kiama (185km south of Sydney) via the Jamberoo Mountain Road.

When to go

The rainforest is generally mild, although it can get quite humid in summer. The waterfalls are at their best in summer, although if you want to see a lyrebird then the breeding season, May to August, is your best bet.

- January: 17–25°C
- July: 8–17°C

Part of the Illawarra escarpment that stretches from Stanwell Tops in the north to Nowra in the south, Budderoo is typical of the dramatic landscape carved from the sandstone plateau, including 100m high cliffs, gorges and waterfalls, of which spectacular Carrington Falls in the northern section of the park is just one.

Most people, however, come here to visit the Minnamurra Rainforest Centre. Suitable for school groups, and people of all levels of mobility, the wheelchair-accessible boardwalk that winds through the forest is also very popular with families. Keep an eye and ear out for the elusive lyrebird, which is quite plentiful

Footbridge at Minnamuura Falls. Image courtesy Tourism NSW.

in the park. Identifying Lyrebird calls can be tricky, as they are great mimics.

Top tracks and trails

Rainforest Loop: this fantastic walk (allow an hour) is on elevated timber boardwalks and paved paths and loops through the warm temperate rainforest at Minnamurra. The first 900m are accessible to wheelchairs, although there are some decent uphills sections, so assistance will be required. There are plenty of rest stops and a viewing platform where you can admire and listen to the sounds of the rainforest—until the next group of school kids on excursion comes along.

The Falls Walk: branching off the popular rainforest loop at around the midway point, the Falls Walk, even though it is mainly boardwalk and paved path, is much more strenuous. There are several steep sections (and plenty of seats) along the way, particularly the first 500m and last 100m. The view of Minnamurra Falls and the canyon at the end is worth it. Allow two hours if you are going to do this and the rainforest loop walk, and make sure you leave the visitor centre no later than 3pm, as the park gates close at 5pm.

Missingham Lookout: a 4km return walk has spectacular views over the Carrington Falls Gorge.

Warris Chair Lookout: an easy 1km walk to a lookout over the very pretty Kangaroo Valley in the Carrington Falls section of the park.

Izzards Lookout: also in the Carrington Falls area, this is another easy 1km walk to a lookout.

Budderoo Track: a 24km return walk through open forest, woodland and heath that traverses the park from south-west to north-east and features some great wildflower viewing in late winter and early spring. Watch out for vehicles on the track.

Best picnic spots

There are picnic tables and toilets at Carrington Falls and Nellies Glen, but by far the most popular (and therefore crowded) spot is beside the kiosk at the Minnamurra Rainforest Centre.

Camping, caravanning and accommodation options

There are no camping facilities within the park. Nearby Kiama (15 minutes away) has a wide range of accommodation and caravanning options.

Contact information

For more information call the Minnamurra Rainforest Centre on (02) 4236-0469 or visit www.environment.nsw.gov.au/NationalParks.

Bundjalung National Park and Iluka Nature Reserve

How to get there

Bundjalung National Park is 50km south of Ballina, 60km north of Grafton off the Pacific Highway on Iluka Road.

When to go

Temperatures are moderate most of the year. March is usually the wettest month but water temperatures are usually good for swimming from November through to April. Expect summer and school holiday crowds.

- January: 20–27°C
- July: 10–19°C

Bundjalung National Park, between Evans Head and Iluka (just across the wide mouth of the Clarence River from Yamba), is a beautiful expanse of undeveloped coastline. The Esk River, the largest untouched coastal river system on the north coast, runs through the southern half of the park, which also contains the World-Heritage listed Iluka Nature Reserve, the largest remaining beachside rainforest in New South Wales.

The southern section is the most popular with lots of grassy picnic areas and beaches—although all beaches are unpatrolled and can be subject to dangerous currents so swim at your own risk. Four-wheel-drive access is permitted along Ten Mile Beach from Shark Bay in the south to just near Black Rocks at low tide.

Black Rocks gets its name from the Coffee Rock formations on the beach, a crumbly chocolate-coloured soft rock formed from ancient river sediments that really does look and feel like spent coffee grounds.

Another highlight is the tea-tree-stained waters of Jerusalem Creek, lined with flowering banksias and tea trees and a great place to go paddling if you have a kayak or canoe as the creek meanders north towards the sea for 8km.

Top tracks and trails

Iluka Nature Reserve: a terrific 2.5km easy walk that spears through the centre of the narrow rainforest strip. Entrance to the southern end of the track is from Long Street; the northern end comes out at Iluka Bluff picnic area.

Jerusalem Creek Walk: a three-hour, 8km return walk along the banks of Jerusalem Creek to its mouth near Black Rocks Camping Area. Sections can be very boggy after rain.

Emu Loop: a 45-minute walk through coastal heath to an old World War II bunker. Keep an eye out for the rare coastal emu and carpets of wildflowers during spring.

Best picnic spots

Most of the picnic areas are in the southern

Sunrise at Black Rocks.

section of the park, near Iluka. Iluka Bluff has a great whale-watching lookout and cultural heritage display in the picnic shelter, the Old Ferry Crossing Picnic Area is on the bank of the Clarence River and a good fishing spot, and there are free gas barbecues at Shark Bay and Woody Head.

Camping, caravanning and accommodation options

Woody Head, just 6km from Iluka town centre, is the most popular camping spot in Bundjalung, with hot showers, a kiosk, great views and room for 103 tents and caravans (no power) and four cabins. Bookings are essential and bookings for the New South Wales/Queensland summer school holidays open on 1 March. Call the campground on (02) 6646-6134.

The Black Rocks campground, roughly mid-way between Evans Head and Iluka, has room for just 26 people in a great little camping area hidden behind the dunes of Ten Mile Beach. BYO firewood.

Contact information

For more information call the Grafton park office on (02) 6641-1500 or visit www.environment.nsw.gov.au/NationalParks.

Crowdy Bay National Park

How to get there

Crowdy Bay is 35km north-east of Taree off the Pacific Highway at Moorland; 5km south of Laurieton (30km south of Port Macquarie).

When to go

Temperatures are moderate most of the year. February and March are usually the wettest months but water temperatures are good for swimming from November through to April.

- January: 18–26°C
- July: 7–17°C

Long stretches of windswept beach, dramatic rocky headlands, rock pools, sand dunes, wetlands, rainforest, heathland and plentiful wildlife make Crowdy Bay National Park a popular family holiday spot, particularly in summer.

In the 1960s author Kylie Tennant lived here in a slab hut built for her by local man Ernie Metcalfe, the subject of her famous book, *The Man on the Headland* (1971). It's one of the park's star attractions, along with the 113m-high Diamond Head, named for the quartz crystals in the cliffs that sparkle in the sunlight (best seen from the sea).

Wildlife is prolific: kangaroos are often seen grazing in the grassy campgrounds; you can see whales from Diamond Head between May and October; it's a known koala habitat and a great spot for bird watching. In spring the coastal plains are blanketed in wildflowers—look out for Christmas Bells between late December and early February.

Top tracks and trails

Diamond Head Loop Walk: this two-hour walk that can be started at either Indian or Diamond Head camping areas featuring panoramic coastal views as you skirt the cliff edges of the headland. Keep small children under strict supervision, as cliff edges are not fenced.

Kylie's Hut: a 3km walk to the historic slab hut that belonged to the author Kylie Tennant.

Metcalfe's Walk: this easy 1.2km-return walk from Indian Head to Kylies Beach is a great place to see koalas in the wild.

Fishermans Track: as the name implies, this steep and narrow 2km return walk from Diamond Head campground to a rock platform at the northern end of the headland is popular with anglers.

Best picnic spots

A favourite picnic spot is Indian Head, although the lace monitors, which can grow to an alarming two metres in length, often prowl the area and can raid food boxes if left unattended. There are also three good picnic areas along Dunbogan Beach at Blackbutt, Cheese Tree and Geebung.

Camping, caravanning and accommodation options

There are three campgrounds in the park and all provide large grassy areas that are suitable for caravans and have access to beaches and cold showers. The largest and most popular is Diamond Head, where facilities include free gas barbecues and it's a very easy walk to the beach. Be prepared to share your camp with the resident mob of kangaroos. Facilities are a bit more basic at Indian Head and Kylies Beach, and beach access involves a bit more walking (3km at Kylies Beach) but they are generally less crowded. BYO drinking water to all three. There is also a walk-in campground near Kylies Hut, 3km from the Kylies Beach campground. All of the campgrounds are very popular during summer and Easter school holidays, so you'll need to book well ahead.

Contact information

For more information call the Port Macquarie park office on (02) 6586-8300 or visit www.environment.nsw.gov.au/NationalParks.

Dunbogan Beach.

Dorrigo National Park

How to get there

Dorrigo National Park is on the eastern outskirts of Dorrigo, 38km west of Coffs Harbour.

When to go

Summer tends to be mild and wet, winter is cooler here than on the coast. Spring is usually dry.

- January: 19–27°C
- July: 7–19°C

Part of the Gondwana Rainforest, Dorrigo National Park is one of the most accessible national parks in the state, proving that you don't have to rough it on long hikes to see some of the country's best World Heritage listed wilderness. With a range of wheelchair accessible boardwalks, it's great for either a quick one-hour visit or you can spend all day here on one of the longer, five-hour walks.

The first place to go is the Rainforest Centre, which has an excellent interpretive display on the history of the area and the types of plants and wildlife you're likely to see

Boardwalk at the Rainforest Centre. Image courtesy Tourism NSW.

while you're here. Straight out the back is Skywalk—a dramatic boardwalk above the rainforest canopy that leads way out over the edge of the escarpment, which rises to 1586m on the western boundary. The boardwalk itself is 70m high. The views of the world heritage wilderness and across to the coast are spectacular.

Other highlights of the park include beautiful waterfalls, lush subtropical rainforest and a wealth of birdlife, including lyrebirds, brush turkeys and whipbirds.

Top tracks and trails

Walk with the Birds: a wheelchair-accessible 110m-long elevated boardwalk with information panels along its length that starts from the Glade Picnic Area.

Satinbird Stroll: a short and easy rainforest circuit (allow 20 minutes) that is also suitable for wheelchairs.

The Wonga Walk: a two-and-a-half-hour sealed walking track through sections of rainforest featuring waterfalls and good views.

Rosewood Creek Track: a two-hour medium

Rainforest vines. Image courtesy Tourism NSW.

Crystal Shower Falls. Image courtesy Coffs Coast Tourism.

walk from the Never Never picnic area that follows the creek to Coachwood Falls. You can add a pleasant extra hour to the walk and follow the zigzag track down to the base of Red Cedar Falls.

Casuarina Falls: another good walk from the Never Never picnic area takes you to the top of the falls and has fantastic views of McGrath's Hump and the Escarpment. Allow 90 minutes.

Blackbutt Track: the park's longest track, 12km return, follows the edge of the escarpment from near the park entrance to the Never Never picnic area.

Best picnic spots

There are three picnic areas in the park: Dorrigo Rainforest Centre; Glade picnic area and the Never Never picnic area, which you can drive to via Dome Road. The track to the Glade Picnic area is suitable for strollers and even wheelchairs, and takes around 20 minutes. There are tables, toilets and barbecue facilities here, but be warned, the brush turkeys are not shy and can smell a picnic a mile away.

The Canopy Cafe at the Rainforest Centre serves light lunches, cakes and a decent coffee. It's open daily, 9am–4pm.

Camping, caravanning and accommodation options

There are no camping grounds in the park, but you can bush camp in remote areas. There is a range of accommodation to suit all budgets in nearby Dorrigo.

Contact information

The Rainforest Centre is open daily, 9am–4.30pm. For more information call the Dorrigo Rainforest Centre on (02) 6657-2309 or visit www.environment.nsw.gov.au/NationalParks.

Skywalk. Image courtesy Tourism NSW.

How to get there

The park straddles the Great Dividing Range approximately halfway between Grafton (104km east) and Glen Innes (79km west).

When to go

During summer you can expect warm days and cool nights; winter nights are frosty and often dip below zero. Weather conditions can change quickly, so always be prepared for the worst.

- January: 13–24°C
- July: -1–12°C

Another World Heritage-listed national park, Gibraltar Range is granite country and a spectacular contrast to the lush, cool rainforests of Washpool National Park, literally just across the road on the other side to the Gwydir Highway.

Deep-sided valleys and striking granite outcrops are the main attraction, many of which form fantastic shapes with balancing rocks that give rise to descriptive names such as Anvil Rock, Old Mans Hat and the Needles. The outcrops are actually the exposed tops of the New England Batholith, a huge underground mass of rock that stretches some 400km from Tamworth to Stanthorpe in Queensland.

There are a number of pretty waterfalls and scenic lookouts—the park's highest point is

Summit Mountain, 1175m above sea level—including Raspberry Lookout and Vinegar Hill, both offering great views over the surrounding wilderness. Keep an eye out for the spotted-tailed quoll and the platypus in the creeks.

Top tracks and trails

Forest Walk: a 90-minute walk past Barra Nulla Cascades through open forest that dips in and out of rainforest gullies before leading to a granite outcrop with good views.

Lyrebird Falls: easy 1km (each way) walk to a small waterfall downstream from Boundary Falls.

The Needles: 6km medium walk following an old stock route to six spectacular granite columns that rise 300 m above the edge of the escarpment, overlooking the Dandahra Gorge.

Gibraltar-Washpool World Heritage Walk: for fit, experienced and well-equipped walkers only, this long-distance track links the Gibraltar Range and Washpool national parks and covers a variety of rugged mountainous terrain. Most walkers allow five days to do the 40km main loop, and include most of the optional side walks, which can add another 40km.

Best picnic spots

Favourite picnic spot is at Mulligans (named after William Mulligan, who surveyed the area for a proposed hydroelectric scheme in the 1920s), where there is a large shelter with free

gas barbecues surrounded by grass trees. It's also within easy stroll of Little Dandahra Creek, a nice place to swim in summer, although it's always icy cold, and Burra Nulla Cascades. There are also picnic facilities at Dandahra, just off the Gwydir Highway and at Raspberry Lookout, which can be a bit exposed.

Camping, caravanning and accommodation options

There are two campgrounds, both suitable for caravans and camper trailers. Mulligans is near Little Dandahra Creek and facilities include cold showers, gas barbecues, firewood and flush toilets. Boundary Falls, on the site of an old sawmill, is a little more basic, but close to some lovely waterfalls. If towing a caravan, there is a very narrow bridge on the road into Mulligans and the sites suit mid-size vans. Larger vans should opt for Boundary Creek, where there is more room to manoeuvre.

Contact information

For more information call the Glen Innes park office on (02) 6739-0700 or visit www.environment.nsw.gov.au/NationalParks.

The Forest Walk. Image courtesy Bill McKinnon.

Hat Head National Park and Arakoon State Conservation Area

Hat Head National Park is 24km east of Kempsey, near the village of South West Rocks.

When to go

Temperatures are mild most of the year. February and March are usually the wettest months but water temperatures are good for swimming from November through to April.

- January: 19–27°C
- July: 11–19°C

Long, sweeping beaches and even longer views are just some of the highlights of this coastal national park south of South West Rocks. Facilities are clustered around Hat Head in the south and Smoky Cape in the north, crowned by the 1891 lighthouse.

Adjoining Smoky Cape is Arakoon State Conservation Area, a popular camping and picnic area overlooking beautiful Trial Bay. Star attraction is the very photogenic sandstone ruin of Trial Bay Gaol. Built in 1877, closed in 1903 and reopened in 1915 to hold internees from Germany during World War I, where they were allowed out onto the beaches during the day but locked up at night—this is a gaol with a view. It's now a museum (open daily 9am-4.30pm) and you can walk through the old cells and grounds.

The licensed restaurant, simply called The Kiosk, is a favourite with locals who come here to linger over a long lunch and soak in the views. Call (02) 6566-7100 for bookings.

Top tracks and trails

Monument Hill: an easy 30-minute walk from Trial Bay Gaol to the summit of Monument Hill with great views of the gaol and Trial Bay and along the coast.

Korogoro Track: a medium 3.2km walk circling the headland (Hat Head) with great coastal views and wildflowers.

Connors Track: this 6.7km trail follows the coastline south of Hat Head to secluded Connors and Third beaches and also offers great coastal views.

Little Bay to Smoky Cape: if you can organise a car pick-up this four hour (10km) one-way coastal walk from Little Bay (in Arakoon) to Smoky Cape is quite hard, but worth it for the views alone.

Best picnic spots

For a picnic table with a view head to Captain Cook's Lookout on the Smoky Cape headland, which has electric barbecues, picnic tables, toilets and jaw dropping views—it's a great

Smoky Cape Lighthouse.

Trial Bay Gaol.

whale watching spot. There's also a great picnic spot near the gaol at Trial Bay with a playground for kids.

Camping, caravanning and accommodation options

There are two campgrounds at Hat Head: Hungry Head is surrounded by heathland but facilities are basic; Smoky Cape is just below the lighthouse. Neither are suitable for caravans and you'll need to bring your own drinking water. For those with a caravan, the campground at Arakoon, in the shadow of the beautiful sandstone gaol, has powered and unpowered caravan sites overlooking the bay and (coin operated) hot showers. You can also stay at the lighthouse at Smoky Cape, either in one of the two self-contained assistant keepers' cottages (both sleep six) or B&B style in the head keeper's house. Views are to die for. Call (02) 6566-6301 or visit www.smokycapelighthouse.com.

Contact information

For more information call the South West Rocks office at Trial Bay Gaol on (02) 6566-6168 or visit www.environment.nsw.gov.au/NationalParks. How to get there

Kinchega National Park

How to get there

Access to the park is 110km south-east of Broken Hill near Menindee. Broken Hill is 1160km north-west of Sydney; 510km east of Adelaide. Rain out here is rare, but when it does fall, unsealed roads quickly become rivers of thick, glue-like mud that can be impassable for days, so always check road conditions before setting out.

When to go

Summer can be very hot and the flies are extremely friendly—winter (although nights can be very cold) is the most pleasant time to travel throughout the area.

- January: 18–34°C
- July: 4–17°C

Amid the vast arid plains, Kinchega National Park is a veritable desert oasis where the Darling River flows into the Menindee lakes, forming three huge bodies of water. This water attracts an amazing wealth of birdlife—flocks of pelicans, groups of ibis, herons, whistling kites, great egrets, and countless others, although during times of extended drought when the Darling stops flowing, some lakes may be dry.

Much of the park was originally Kinchega Station, once one of the biggest pastoral stations in the west. Established in 1850, the station had important links to European explorers; Charles Sturt camped here on his search for the inland sea and, in 1860, Burke and Wills stayed at Maidens Hotel in nearby Menindee at the beginning of their ill-fated trip that ended at Cooper Creek. William Wright, the man who has been blamed for a large part of the tragedy, was a station manager at Kinchega before he joined their party. By 1967, when the station lease expired and it became a national park, more than six million sheep had been shorn in the original 62-stand woolshed—built in 1875. It's now one of the park's most visited attractions.

The park is also rich in Aboriginal heritage and there are several sites in the park, including middens and scarred trees, where bark was removed to make canoes.

Top tracks and trails

Lake Cawndilla: take a walk along the lake shore from the campground. Bird and wildlife life is at its most prolific at sunrise and sunset.

Tourist Drives: there are two great self-guided heritage drives around the lakes and along the Darling River inside the park.

Best picnic spots

Watching the sun sink into the lake against the silhouettes of the drowned river red gums in the water (a photographers dream) with a cold drink is one of the delights of a stay in Kinchega.

Camping, caravanning and accommodation options

The campsites along the bank of the Darling River are some of the best in the state. Facilities are basic, but the campsites are spread along the bank out of sight of each other. The lakeside camping at Lake Cawndilla (popular with groups) and Emu Lake have the best sunset show around. There are gas/ electric barbecues at Cawndilla; the other two campgrounds have wood barbecues but you'll need to bring your own wood and drinking water. Hot showers and bore water are available at the Shearer's Quarters at the woolshed, which sleeps up to 24 in bunk beds—BYO linen.

Contact information

For more information call the Broken Hill park office on (08) 8080-3200 or visit www.environment.nsw.gov.au/NationalParks.

Sunset at Cawndilla Lake. Image courtesy Tourism NSW.

Boating is a popular pastime on the lake. Image courtesy Tourism NSW.

13 Kosciuszko National Park

How to get there

The park is 10km from Jindabyne; 15km from Adaminaby; 15km from Tumut and 70km from Cooma. If you are driving a 2WD, snow chains must be carried between 1 June and 10 October.

When to go

Summer can be warm and dry, but nights can get very cold. Expect snow during winter.

- January: 10–25°C
- July: -2–11°C

Alpine New South Wales stretches from the ACT to the Victorian border along the spine of the Great Dividing Range. Kosciuszko National Park encompasses most of the area including Australia's highest peak, Mt Kosciuszko (2228m). In winter the area is a magnet for lovers of snow sports; in summer, fishing, bushwalking and mountain biking reign supreme.

The park is home to several historic cattleman's huts and Yarrangobilly Caves, among the most richly-decorated limestone caves in Australia. There is also a thermal pool with water a constant 27°C. Take a self-guided

Sunrise over the range. Image courtesy Bill McKinnon.

tour of Glory Hole Cave between 10am-4pm (daily), or join one of the guided tours of the other caves.

Gold was discovered at Kiandra in 1859, sparking one of the shortest gold rushes in Australian history—from November 1859 to March 1861. At its height there were 10,000 people on the diggings. Today all that remains are a few ruins covered by wildflowers and some display boards telling the story.

Top tracks and trails

Mt Kosciuszko: take the chairlift to the top of Crackenback from Thredbo village and walk the six-kilometre easy track to the top of Mt Kosciusko.

Dead Horse Gap: 10km walk that takes you from the chairlift across the mountain and then back to Thredbo village through stands of snow gums and along the Thredbo River.

Snow Gums Boardwalk: a 15-minute stroll that starts at the Charlotte's Pass lookout that has great views of Australia's highest peaks.

The Summit Walk: a 9km, three-hour difficult walk that follows the old road to the summit of Mount Kosciuszko from Charlotte's Pass.

Main Range Track: a challenging two-hour walk from Charlotte's Pass to Blue Lake lookout.

Best picnic spots

There are dozens of great picnic sites scattered throughout the park. Favourites include Thredbo River (gas barbecues), Sawpit Creek (starting point of three walks) and Scammell's Lookout, which has a knock-out view of the western face of the main range.

Camping, caravanning and accommodation options

Walk-in camping is permitted virtually anywhere in the park, but you'll need to be out of sight of the roads and well away from watercourses. Most of the official campgrounds in the park are very basic and do not have drinking water.

There are some nice summer camping spots at Tom Groggin on the banks of the Murray and beside Swampy Plain River at Geehi, 31km south of Khancoban. Three Mile Dam, near the Mount Selwyn ski fields in the north of the park, provides good high altitude camping and further north still, Talbingo and Blowering Reservoirs provide exposed camping with good views over the water.

Kosciuszko Mountain Retreat, has powered caravan sites set amongst the snowgums. The Retreat is 14km north-west of Jindabyne at Sawpit Creek. Tel: (02) 6456-2224. There is a range of accommodation at Thredbo, see www.thredbo.com.au.

Contact information

For more information call the Jindabyne park office on (02) 6450-5600 or visit www.environment.nsw.gov.au/NationalParks.

Snowgum. Image courtesy Tourism NSW.

Ku-ring-gai Chase National Park

How to get there

Ku-ring-gai National Park is on the northern outskirts of Sydney. Best access is via Bobbin Head Road at North Turramurra, via Terry Hills to Cottage Point and beyond to West Head, or via ferry from Palm Beach. Ferry services leave Palm Beach Wharf for The Basin, every hour on the hour. You can also access to park by train (Berowra, Cowan, Brooklyn or Mount Ku-ring-gai stations) and suburban bus (185, 190) from Wynyard in Sydney's city centre.

When to go

Temperatures are mild most of the year. Late summer and early autumn can be stormy.

- January: 17–28°C
- July: 5–17°C

On the northern edge of Sydney's suburban sprawl, Ku-ring-gai Chase National Park is where the Hawkesbury River seeps into the sea in a maze of winding waterways. The sheltered beaches and sandstone ridges make it a popular place for a summertime picnic.

Highlights include the sandy beach and lagoon at The Basin, the view from West Head lookout, Aboriginal rock engravings, middens, axe grinding grooves and cave drawings. Barrenjoey Lighthouse (on the Palm Beach side of Pittwater) is open for tours every Sunday, between 11am and 3pm.

Top tracks and trails

Sphinx Track: a three-and-a-half-hour return walk to Bobbin Head from the park entrance gates at North Turramurra. It's named after a sandstone miniature of the Egyptian sphinx, carved by a returned serviceman in the 1920s. Keep an eye out for Aboriginal middens along the way.

Resolute Track: a 7km (three hour) walk around West Head that passes several Aboriginal rock engravings and down a steep slope to an Aboriginal occupation site in a cave.

Jerusalem Bay Track: part of the 250km Sydney to Newcastle Great North Walk, this 5km section starts at Cowan train station and leads down a fairly steep descent to beautiful Jerusalem Bay with some spectacular views along the way.

The Basin Track and Mackerel Track: allow two and a half hours for this walk to one of the park's most popular spots, The Basin, from West Head Road. There is a wooden walkway near the start of the track that leads to one of the best Aboriginal engraving sites in the park. From The Basin you can walk around the shoreline to Currawong Beach and Mackerel Beach before heading back up the Mackerel Track which links up with the Basin Track.

Best picnic spots

Akuna Bay, which has a marina and boat hire, is a popular picnic spot, as is The Basin

Lookout at West Head.

and Bobbin Head, a good fishing spot with a marina, mangrove boardwalk, playground, cafes, free barbecues and plenty of picnic tables. There are also barbecues and shelters near West Head at Resolute Picnic Area.

Camping, caravanning and accommodation options

The Basin campground is the only camping place in the park, but has space for 400 people. Facilities include gas/electric barbecues, flush toilets, cold showers, and drinking water and it's a great place for swimming, bushwalking and bird watching. Access is via the 2.8km walk from West Head or by ferry from Palm Beach. Bookings are essential.

Contact information

For more information call the Sydney North office on (02) 9472-8949 or visit www.environment.nsw.gov.au/NationalParks.

How to get there

Kwiambal is 90km north of Inverell, via Ashford village. Access involves sections of unsealed roads that are in good condition but could become tricky after wet weather as there are some (usually dry) creek crossings.

When to go

Summer is warm and the nights are pleasantly cool. Winter can be very cold. Spring is great for wildflowers.

- January: 18–31°C
- July: 2–17°C

Macintrye River. Image courtesy Bill McKinnon.

Kwiambal National Park is one of the more stunning parks in the north west. On the junction of the Macintyre and Severn Rivers, this park has some of the best swimming holes and river gorge scenery you'll see east of the Kimberley. Both rivers are also good for fishing: Murray cod, golden perch and catfish are the common catches.

The main picnic and camping area is a great place to swim (although the current in middle of the river moves quite fast the sandy river beaches are calm enough). Fish, rock-hop or just sit and watch the early morning sun warm the pale river rocks. Outside of holiday season, you'll propably be sharing the campground with just a couple of others, if anyone at all.

Top tracks and trails

Macintyre Falls: there is a lookout perched high above the gorge with fabulous views down river and a 600m boardwalk down the side of the rockwall to a wide, deep plunge pool. After winding down what seems like hundreds of steps the swim is just what the doctor ordered. Trouble is, once you get back to the top, you'll wish you were back in the water again.

Junction Walk: this 7km (return) walk, which leaves from the camping area, follows a disused dirt road through the woodlands to the junction of the two rivers. It's a fairly easy walk, although there are two steep hills, one at each end. The swimming at the end makes up for the up-and-down-again slog. Pack a cut lunch

Cool off in one of the many waterholes. Image courtesy Bill McKinnon.

and a good book—you could easily spend the day here lazing around in the shade on the beach. On the return leg take the branch track to Dungeon Lookout, high above the rocky gorge on the Severn River.

Best picnic spots

Favourite picnic sites are the riverside campground at Lemon Tree Flat and Macintyre Falls lookout, both of which have access to swimming holes.

Camping, caravanning and accommodation options

The camping area is at Lemon Tree Flat, a shady sprawling grassed area beside the Severn River. Here, you camp under wind-twisted gums in the shadow of the high granite walls of the river gorge, with campsite views of huge boulders balancing precariously above the eddying water. Most of the camp sites involve hauling your gear 50m or so from your car to your camp site, although you can camp beside your vehicle if you wish—it's just much nicer down the slope towards the river. There are six (unpowered) caravan sites. Bring your own firewood and water—the river water seems clean and clear, but you should boil it thoroughly before you use it.

Contact information

For more information call the Tenterfield park office on (02) 6736-4298 or visit www.environment.nsw.gov.au/NationalParks.

Lord Howe Island

How to get there

Part of New South Wales, Lord Howe Island lies approximately 600km north-east of Sydney and south-east of Brisbane, at the same latitude as Port Macquarie. Unless you've got your own yacht, you'll need to fly and there are regular services from Sydney most days, weekend services from Brisbane and summer services from Port Macquarie. Flight time is just under two hours.

When to go

Temperatures are lovely most of the year, with a mild winter, although weather is very changeable due to the island's location in the middle of ocean.

- January: 20–25°C
- July: 14–19°C

Just 11km long and barely two kilometres at its widest point, world-heritage-listed Lord Howe Island is home to the world's most southerly coral reef, pristine beaches where kingfish swim around your ankles, beautiful kentia palm forests, a vast array of rare birdlife and one of the most challenging bushwalks in Australia, the climb to the summit of Mount Gower.

Two thirds of the island is a Permanent Park Preserve and the surrounding waters are a Marine Park containing around 450 species of fish (around one-tenth are unique to the area), 90 species of coral, green and hawksbill turtles and countless species of algae and molluscs. You can snorkel out to the reef from the beach. For those who prefer to stay dry there are also a number of glass bottom boat tours available.

The island is also home to more than 130 species of bird, including the Lord Howe woodhen—this olive-brown flightless bird was on the brink of extinction 25 years ago and is one of the rarest birds on earth with less than a dozen nesting pairs left. Those that survived the impact of the introduction of pigs on the island by sailors in the late 18th century did so mainly atop the summit of Mount Gower, where the wild pigs could not reach them. Now that the feral pigs have been eradicated, the woodhen has made a comeback.

Top tracks and trails

Mount Gower: the climb to the summit is not for the unfit or those with a fear of heights or dodgy knees. It's a 10-hour return climb from sea level to 875m and involves lots of ropes and narrow ledges. But, if you're at the top when the clouds break, it really is like being on top of the world. The walk is only open to those who go with a licensed guide. Contact Jack Shick on (02) 6563-2218 or visit www.lordhoweisland.info/services/sea.html.

The Clear Place: an easy one-hour return walk through a forest of kentia palms and

Banyan trees to a lookout on the north-eastern side of the island.

Best picnic spots

Pack a picnic dinner and head to Ned's Beach at sunset, where you can laugh as you watch the shearwaters (mutton birds) crash-land into the kentia palm forest behind you.

Camping, caravanning and accommodation options

No camping is permitted on the island and visitor numbers are limited to 400 at any one time. There are 17 properties with prices to suit a range of budgets. See www.lordhoweisland.info for more details.

Contact information

For more information call 1800 240 937 or visit www.lordhoweisland.info.

Mt Gower and Mt Lidgbird.

Snorkelling the rock pools. Image courtesy Tourism NSW.

Banyan Tree, Lord Howe Island. Image courtesy Tourism NSW.

How to get there

Morton National Park is approximately 20km west of Nowra. To get to Fitzroy Falls take the Nowra Road from Moss Vale or take the Princes Highway from Nowra to the Southern Highlands via the very scenic Kangaroo Valley.

When to go

Best months to visit are March/April and September/October when wildflowers are at their best and weather is usually mild and dry.

- January: 13–25°C
- July: 5–11°C

Morton National Park in the mountains behind Nowra is the place to go for sandstone scenery on a grand scale. Essentially a flat plateau dissected by deep gorges, there are dozens of great lookouts and three spectacular waterfalls that plunge off the plateau into rainforest gullies; Tianjara Falls off the Nowra-Braidwood road and Fitzroy Falls and Belmore Falls in the northern section of the park. To the south, George Boyd lookout, Little Forest Plateau and Pigeon House Mountain offer views of the coastline and across the Budawang wilderness area and are accessible only by foot and for well-equipped experienced hikers only. On the western side at Tallong there are wonderful views of the Shoalhaven Gorge from Badgerys and Longpoint lookouts.

Most of the visitor facilities and walking tracks are clustered around Fitzroy Falls, where there is a large visitor's centre with interactive displays and a cafe, as well as several wheelchair accessible boardwalks leading to lookouts over the falls.

The fire trails that cut through the park are popular with mountain bikers and four-wheel-drivers, although you will need a permit to drive some tracks and most are dry-weather roads only.

Top tracks and trails

Pigeon House Mountain: the climb to the top of Pigeon House Mountain is one of the most popular walks on the south coast. Graded as difficult, it's a four-hour return climb that involves ladders at the top. Your reward is magnificent panoramic views of the rugged cliffs and gorges carved by the Clyde River and its tributaries. On a clear day, you can see the coastline from Point Perpendicular in the north to Mount Dromaderry in the south.

Belmore Falls: an easy 45-minute walk around the escarpment with several good lookouts along the way giving great views of Belmore Falls.

East Rim Wildflower walk: a lovely two-hour walk from the Visitor Centre at Fitzroy

Falls with many interpretive boards relating to the wildflowers found along the track. Spectacular lookouts provide views over the valley below the escarpment.

Best picnic spots

The most popular (and sometimes crowded) picnic spot is at Fitzroy Falls, where you'll find barbecue facilities as well as a café. Other good picnic spots in the park include Belmore Falls and Pigeon House.

Camping, caravanning and accommodation options

Gambells Rest campground in the Bundanoon section of the park has 10 sites (suitable for caravans and trailers), but you'll need to book first with the Fitzroy Falls Visitors Centre. Facilities include picnic tables, gas/electric barbecues, flush toilets, hot showers and drinking water. You can bush camp (backpack only, no car-based camping) anywhere in the park provided you camp more than 300m from roads—a popular option for those walking in the Budawang wilderness section of the park.

Contact information

For more information call the Fitzroy Falls Visitor Centre on (02) 4887-7270 or visit www.environment.nsw.gov.au/ NationalParks.

Fitzroy Falls. Image courtesy Tourism NSW.

Mungo National Park

How to get there

Mungo National Park is 85km south-east of Pooncarie; 316km south of Broken Hill. All roads in and around the park are closed after rain.

When to go

Winter is the most pleasant time to visit and the best season for photography, as the light is at its clearest.

- January: 18–34°C
- July: 4–17°C

At the centre of Willandra Lakes World Heritage area, Mungo National Park is an important place for local Aboriginal groups. 15,000 years ago this vast, flat plain was a huge lake. Along the eastern shore of the ancient lakebed is a 22km crescent-shaped wall of sand and clay eroded into weird and fantastic formations. Called the Walls of China by Chinese station workers in the 19th century, the lunette has preserved countless Aboriginal campfires, cooking hearths and burials. It was here that the oldest recorded cremation in the world was found—an Aboriginal woman more than 40,000 years old. Skeletons of ancient megafauna and Tasmanian tigers have also been found here.

The best way to gain an insight into the cultural significance of the area is to join one of the Harry Nanya tours. Led by Aboriginal guides, you'll learn how the original owners of this land lived and hunted as well as the dreamtime creation stories associated with the area. There are a range of full and half-day tours as well as sunset tours—the park is particularly beautiful in the evening when the white sand lunette changes colour and glows in the light of the setting sun. For bookings or more information, call (03) 5027-2076.

Another must-see sight is the old Mungo Woolshed, built in 1869.

Top tracks and trails

Mungo Drive Tour: this 70km, one-way driving loop around the park is a must do. The track crosses the lake floor to the Walls of China, before heading over the dune to the mallee country and then around the north-east shore of the lake. It's also popular with mountainbike riders—just make sure you carry lots of water.

Foreshore walk: this one-hour return walk starts near the Mungo Woolshed and cuts across a small section of the lake bed to climb a dune on the western shore.

Best picnic spots

Best picnic spot is at the Walls of China viewing platform, where you can gaze out at the striking formations. Best time to do this is at sunset, when the walls glow deep red in the setting sun. There are also picnic tables overlooking the dry lake bed at Mungo Lookout and good shade at Rosewood rest area.

Camping, caravanning and accommodation options

There are two campgrounds in the park. The Main Camp has 33 sites and is suitable for caravans. Facilities include gas/electric barbecues and toilets. There are hot showers at Mungo Visitor Centre, 2km away and firewood is available for purchase ($5 per 25-litre bin). The smaller, more secluded Belah campground is at around the halfway point on the Mungo Drive Tour, but is not suitable for trailers or caravans. Just outside the park boundary, Mungo Lodge offers motel-style accommodation and self contained cottages. Tel: (03) 5029-7297; www.mungolodge.com.au.

Contact information

For more information call the Buronga park office on (03) 5021-8900 or visit www.environment.nsw.gov.au/NationalParks.

The striking formations of the Walls of China. Image courtesy Tourism NSW.

How to get there

Murramarang National Park stretches south of Bawley Point (10km south of Ulladulla) to Durras, 10km north of Batemans Bay.

When to go

Temperatures are moderate most of the year. Water temperatures are usually good for swimming from November through to April.

- January: 16–25°C
- July: 6–16°C

The rugged coastline between Ulladulla and Bateman's Bay make Murramarang National Park one of the state's most popular parks in the summer holiday season with beautiful beaches, rock platforms, spotted gum forests, rainforest gullies and lovely Durras Lake, a popular fishing and canoeing spot. There's beachfront cabin accommodation, good snorkelling, swimming and surfing and a range of bushwalks. Keep an eye out for eastern grey kangaroos on the beaches.

Murramarang Aboriginal Area near Bawley Point protects one of the largest middens on the south coast, although signposting is non-existent and it can be hard to find.

Not part of Murramarang National Park, neighbouring Cullendulla Creek Nature Reserve on the northern outskirts of Batemans Bay protects one of the largest stands of mangroves south of Sydney and has significant Aboriginal middens and burial sites, and is well worth a visit.

Top tracks and trails

Depot Beach Rainforest Walk: a short 2km loop through coastal rainforest behind Depot Beach.

Discovery Trail and Lake Walk: easy 8km walk through the rainforest around the shoreline of Durras Lake.

Pretty Beach to Pebbly Beach: a very pretty four-hour (9km) walk that takes you through rainforest to the top of Durras Mountain (283m), with spectacular views of the ocean and offshore islands.

Wasp Head Walk: easy 40-minute walk though casuarina forest to Emily Miller Head, where you'll get great views of the rocky cove and out towards Wasp Island.

Mangrove Walk: 2km interpretive boardwalk through the mangroves and across the dunes at Cullendulla Creek Nature Reserve.

Best picnic spots

There is a nice grassy picnic area with tables overlooking Depot Beach, but you'll need to bring your own barbecue or stove. Pebbly Beach has a large picnic area with shelters and gas barbecues and is a good place for swimming and wildlife watching with lots of kangaroos in the early morning and at sunset.

Emily Miller Beach. Image courtesy Eurobodalla Coast Tourism.

Camping, caravanning and accommodation options

There are several good camping areas within the national park and countless commercial caravan parks and holiday accommodation options in surrounding towns of Durras Lake and Bawley Point. The largest campground, Pretty Beach, has 70 sites (including powered caravan sites) and facilities include hot showers. Pebbly Beach is the best place to go to see kangaroos on the beach and has 20 sites, cold showers and gas barbecues, but is not suitable for caravans. Depot Beach is another good spot and also has powered caravan sites and hot showers. The Lakesea Holiday Park at South Durras offers easy access to the beach and the lake and has a range of accommodation, from powered caravan sites to self-contained cabins and brand new four-star elevated two-bedroom seaside cabins with private balconies (www.lakesea.com.au). Bookings are essential at all campgrounds and holiday parks during the summer holiday season.

Contact information

For more information call the Depot Beach park office on (02) 4478-6582 or the Pebbly Beach office on (02) 4478-6023; or visit www.environment.nsw.gov.au/NationalParks.

Mutawintji National Park

How to get there

Mutawintji is 130km north-west of Broken Hill along the unsealed road to Tibooburra. Roads are closed after rain.

When to go

Summer can be extremely hot and uncomfortable—winter (although nights can be very cold) is the most pleasant time to visit.

- January: 18–35°C
- July: 4–17°C

Mutawintji is spectacular gorge country and of huge significance to the Malyankapa and Pandjikali people, who used to gather here in groups of more than 1000 to preform initiation, rainmaking and other ceremonies, producing one of the best collections of Aboriginal art in New South Wales. The area is still used for meetings and other cultural activities.

The Mutawintji Local Land Council conducts tours to the Mutawintji Historic Site, where your guide will show you Aboriginal rock art that dates back more than 8000 years, as well as explain the significance of the area and the many uses of the flora and fauna of the park. The entire park was returned to its Aboriginal owners in 1998 and entry to the Historic Site section is now by guided tour only on Wednesday and Saturday mornings from April to October at 11am. No bookings are necessary, just meet at the visitor centre.

You can also take a self-guided tour of the Homestead Creek Gorge to Wright's Cave where you can see more examples of engravings and stencils, or the longer walk to Old Mootwingee Gorge, a delightful swimming hole surrounded by towering red cliffs.

Top tracks and trails

Thaaklatjika Mingkana Walk: a short 500m walk, easy enough to be suitable for wheelchairs, winds through the gorges to Thaaklatjika (Wright's Cave). This large, rocky overhang covered in Aboriginal paintings, stencils and engravings, and some fascinating early colonial graffiti that includes a blue triangle painted by William Wright (of Burke and Wills fame—he was leader of the back-up party that famously abandoned the camp at the Dig Tree just hours before the ill-fated explorers returned) with his initials inside.

Old Mootwingee Gorge Walk: a 3km walk of medium difficulty into one of the park's most picturesque gorges, ending at a peaceful rock pool enclosed by towering rusty red cliffs.

Sunset Ridge Trail: a five-hour walk that includes several steep sections that takes you to the top of a ridge overlooking the vast desert plains and beautiful Bynguano Range.

It's wonderful at sunset, but the walk back can take up to two hours to complete and night falls quickly, so take a torch.

The Homestead Gorge Trail: a leisurely three-hour walk between the craggy cliffs of Homestead Creek, and into the Homestead Gorge. Keep an eye out for Aboriginal engravings.

Bynguano Range: a hard three-and-a-half-hour (5.5km) walk branching off from the Homestead Gorge Trail that offers fantastic views of the gorges. For experienced walkers only.

Best picnic spots

There are picnic facilities at Homestead Creek and at the Visitor Centre. Both have gas barbecues.

Camping, caravanning and accommodation options

Homestead Creek camping ground has 50 sites, and is suitable for caravans, although sites are unpowered. Facilities include picnic tables, gas/electric barbecues, flush toilets and hot showers. Bring your own firewood from Broken Hill.

Contact information

For more information call the Broken Hill park office on (08) 8080-3200 or visit www.environment.nsw.gov.au/NationalParks.

Rockholes at Old Mootwingee (Mutawintji) Gorge.

Mutawintji Historic Site.

How to get there

Myall Lakes National Park is east of Bulahdelah, around 235km north of Sydney via the Pacific Highway and The Lakes Way. The vehicle ferry at Bombah Point operates from 8am to 6pm every day. There are crossings every 30 minutes (fees apply).

When to go

Generally, the water in the lakes and ocean is warm enough for swimming between September and April.

- January: 18–27°C
- July: 7–19°C

Myall Lakes National Park contains the largest coastal lake system in New South Wales, as well as extensive sand dunes and stretches of rainforest. In spring, the heathlands are ablaze with scented wildflowers, banksias, flannel flowers, lilies and flowering gums. Despite the annual human summer holiday invasion there is an abundance of wildlife as well—kangaroos, wallabies, possums, bandicoots, gliders, echidnas, goannas and a wide variety of birdlife.

Children can splash about in the clear shallows and there are dozens of great places to jump in a canoe for a leisurely paddle around the edge of the lake. If you don't have your own kayak or canoe you can hire one from the Lakeside Coffee Lounge and Boat Hire at Pacific Palms. Tel: (02) 6554-0309.

At the northern end of the park the 15m-high Sugarloaf Point Lighthouse stands on a remote and dramatic headland east of Seal Rocks village. It was completed in 1875 and is a great place for whale watching between May and November.

Top tracks and trails

Mungo Brush Rainforest Walk: an easy 30-minute loop through littoral rainforest. Keep an eye out for koalas.

Yacaaba Headland Walk: a 30-minute walk to the largest headland of Port Stephens and has some great views along the way. The last section to the top of the headland is steep.

The Mungo Track: 22km track from Hawks Nest up to Mungo Brush. It forms part of the 220km Tops to Myall Heritage Trail from Barrington Tops to Hawks Nest/Tea Gardens.

Best picnic spots

Mungo Brush is one of the most popular spots in the park. It's a shady, lakeside camping and picnic spot with electric barbecues and picnic tables, where pelicans lazily fish in the shady shallows as black swans gracefully glide by and opportunistic goannas prowl the grassy clearing once the visitors have packed up for the day.

Sugarloaf Point. Image courtesy Tourism NSW.

Camping, caravanning and accommodation options

There are 11 campgrounds scattered across the park, as well as nine boat-based campsites that are only accessible by boat. The largest, and most popular campground is Mungo Brush, which has 80 sites, and is suitable for caravans. Neranie Head, Korsmans Landing, Yagon, Banksia Green, Bungaree Bay, The Wells, White Tree Bay, Dees Corner and Bungaree Bay are also suitable for caravans. No drinking water is available at any of the campgrounds, so make sure you bring your own. No bookings are taken at any campgrounds—all camping is on a first-come-first-served basis and all are very popular during summer and school holidays. Also good are the shady waterfront sites at

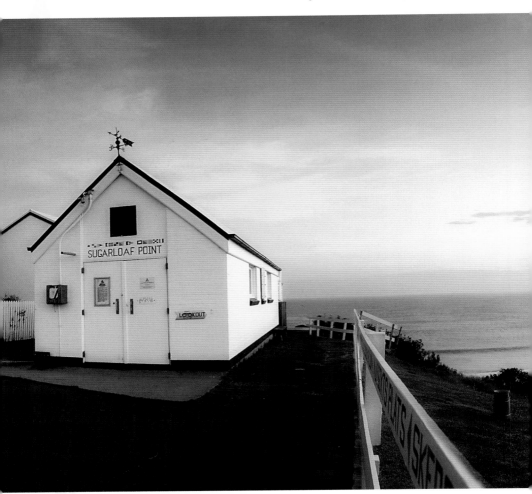

Sugarloaf Point Lighthouse. Image courtesy Tourism NSW.

Myall Shores Resort, which has a restaurant, pool and a range of activities and facilities. Tel: 1300 769 566.

Contact information

For more information call the Pacific Palms office on (02) 6591-0300 or visit www.environment.nsw.gov.au/NationalParks.

How to get there

The Namadgi Visitor Centre is 2km south of Tharwa on the Naas Road, around 35km from Canberra.

When to go

Be prepared for cool evenings in summer and snow and sub-zero temperatures in winter.

- January: 12–26°C
- July: 0–10°C

This national park on the southern outskirts of the national capital covers more than half of the ACT. Together with neighbouring Kosciuszko National Park, the Bimberi and Scabby Range nature reserves and Brindabella National Park, Namadgi National Park forms a huge swathe of high country wilderness.

It's always been a place of importance to the local aboriginal people, the Ngunnawal, who called these rugged mountains 'Namadgi' and who have—according to archaeological evidence found at a rock shelter at Birrigai just north of the national park—been living in the area since the last ice age, more than 21,000 years ago. Most likely, they came to these snowy peaks to feast upon the bogong moths that congregate in the rocky crevices each spring.

One of the park's best (and most accessible) rock art sites is at Yankee Hat, named after a nearby mountain that is supposed to look like a colonial American hat. The rock art gallery is in the overhang of a huge weathered granite boulder, its lower sides covered in vibrant white and ochre paintings of human figures, kangaroos, wombats, koalas, dingos and birds. Carbon dating of campsite remains in the shelter show that Aboriginal people began using the shelter more than 800 years ago, and there is even evidence from nearby sites that indicate they were using the area as a campground and gallery as long as 3700 years ago.

The wide open grasslands of Namadgi is one of the best places to see wild kangaroos and the 'Valley of 1000 Kangaroos' in nearby Gudgenby lives up to its descriptive name.

Top tracks and trails

Yankee Hat: easy 6km walk to Yankee Hat rock art site. Great for family trips with kids or grandparents in tow, the trail meanders through open grasslands past mobs of eastern grey kangaroos and along boardwalks skirting the edge of the Bogong Swamp.

Square Rock: 8km return walk through sub-alpine forest and snowgum woodlands to Square Rock, a fantastic outcrop of large boulders and great views of the Tidbinbilla Ranges.

Horse Gully Hut: 16km return walk through the remote Naas Valley.

Best picnic spots

There is a good picnic shelter at Bulls Head, and there are also good picnic facilities near the visitor centre. A personal favourite however, is at Yankee Hat, where you're pretty much guaranteed to see kangaroos, whatever the time of day.

Camping, caravanning and accommodation options

There are three designated campsites within the park: Orroral Valley, Honeysuckle Creek and Mt Clear all have a three-night limit. All have only basic facilities including pit toilets, picnic tables and fireplaces. There are no designated caravan sites, although small campervans are okay at Honeysuckle. Bush camping is allowed anywhere within the park away from roads. Camping permits are required when camping in the Cotter catchment (as it is part of Canberra's water supply), and some areas are totally banned. Permits are available from the Namadgi Visitor Centre.

Contact information

For more information call the Namadgi Visitor Centre on (02) 6207-2900 or visit www.australianalps.deh.gov.au.

Kangaroos on the track to Yankee Hat.

How to get there

The park lies north of the Oxley Highway, between Wauchope, Armidale and Walcha. Apsley Gorge and Tia Falls are just off the Oxley Highway; Dangars Gorge and Falls are 22km south-east of Armidale along the Dangersleigh Road; to get to Wollomombi follow the Waterfall Way 38km east of Armidale.

When to go

During summer you can expect warm days and cool nights; winter nights are frosty and can dip below zero. Weather conditions can change quickly, so always be prepared for the worst.

- January: 13–28°C
- July: 5–12°C

Situated east of Armidale and Walcha, the world-heritage Oxley Wild Rivers National Park encompasses more than 500km of rivers, which fall from the New England Escarpment in spectacular waterfalls then flow through dramatic gorges and valleys to join the mighty Macleay River.

The sixth largest wilderness area in the state with the largest area of dry rainforest in New South Wales, attractions include Wollomombi Falls, which is often quoted as Australia's tallest waterfall, but this is only so if measured from its highest point, where the land has a much gentler gradient and the water does not truly 'fall'. Other falls include Apsley Falls, Tia Falls, Dangars Falls, Gara Falls, Bakers Creek Falls and Chandler Falls.

Top tracks and trails

Apsley Gorge Rim Walk: 30-minute walk around the gorge rim with two fantastic lookouts.

Tia Falls Walk: 45-minute walk to Tia falls lookout. The longer, 5km Tiara walk crosses the Tia River by footbridge and continues along the western side of the gorge, ending at Tiara Lookout.

Wollomombi Walk: this 4km return walk crosses the Wollomombi River and continues around the rim of the gorge to Chandler Falls.

Chandler View Circuit Walk: a two-hour (6km) medium loop walk from the Long Point picnic ground, with views over the Chandler River.

Salisbury Waters Walk: a hard 14km, eight-hour gorge walk from Dangars Falls and along the ridge to Sarum Hill Lookout before descending 500m to Salisbury Waters.

Youdales Hut: 4WD track to a slab-sided mustering hut in the Kunderang Gorges. Access is via Kangaroo Flat Road, (off the Oxley Highway 55km from Walcha). The trail is steep and you'll need to use low range, and trailers are not permitted. Contact the Walcha office for a permit and key.

Best picnic spots

There are more than a dozen good picnic spots throughout the park, almost all boasting knockout views and waterfalls. Best bets include Dangars Gorge and Falls, Wollomombi Falls, Apsley Falls and Tia Falls.

Camping, caravanning and accommodation options

There are eight campgrounds scattered throughout the park. Unpowered (small) caravan camping is available at Tia Falls, Apsley Falls and Green Gully (just off the Waterfall Way) where there are lookouts over the Chandler and Wollomombi Rivers. Youdales Hut and Riverside are both 4WD only and both need a permit and key—contact the Walcha office. Dangars Gorge, Budds Mare and Long Point campgrounds are accessible by 4WD vehicles but campsites are a short walk away from the car park.

Contact information

For more information call the Armidale park office on (02) 6738-9100, the Walcha office on (02) 6777-4700 or visit www.environment.nsw.gov.au/NationalParks.

Apsley Falls.

Wollomombi Falls. Image courtesy Tourism NSW.

Royal National Park

How to get there

The Royal is just south of Sutherland, on the southern outskirts of Sydney. Best access is via the Princes Highway, south of Loftus, or via McKell Avenue at Waterfall. You can also take a ferry from Cronulla to Bundeena. Park gates are locked at 8.30pm each day.

When to go

Temperatures are mild most of the year. Late summer and early autumn can be stormy.

- January: 17–28°C
- July: 6–16°C

Australia's first national park, The Royal National Park is the world's second oldest national park, founded in 1879. (Yellowstone in the USA is seven years older.) Just 32km south of Sydney, the park features a diverse range of flora and fauna, riverside picnic areas, surf beaches, cliff-top heathland walks and rainforest cycle tracks.

The twisting, narrow Lady Wakehurst Drive will take you through the heart of the park, winding through eucalypt forests, over windswept heathlands and across low-level river weirs. Side tracks spear off to beaches and lookouts and there are dozens of great picnic

Lady Wakehurst Drive. Image courtesy Tourism NSW.

and swimming spots along the way. The park is a very popular place on sunny weekends, when traffic snarls can be frustrating. If you can time your visit for a weekday, however, you'll pretty much have the park to yourself.

Top tracks and trails

Bungoona Path: an easy 30-minute walk (wheelchair accessible) to a lookout with great views over the Hacking River.

Forest Path: a 4.5km loop through rainforest. It starts near the southern end of Lady Carrington Drive.

Lady Carrington Drive: one of the park's early carriageways, it's now closed to vehicles and the 10km track is now a great walking track. If possible, arrange a vehicle pick up at one end to avoid retracing your steps.

Curra Moors Loop Track: a good walk to do in spring when the wild heath flowers are blooming. 10km, allow three hours.

Werrong Beach Track: a rather challenging short walk (2km) to a secluded beach. Don't go if nudity offends, however, as it's the only authorised nude bathing area in the park.

Karloo Track: 5km, medium walk to Karloo Pool, a good swimming area.

The Coast Track: two-day 26km coastal walk along the cliffs, beaches and escarpments from Bundeena to Otford. Camp overnight at North Era.

Best picnic spots

There are many picnic spots in the park, but the popular Audley Weir, has gas/electric barbecues, boat hire and a kiosk, as do Garie Beach and the Wattamolla picnic area. For a slightly wilder picnic, head to Bola Creek, Currawong Flat, Iron Back Flat or Warumbul. Governor Game lookout has great views as well as picnic tables.

Camping, caravanning and accommodation options

There are three campgrounds in the park. The largest is Bonnie Vale, which has 74 sites and some good swimming. It's suitable for caravans and facilities include flush toilets and hot showers. North Era and Uloola Falls are both walk-in only, and you'll need to carry in your own drinking water. Bookings are essential at all three and fees are payable in advance. You can also stay at Weemalah Cottage, a three-bedroom house on the shore of the Hacking River. It sleeps eight.

Contact information

For more information call the Sydney South office on (02) 9542-0648 or visit www.environment.nsw.gov.au/NationalParks.

Sturt National Park

How to get there

Sturt National park is 335km north of Broken Hill via the partly paved Silver City Highway and 400km west of Bourke. Tibooburra is the closest town. 4WD is recommended to explore the best of the park. Rain out here is rare, but when it does fall, unsealed roads quickly become rivers of thick, glue-like mud that can be impassable for days, so always check road conditions before setting out. Travelling on roads that have a 'closed road' sign, even if you are in a four-wheel-drive vehicle, may incur a fine of up to $1000.

When to go

Summer temperatures are often well into the 40s, so the best time to visit is during winter, when nights are very cold but days are warm.

- January: 19–37°C
- July: 5–17°C

The far north-western corner of New South Wales is a great introduction to the outback, where endless red dust plains studded with salt bush and mulga seem to stretch on forever under cloudless blue skies, and mobs of kangaroos and emus and cackling galahs are the only signs of life. The most dramatic features of this outback park are the startling jump-ups, flat mesa-like mountains that rise dramatically from the surrounding plains. After rain, the dry plains transform into a sea of green.

A desert dune. Image courtesy Tourism NSW.

Another highlight is Cameron Corner, where New South Wales, South Australia and Queensland meet amongst the red dunes and wide brown gibber plains of the Strezlecki Desert. If you are lucky enough to be here after the rain has been and gone, the dunes are carpeted in yellow and white daisy-like wildflowers. There's not much at Cameron Corner—just the Corner Store on the Queensland side. But like all good corner shops it sells everything—fuel, basic mechanical gear, food supplies, snacks, cold beer and souvenirs. Stop and chat awhile with the owners, who can update you on local road conditions.

Top tracks and trails

The Gorge Loop Road: driving loop around Mt Wood Homestead and shearers quarters, the

Gibber and Mitchell Grass Plains, Twelve Mile Creek Gorge and old pastoral remains.

The Jump-Ups Loop Road: scenic drive with great views of the 150m-high plateau (Mesa) and the granite strewn plains.

Best picnic spots

The four campgrounds each have picnic tables, free gas barbecues and toilets. Personal favourite is Fort Grey where explorer Charles Sturt built a stockade in 1845, although little remains today.

Camping, caravanning and accommodation options

There are four campgrounds in the park and all areas are accessible to caravans and 2WDs via dry-weather dirt roads. Dead Horse Gully is set amongst large granite boulders not far from Tibooburra; Olive Downs is on top of the 'Jump-Up' Range; Fort Grey is in the western part of the park among the sand dunes and near the shores of the ephemeral Lake Pinaroo, and Mount Wood is near historic Mount Wood Homestead on the eastern side of the park. Bring your own water and be aware that no wood fires are permitted in the park. If you are part of a group you can stay at Mount Wood Homestead (up to 15 people) or the shearing quarters (up to 38 people).

Contact information

For more information call the Tibooburra park office on (08) 8091-3308 or visit www.environment.nsw.gov.au/NationalParks.

Sydney Harbour National Park

How to get there

Tours to Fort Denison depart Circular Quay (wharf 6) daily with Matilda Ferries, who also operate a ferry service to Shark Island www.matilda.com.au. To get to Q Station follow North Head Scenic Drive from Manly.

When to go

Temperatures are mild most of the year. Late summer and early autumn can be stormy.

- January: 17–28°C
- July: 5–17°C

Sydney's stunning harbour is a massive drowned valley extending over 55 square kilometres with more than 240km of foreshore. Multi-million dollar apartments and mansions line the water's edge, but the real beauty of Sydney's harbour is that Sydney Harbour National Park protects the islands and vast swathes of foreshore, offering a rare chance to go bush in the heart of the city.

Unpack a picnic at historic Nielsen Park beside Shark Beach where you can swim inside a shark-netted enclosure or follow one of the many walking trails to beautiful beaches and spectacular lookouts.

Take a ferry trip from Circular Quay to the former convict prison island of Fort Denison, once known as 'Pinchgut' due to the meagre rations served there. The round Martello Tower, erected to defend Sydney against a possible attack by Russian warships (which never eventuated), was one of the last to be built in the world.

Spend an afternoon soaking up the views from Shark Island or explore the often tragic history of the Old Quarantine Station (now known as Q Station) near North Head at Manly. Take a walk around South Head for breathtaking clifftop views across the harbour entrance or head to Bradley's Head on the north side for fantastic city and Opera House views.

Top tracks and trails

Manly Scenic Walkway: a four-hour 9.5km coastal walking trail from The Spit to Manly. Highlights include beaches, historic Grotto Point Lighthouse, Aboriginal sites, pockets of subtropical rainforest and sweeping views of the harbour and city skyline.

Hermitage Foreshore Track: 1.5km easy harbourside stroll from Nielsen Park along the western edge of Vaucluse in eastern Sydney. Great views across the harbour and Shark Island.

Bradleys Head and Chowder Head walk: 5km walk from Taronga Zoo wharf following the shoreline to Chowder Head with fantastic city views.

Best picnic spots

There are dozens of great picnic spots in Sydney Harbour National Park where you can watch the world sail by. Favourites include Shark Island, where you usually have the island largely to yourself but you'll need to book, and lovely Neilson Park and nearby Parsley Bay, both of which have netted swimming enclosures, cafe or a kiosk and large grassy picnic areas.

Camping, caravanning and accommodation options

Camping is prohibited in Sydney Harbour National Park. If you really want to camp out in the middle of the harbour you can pitch a tent on the former shipbuilding yard at Cockatoo Island, but it's not exactly a wilderness experience www.cockatooisland.gov.au. The first and second class quarters of the old Quarantine Station have been turned into a stylish hotel. See www.qstation.com.au.

Contact information

For more information call the Sydney office on (02) 9247-5033 or visit the information centre at Cadmans Cottage at Circular Quay for tour bookings and information on how to get to Sydney Harbour islands www.environment.nsw.gov.au/NationalParks.

South Head. Image courtesy Tourism NSW.

Warrumbungle National Park

How to get there

Warrumbungle National Park is 35km west of Coonabarabran.

When to go

The Coonabarabran district enjoys four distinct seasons—hot summers, cold winters, very pleasant autumn and spring, which is the best time to visit. Walking can be very hot in summer. Camping areas are busy during spring and autumn school holidays, Easter and the October long weekend.

- January: 16–32°C
- July: 0–15°C

Warrumbungle means 'crooked mountains' in the Kamilaroi language and this park, one of the state's most popular, has plenty, with forested ridges, rocky spires, domes and deep gorges. Most of the park was once a huge shield volcano and this once restless land has produced some fantastic rock formations, the most famous of all being the Breadknife, a 600m-long, 100m-high sliver of rock that was formed when magma forced its way through a long crack in the bedrock.

The Warrumbungles has some of the country's best, and most adventurous, rock climbing routes. There are four main climbing areas—Crater Bluff, Belougery Spire, Touduron and Bluff Mountain. You'll need to register

The Breadknife, Grand High Tops.

at the visitor centre before you get started. Climbing is permitted everywhere except the Breadknife and Chalkers Mountain.

Expect to see plenty of kangaroos, wallabies and emus; there is also a healthy population of koalas. The park is famous for its clear atmosphere and views of the night sky are exceptional.

Top tracks and trails

Grand High Tops Track: a terrific four-hour (12.5km) walk that involves a long, steep climb up to the base of the Breadknife and beyond to the Grand High Tops, but the panoramic views make the hard slog worthwhile. Recent track upgrades and new staircases make the walk much easier than it used to be. An alternative route back down to Spirey Creek follows the other side of the Breadknife with close-up views of its western face. If you only have time for one walk, make sure this is it.

Fans Horizon: a two-hour walk from Spirey Creek to Balgatan—it has more than 1000 steps so it's not great for those with dodgy knees. The views at the lookout cover most of the Grand High Tops including the Breadknife, Belougery Spire and Crater Bluff.

Whitegum Lookout: easy 1km return wheelchair accessible walk to a lookout. Spectacular at sunset.

Best picnic spots

The Canyon Picnic Area is set in the bush with picnic tables, water, electric barbecues and toilets. It is the starting point for the 1km Wambelong Nature Track, and is good for koala spotting. There are also picnic tables at Whitegum lookout.

Camping, caravanning and accommodation options

Camp Blackman has 70 individual campsites, including 32 powered sites suitable for caravans and motorhomes. Facilities include hot showers, amenities block and shelters with gas/electric barbecues. The much more basic, but usually less crowded, Camp Wambelong is a large, open grassy area (popular with kangaroos) beside the creek and is suitable for caravans, but there are no picnic tables. Camp Walaay has five group sites and bookings are essential. All other campgrounds, including Balor Hut at the base of The Breadknife, are walk-in only and you must register at the visitor centre before setting off. BYO firewood.

Contact information

For more information call the Coonabarabran park office on (02) 6825-4364 or visit www.environment.nsw.gov.au/NationalParks.

Washpool National Park

How to get there

The park straddles the Great Dividing Range approximately halfway between Grafton (93km east) and Glen Innes (78km west). It is almost directly opposite Gibraltar Range National Park on the western side of Gwydir Highway.

When to go

During summer you can expect warm days and cool nights; winter nights are frosty and often dip below zero. Weather conditions can change quickly, so always be prepared for the worst.

- January: 13–24°C
- July: -1–12°C

Part of the Gondwana Rainforests of Australia, this world heritage park has some of the most beautiful cool temperature rainforest in the country. Largely a wilderness area, Washpool National Park features steep gorges and deep-sided valleys, clear boulder-strewn creeks with tumbling waters, moss covered trees, lush ferns and some of the most diverse and least disturbed forest in New South Wales, including the world's largest stand of coachwood trees and beautiful specimens of old growth red cedar.

The four-hour Washpool Walk is one of my favourite short walks, a mini-wilderness trek through gorgeous rainforest that will make you feel like you have entered a whole new world. Most of the walks in the park follow beautiful creeks and offer a cool respite from summer temperatures. There is a range of wilderness walks for experienced, well-equipped walkers.

Keep an eye out for kolas, spotted quolls, wallabies and potoroos. The park is rich in birdlife, including the powerful owl and lyrebirds, their strange calls echoing through the bush during daylight hours. Great mimics, the lyrebird is capable of imitating almost any sound—during our visit to the park they seemed intent on replicating the sound of an unattended car alarm!

Top tracks and trails

Washpool Walk: excellent four-hour walk through the rainforest to Summit Falls and Washpool Lookout. Highlights include beautiful creek-side walking and giant red cedar trees.

Coombadjha Nature Stroll: easy half-hour rainforest loop along the banks of Coombadjha Creek.

Granite Loop Walk: easy 700m walk through dry open forest and rocky granite outcrops to Granite Lookout, which looks out over the densely forested south-east section of the park.

Best picnic spots

Favourite picnic spot is at Coachwood, a lovely rainforest clearing near Coombadjha Creek and starting point for both walks. Facilities include picnic tables, gas/electric barbecues, a wet weather shelter and toilets. The Granites picnic area is close to the Gwydir Highway and has good access to Granite Lookout.

Camping, caravanning and accommodation options

There are two campgrounds in the park; Coombadjha is a walk-in only camp, although it's only a few hundred metres from the car park at the end of Coachwood drive; nearby Bellbird campground has good individual sites suitable for caravans and trailers, although sites can be a bit damp as they do not receive much sun. There is a good cooking shelter with gas/electric barbecues. Most sites also have a wood fireplace and there is usually a good supply of chopped wood available, although in busy times you should bring your own. Beware of fearless scrub turkeys who will raid your food supplies if you turn your back for half a minute.

Contact information

For more information call the Glen Innes park office on (02) 6739-0700 or visit www.environment.nsw.gov.au/NationalParks.

Summit Falls.

Coombadjha Creek. Image courtesy Bill McKinnon.

Werrikimbe and Willi Willi National Parks

How to get there

Werrikimbe is between Wauchope and Walcha in the mid-north coast hinterland. Best access is via Hastings Valley Way from Wauchope. From the west, you can access the park via the Oxley Highway from Walcha. Wilson River in Willi Willi is also accessed via the Hastings Valley Way (52 km from Wauchope).

Crossing the Forbes River.

When to go

These temperatures are for Wauchope, but expect much cooler temperatures in the mountains.

- January: 17–27°C
- July: 5–19°C

If you really want to escape the maddening crowds, then the World Heritage listed Werrikimbe National Park is the place to do it. One of the first high country rainforest parks to be reserved in New South Wales, this is truly a wilderness park and, together with adjoining Willi Willi, Oxley Wild Rivers and Cottan-Bimbang national parks, it protects a huge tract of the pristine rainforests and sub-alpine forests that straddle both the eastern and western sides of the Great Dividing Range.

Top tracks and trails

Waterfall Walk: great 3.6km rainforest walk to a waterfall and pool from the Wilson River picnic area. Keep an eye out for the majestic strangler figs along the way.

King Fern Walk: easy 2km stroll through Antarctic Beech rainforest from the Plateau Beech camping area.

Mooraback Trail: 7km medium walk from the camping area past platypus pools (home to several platypus) before heading to the source of the Hastings River, Racecourse Swamp.

Werrikimbe Trail: a challenging 19km walk through the wilderness from Cobcroft Road to the Racecourse Swamp with several steep sections. You can camp at around the halfway mark, where there is a large grassy area beside a pool on the Hastings River, but no facilities.

Racecourse Trail: a 25km four-wheel-drive track across the top of the park from

The Racecourse Trail.

Mooraback to Brushy Mountain. It's steep and rocky in sections, and the Forbes River crossing can be tricky after rain, when the track can also become very boggy. Highlights of the trail include beautiful forests with fern understoreys, stands of snow gums, and, during spring, masses of blooming heathland flowers and other wildflowers.

Best picnic spots

There is a good picnic area at Cobcroft and at the three campgrounds, but you'll be hard pressed to find a better picnic spot than Wilson River in Willi Willi, where there are two picnic shelters, barbecues, toilets and three walking tracks. The river is a great place to swim and there are still a few red cedar trees that somehow managed to escape the timber getters in the late 19th and early 20th centuries.

Camping, caravanning and accommodation options

Willi Willi is a day use area only, but there are three small campgrounds in Werrikimbe. Brushy Mountain is the largest with 12 large grassy sites set amongst gum trees and has a large cooking shelter. Mooraback is much more basic and has just five sites but it's a good place to see kangaroos and platypus. Plateau Beech has five walk-in sites and is at the start of a walking trail that winds through Antarctic beech forest. None of the campgrounds are suitable for caravans and you'll need to bring your own firewood to all three.

Contact information

For more information call the Port Macquarie park office on (02) 6586-8300 or visit www.environment.nsw.gov.au/NationalParks.

Yuraygir National Park

How to get there

Yuraygir National Park is roughly an hour's drive north of Coffs Harbour (42km) or 45 minutes south of Grafton (39km).

When to go

Temperatures are moderate most of the year. March is usually the wettest month but water temperatures are usually good for swimming from November through to April. Expect crowds in summer and school holidays.

- January: 20–27°C
- July: 10–19°C

Yuraygir National Park protects the longest stretch of undeveloped coastline in New South Wales—60km of rocky headlands, cliff-top lookouts and deserted beaches flanked by wetlands and forests. The Sandon River claims to be the cleanest river in the state and according to the ranger these isolated and empty beaches are one of the few places in the country where you'll see emus on the beach.

Check out the astonishing views from the lookouts at Red Cliff on the headlands south of Lake Arragan and wander the pebbly beach beneath the (you guessed it) red cliffs at low tide, exploring countless rockpools. Launch a canoe and paddle the many lakes and waterways, go for a swim at Illaroo and Sandon beaches, snorkel in the huge rockpools at Sandon Bluff or catch a wave at Angourie, famous for its right-hand point break.

This section of the coast has always been popular with anglers and you can still find collections of fishing shacks that were built before the park was declared in 1980, especially around the mouth of the Sandon River and at Wooli. Best catches include jewfish, drummer, tailor, bream and groper.

Top tracks and trails

Rocky Point Track: 45-minute walk following the coastline from Illaroo camping area to Rocky Point.

Freshwater Track: 4km walk linking the northern end of Pebbly Beach to Freshwater Beach.

Wilsons Headland Walk: one-hour easy walk with fantastic ocean views and great wildflowers in spring.

Angourie Walk: terrific 10km (three hours) coastal walk linking Mara Creek in the north with Lake Arragan in the south. Highlights include the views from Point Dirrigan lookout (watch out for dolphins) and coastal caves on the southern side of Shelley Headland.

Best picnic spots

All the camp grounds also have good picnic facilities and most have easy access to beaches and/or waterways. Angourie Bay and Wilson

Headland are also nice spots to lay out the picnic rug, but you'll need to bring your own stove.

Camping, caravanning and accommodation options

Yuraygir is a popular camping spot, especially in summer, and there are six campgrounds. In the southern section, Pebbly Beach has 60 sites but is 4WD only and Station Creek (good swimming and canoeing) has 20 sites and is suitable for caravans; in the mid-section of the park you can camp at Boorkoom (no caravans) or at the much larger Illaroo campground, which has 60 open sites, gas/electric barbecues and is OK for caravans; just further north is Sandon River, a popular spot with fishos (also OK for small caravans) and in the northern section you can camp on the headland at Lake Arragan and Red Cliffs (65 sites and suitable for caravans) or walk in to Shelly Head (5 sites).

Contact Information

For more information call the Grafton park office on (02) 6641-1500 or visit www.environment.nsw.gov.au/NationalParks.

Sandon Beach.

31

Jervis Bay National Park & Marine Park

This national park 25km south of Nowra fringes Jervis Bay and is rich in Aboriginal heritage and includes wetlands, Lake Wollumboola and borders Booderee National Park. The bay offers beaches, rocky platforms and reefs, extensive sea grass beds, estuaries and deep-water cliffs with caves. Dolphins are often seen in the bay. Scuba diving, swimming, surfing, boating and fishing are all popular in the marine park and it is a great place to take a whale-watching cruise from June to November. Camping is not permitted but you can camp at Green Patch in Booderee National Park.

Jervis Bay. Image courtesy Tourism NSW.

32
Mann River Nature Reserve

You can free camp beside the Mann River at this great little nature reserve at the foot of the 'Big Hill' just off the Old Glen Innes to Grafton Road, a 180km unsealed road that was built in the late 1800s to connect the tablelands and the river port of Grafton. It's unsuitable for caravans and very narrow in places, but a highlight is a 20m tunnel through the rock. The reserve is a terrific place for picnics and cooling off in the large waterholes, although the water can be surprisingly cold and deep.

33
Montague Island Nature Reserve

A granite lighthouse stands sentinel above the island 9km offshore from Narooma, watching over the colonies of Australian and New Zealand fur seals and 8,000 pairs of little penguins that live here. You'll also find crested terns, silver gulls and three different species of shearwaters here during the nesting season and it is a great spot to watch whales between September and November. The National Parks and Wildlife Service (NPWS) run four-hour tours out to the island, where you'll learn about the history of the island and the lighthouse, the Aboriginal heritage and wildlife. Night-time tours include an hour or two of penguin watching. Tours depart Narooma Wharf daily (depending on the weather). You can also stay overnight in the lighthouse keeper's cottage. Tel: (02) 4476-0800 for bookings.

34
Mount Kaputar National Park

The Nandewar Range is a dramatic landscape of volcanic plugs and lava terraces. The highest peak, Mt Kaputar, is 1510m and has superb views from the summit, as do many other lookouts in the park. A highlight is Sawn Rocks, a 40m basalt cliff face featuring perpendicular-octagonal shaped rocks, resembling a giant series of organ pipes. The park is 57km east of Narrabri.

35
New England National Park

A wilderness park 85km east of Armidale on the Waterfall Way featuring world heritage rainforests on the edge of the Great Escarpment. Point Lookout, Banksia Point and Wrights Lookout all offer spectacular wilderness views (although more often than not the lookouts are shrouded in mist) and walks. Three cabins are available for accommodation. Tel: (02) 6657-2309 for bookings.

36
Nightcap National Park

This world heritage rainforest 35km north of Lismore is on the southern edge of the 20 million-year-old Mount Warning volcano. In 1979 a determined group of conservationists saved the rainforest area, including Protestors Falls. There are some beautiful drives to Mt Nardi and Minyon Falls, some great lookouts and numerous good picnic areas. No camping.

New England National Park. Image courtesy Tourism NSW.

37
Wingham Brush Nature Reserve

This nature reserve right in the heart of the town of Wingham near Taree protects a rare patch of remnant of subtropical floodplain rainforest. It is one of the state's most significant maternity sites for the endangered grey-headed flying fox. There's a boardwalk inside the dense thicket of rainforest that winds around huge fig trees and underneath thousands of roosting bat-like creatures hanging upside down from the canopy branches overhead (wear a hat!).

38
Yengo National Park

One of the state's great wilderness parks stretches for more than 70km from Wisemans Ferry to the Hunter Valley. It's a wild area of steep gorges and rocky ridges, part of the Greater Blue Mountains World Heritage area, but the northern section, near Broke, is one of the state's least known and least visited national parks. The 4WD-only Old Settlers and Yengo tracks in the northern section of the park wind their way along the tops of two sandstone ridges above steep rocky gorges. There are some great Aboriginal rock carvings, lots of wildlife and extensive wilderness views.

Rainforest tree at Wingham Brush.

Queensland

Five of Australia's 16 World Heritage listed areas are in Queensland, the 'sunshine state'. Coupled with a varied array of national parks, they make Queensland one of the most naturally diverse places on the planet.

Whether you're looking to camp on an uninhabited tropical island, explore vast underwater coral gardens, negotiate desert dunes, ford swollen rivers and tackle challenging outback tracks, wander through ancient rainforests and discover hidden gorges, learn about Aboriginal culture and heritage or just want to watch the wildlife, there's a national park in Queensland that can provide precisely the type of wilderness experience you're looking for.

Most of Queensland's national parks are free to enter, although camping fees apply in some parks, and many, such as the coastal islands, need to be booked well in advance. You can book most camping spots online. At around $5 per adult per night, Queensland's parks are some of the best value in the country. Some parks, such as the three sand islands (Bribie, Moreton and Fraser) require a vehicle permit, which must be obtained before arriving at the park. Unlike other states, Queensland does not offer park passes for extended touring.

Some parks are very well developed, with (usually cold) showers, wheelchair accessible facilities and free (or coin-operated) gas or electric barbecues; others offer little more than a bush clearing and pit toilets. Not all supply drinking water, so you will need to be self sufficient, carry a fuel stove and you'll usually have to carry out all rubbish with you.

Like the Northern Territory, some parks are extremely remote and can only be accessed by a high clearance four-wheel drive during the dry season, May to October. Always check local road and track conditions with rangers or police before travelling. Be aware that conditions can change rapidly after rain, when flash flooding can close roads for several days.

For more information about parks and reserves in Queensland, call the Queensland Parks and Wildlife Service (QPWS) on 13 13 04 or visit www.epa.qld.gov.au/parks_and_forests.

1 Barron Gorge National Park

How to get there

The upper section of the Barron Gorge National Park is 27km north-west of Cairns, near the village of Kuranda on the Atherton Tableland. The lower section of the park, around Lake Placid, is 19km from Cairns via Kamerunga Road.

When to go

During the wet season, from December to April, there are heavy, frequent downpours. Winter is warm, sunny and dry.

- January: 18–29°C
- July: 10–22°C

Not all national parks are hard to get to. Barron Gorge National Park protects some of the most accessible rainforest close to Cairns in the highlands near Kuranda and can be accessed via tourist railway and cable car from Cairns, as well as by road.

Part of the Wet Tropics World Heritage Area, the Barron River winds 60km across the Atherton Tableland and rainforest before entering the deep sided Barron Gorge, before tumbling over the edge at the 250m-high Barron Falls, which have now been harnessed to supply hydro-electric power and only flow after heavy rain, or by scheduled release. You can take a free tour of the Barron Gorge Hydro-Power Station, which was built in 1935 and was Australia's first underground power station. Tel: (07) 4036-6955 for tour details.

The 34km Kuranda Scenic Railway, one of the most scenic railway lines in the country, was built between 1886 and 1891. It snakes its way up from Cairns climbing more than 300m through tropical rainforest, passing through 15 tunnels, around 98 curves and across 40 bridges and includes a photo stop on the bridge stretching over the Barron River Falls.

The Skyrail cablecar is a spectacular 7.5km journey over the rainforest canopy from the top of the escarpment down to Cairns. Enjoy the view over the gorge and falls from Wright's Lookout or the elevated boardwalk through the forest at Barron Falls lookout.

Top tracks and trails

Barron Falls lookout: wheelchair accessible elevated boardwalk through the rainforest down to the lookout with great views of Barron Falls.

Wrights lookout: an easy 1km walk from the carpark at Barron Falls to Wrights lookout for fantastic views over the Barron Gorge and down to the coast.

Douglas track: follow the trail of the 19th century gold prospectors through the Barron Gorge valley. Named after the native trooper Sub-inspector Douglas, who founded the track in 1876, it was the main access through the

Barron Falls. Image courtesy Tourism Queensland.

valley until the railway line from Cairns to Myola was opened in 1887. Allow between four and six hours each way.

Smiths track: another historical route linking the inland goldfields with the coast, this track features magnificent stands of tall rainforest, exposed ridges with extensive views and open woodlands. It's 9km one-way and there are some very challenging sections.

Best picnic spots

The only picnic facilities in the park are beside Lake Placid, in the lower section of the park, where you can walk along the lake for views of the gorge.

Camping, caravanning and accommodation options

Barron Gorge National Park is day use only, but you can camp in Speewah Conservation Park on the park's western edge. There is a range of accommodation options in Cairns, Kuranda and Mareeba. A favourite is the safari tents overlooking the lily-covered lagoon at Mareeba wetlands. Tel: (07) 4093-2514 or www.mareebawetlands.com.

Contact information

For more information call QPWS on 13 13 04 or visit www.epa.qld.gov.au/parks_and_forests.

How to get there

Brampton Island is 32km north of Mackay. Access is via private boat or via a commercial service operated by Brampton Island Resort.

When to go

Summer can be warm, wet and humid, winter is temperate and drier. December through to February is the best time to see turtles. Stinger season runs every year from October through to May. Swimming is not recommended during this time as Box Jellyfish and the Irukandji Jellyfish are prevalent in the waters and their stings can cause acute pain and serious illness. Box jellyfish can cause death in previously well humans in as little as three minutes.

- January: 23–30°C
- July: 13–21°C

Brampton Islands National Park, 32km off-shore from Mackay at the southern end of the famous Whitsunday Island Passage, is part of the Cumberland Group of Islands and consists of Brampton and Carlisle Islands.

Brampton Island, the larger of the two islands, has 12 long sandy beaches—seven being easily accessible via walking trails—and clear, shallow water full of colourful fish and coral. Turtles feed in the surrounding marine park waters and the islands are important turtle rookeries.

There is a resort on Brampton, but neighbouring Carlisle Island is entirely national park. You can walk between the islands during low tide and the resort offers their guests guided tours (by boat) as well. Highlights include rainforest and melaleuca stands in the island's interior.

The resort also runs a range of guided tours including a variety of cruises around the twin islands. One of the more popular is the two-hour Sunset Champagne and Cheese Cruise, where you'll often see dolphins, or if you're really lucky, whales, as you toast the sunset before dinner back at the resort.

Top tracks and trails

Brampton Island circuit: a fairly easy two-hour walk into beautiful rainforest, along most of the beaches of the island and to lookouts with spectacular views of the Whitsunday Passage.

Brampton Peak: allow three hours return to the resort for the climb up the island's highest point (214m above sea level). There's some steep sections but the views are worth it.

Carlisle Island crossing: it will take around 40 minutes to wade across to Carlisle Island at low tide: make sure you leave enough time to get back before the tide turns.

Best picnic spots

Pick a beach, any beach. If you want tables and toilets, head to the campground on Carlisle Island or Western Bay and Dinghy Bay West on Brampton.

Camping, caravanning and accommodation options

You can camp at Western Bay (eight sites) on Brampton and on Carlisle (12 sites). Neither area has any facilities other than toilets and tables and there is no public access to the Brampton Island resort for non-guests so make sure you have adequate supplies. Bookings are essential.

Brampton Island resort has a range of room styles; the best are the Ocean View Rooms. They are right on the beach, and have all the mod cons you would expect (king-size bed, flat screen TV, DVD and CD player, espresso machine) but the pièce de résistance is the hammock on the patio—who needs anything more? There's a spa, restaurant and a range of activities and watersports.

Contact information

For more information call QPWS on 13 13 04 or visit www.epa.qld.gov.au/parks_and_forests. For information on Brampton Island Resort visit www.brampton-island.com or call 1300 134 044.

Views along the Brampton Island circuit walk. Image courtesy Voyages resorts.

Brampton Island. Image courtesy Voyages resorts.

Carnarvon Gorge, Carnarvon National Park

How to get there

Carnarvon Gorge is 740km north-west of Brisbane via Roma. The last 23km section of the road is unsealed and can become impassable after rain.

When to go

Best time to visit is the cooler months between April and October.

- January: 21–35°C
- July: 6–23°C

The Moss Garden.

An oasis in the semi-arid heart of Queensland between Roma and Emerald, Carnarvon Gorge is a steep-sided gorge of towering white sandstone cliffs with lush side gorges full of hanging gardens of mosses and ferns, icy swimming holes and sinuously curved ravines with walls so close you can reach out and touch both sides of the gorge at once.

Boulder-strewn Carnarvon Creek winds through the gorge and the sandstone overhands are decorated with some of the finest Aboriginal rock art in the country including rock engravings, ochre stencils and freehand paintings at Cathedral Cave, Baloon Cave and the Art Gallery.

Top tracks and trails

Boolimba Bluff: from the visitors centre at the main entrance to the park, you can follow the 3km Boolimba Bluff track, one of the few easily accessible lookout tracks, climbing to the top of the 200m high cliffs that form the walls of the gorge. It's a hot, steep walk and best done in the morning.

The Moss Garden: water drips down the sandstone walls of a natural amphitheatre, transforming the walls into a hanging garden of mosses, ferns and liverworts. Beyond the wallpaper carpet of green is a waterfall, surrounded by tree ferns. 7km return.

Ward's Canyon: a short climb leads to a hidden

gully full of the largest fern in the world, the ancient King Fern. A short, steep track winds around a small waterfall. 9.2km return.

The Art Gallery: under an overhanging rock face is an ancient Aboriginal rock gallery adorned with more than 2000 engravings, ochres stencils and free-hand paintings. Beneath the art is an excellent interpretive display that explains its significance. 10.8km return.

Boowinda Gorge: just beyond Cathedral Cave is one of the Gorge's least visited spots, but also one of its most spectacular—the curving sculpted side gorge of Boowinda. There's no track, so you'll need to rock hop, but it is quite different to the rest of Carnarvon Gorge as the walls close in ever tighter, until finally you can reach out and touch both sides at once.

Ancient art at The Art Gallery.

Best picnic spots

There's another staggering display of rock art at Cathedral Cave, where there are picnic tables under the shade of the overhang—a great place to unwrap your picnic lunch. The return trip is 18.2km. There are also very welcome picnic tables and a toilet at Big Bend, the end of the walking track.

Camping, caravanning and accommodation options

You can camp in the visitor area only during the Easter, June/July and September/October Queensland school holidays. Bookings are essential. A small hike-in camping area is located at Big Bend, 9.6km from the information centre.

Carnarvon Gorge Wilderness Lodge, just outside the park entrance, has air-conditioned safari tents, complete with ensuite and shady verandah and a licensed restaurant. Tel: (07) 4984-4503 or visit www.carnarvon-gorge.com.

Contact information

For more information call QPWS on 13 13 04 or visit www.epa.qld.gov.au/parks_and_forests.

4 Chillagoe-Mungana Caves National Park

How to get there

Chillagoe is 215km west of Cairns. The road is sealed except for the last 16km, which may become impassable after rain. The park is spread over the Chillagoe area; the Royal Arch Cave is 7km south-west of Chillagoe while the Donna, Pompeii, Bauhinia and Trezkinn caves are 1.5km from the centre of town. Another cave, The Archways, is at Mungana, 15km north-west of Chillagoe.

When to go

The best time to visit is the cooler months between April and October. Winter is usually dry, summer can be very hot and humid.

- January: 21–33°C
- July: 10–27°C

Chillagoe limestone outcrops.

There are more than 600 limestone caves in the Chillagoe area, and the only place in tropical north Queensland where you'll find richly decorated caves. 450 million years ago the entire area around Chillagoe was covered by an inland sea, rich in coral. When sea levels dropped, and the earth crust shifted, the limestone and coral reefs began to buckle and bulge, forming the rocky outcrops and bluffs that stud the landscape around the town.

Meanwhile, remaining limestone has been weathered, dissolved and reformed by water to create spectacular caverns and passages, decorated by stalactites, stalagmites and flowstones. There are five caves open for viewing, each one unique in its own way. The Royal Arch cave is the biggest, a series of 13 chambers spread along a 1.5km passage with roots from trees and patches of light reaching into the caves and lots of bending and squeezing through tight passages. The smaller Donna Cave, accessed by a long steep stairway, is the prettiest, with dozens of magnificent limestone formations. If you are pressed for time Trezkinn Cave is quite short, basically a steel catwalk encircling a central mass of limestone, but it also has lots of decorations, including the massive 'chandelier', a spectacular formation that really does look like a mountain of melted wax. There are also two self-guided caves, but you will need to bring your own torch.

Inside Chillagoe Caves. Image courtesy Tourism Queensland.

Top tracks and trails

Balancing Rock: a short walk up to a rock formation called Balancing Rock, which is just as is sounds—a huge boulder balancing precariously on its point, looking set to tumble at the first hint of a breeze onto unsuspecting sightseers below.

The Archways: 15km beyond town is an open daylight self-guided cave system with maidenhair ferns growing in the passageways and an Aboriginal art site with a number of interesting paintings on the cave walls. Allow 45 minutes.

Best picnic spots

There are picnic tables at Donna and Royal Arch car parks and at the Mungana Aboriginal art site.

Camping, caravanning and accommodation options

No camping is permitted in the national park, but there is a range of accommodation available in Chillagoe. Best bet is Chillagoe Observatory and Eco Lodge, which has a licensed restaurant, campground with powered sites and observatory that runs guided tours of the night sky, weather permitting. Tel: (07) 4094-7155.

Contact information

For more information call QPWS on 13 13 04 or visit www.epa.qld.gov.au/parks_and_forests. Buy your cave tickets at The Chillagoe Hub, which also features displays on the geology and history of the area, 23–24 Queen Street, Chillagoe. www.chillagoehub.com.au.

How to get there

Conway National Park is approximately 30km east of Proserpine.

When to go

Best time to visit is the cooler months between April and October. Summer is the wet season and high humidity can make walking uncomfortable. Conway State Forest is closed during the wet season, November through to April. Marine stingers are present in the coastal waters between October and May.

- January: 22–31°C
- July: 11–24°C

Along with the adjoining Conway State Forest, Conway National Park is a wild and undeveloped area of dense tropical rainforest and ragged peaks with steep, rocky cliffs, mangroves, damp gullies, pretty creeks and coastal ridges overlooking the scenic Whitsunday Passage.

Birdlife is prolific, including the Australian brush turkey and the orange-footed scrubfowl and you'll see their large mounds everywhere. Keep an eye out for the endangered Proserpine rock-wallaby and the brilliant blue flashes of Ulysses butterflies.

A highlight is swimming in the crystal clear cool water below Cedar Creek Falls at the edge of Conway National Park, where a 12m high waterfall cascades into a beautiful

Cedar Creek Falls. Image courtesy Tourism Queensland.

plunge pool and long-necked turtles poke their heads above the surface to check you out as they float by.

Top tracks and trails

Whitsunday Great Walk: the 30km, three-day walk winds through Conway State Forest, starting at Brandy Creek and finishing at Airlie Beach. It follows sections of old logging roads, at times weaving through giant stands of strangler figs and tulip oaks. Highlights include panoramic views of Shute Harbour, Connonvale and the Whitsunday Islands, majestic stands of Alexandra palms, seasonal creeks and pools surrounded by lush tropical rainforest. It has some long, steep sections and can be very slippery when wet.

Kingfisher Circuit: a moderate 2km return walk in Conway State Forest through beautiful rainforest as you wind down into a moist valley.

Mt Rooper: spectacular Whitsunday Passage and island views from the lookout (2.4km). A 2km-long track connects to the Swamp Bay track where open forest gives way to lowland rainforest and a lookout over Swamp Bay. Keep an eye out for interpretive signs that detail how Aboriginals used many of the plants in this area.

Coral Beach track: a popular 2km loop from the Coral Beach carpark, about 4km east from Conway National Park picnic area along Shute Harbour Road and Whitsunday Drive. For good views across the Whitsunday Passage climb the 700m up to The Beak lookout at the beach's south-eastern end.

Best picnic spots

Conway picnic ground has wheelchair accessible toilets and electric barbecues—the gates are opened at 7.30am and locked at 6pm. There are also picnic facilities at Swamp Creek.

Camping, caravanning and accommodation options

The only camping site within the national park is a walk-in bush camp beside the pebble and coral beach at Swamp Bay. Overlooking Daydream (West Molle) Island, it's a 2km walk from the Swamp Bay/Mt Rooper carpark. Take a fuel stove for cooking, as open fires are not permitted and no drinking water is provided, so make sure you bring your own. There are also four walk-in campsites along the Whitsunday Great Walk in neighbouring Conway State Forest. A wide range of accommodation to suit all budgets is available in nearby Airlie Beach.

Contact information

For more information call QPWS on 13 13 04 or visit www.epa.qld.gov.au/parks_and_forests.

How to get there

The park is split into two sections: Mossman Gorge, near the town of Mossman 80km north of Cairns; Cape Tribulation, 138km north of Cairns. The Daintree River ferry operates daily (except Christmas Day and Good Friday (6am-midnight). Roads may be closed after heavy rain.

When to go

During the wet season, from December to April, there are heavy, frequent downpours. Stinger season runs every year from October through to May and swimming is not recommended during this time as Box Jellyfish and the Irukandji Jellyfish stings can cause acute pain and serious illness, even death. Winter is warm, sunny and dry.

- January: 23–37°C
- July: 16–30°C

There are two main reasons that thousands of visitors head to Far North Queensland (FNQ) each year: the rainforest and the reef. The World Heritage Wet Tropics area covers around 900,000 hectares of rainforest wilderness along the eastern escarpment of the Great Dividing Range between Townsville and Cooktown. At Cape Tribulation, north of Port Douglas, two world heritage areas come together when the reef meets the rainforest

along the coast making this area one of the best places to access the reef.

Mossman Gorge cuts through dense rainforest and is one of the most popular spots in the Wet Tropics World Heritage Area. Part of the traditional lands of the Kuku Yalanji people, the park is also home to a prolific range of birdlife, the vivid Ulysses butterfly, freshwater turtles and platypus in the creeks. Take care around the water as the boulders are often slippery and the river is fast flowing.

Cape Tribulation is the coastal section of the park and features a variety of habitats including rainforests, mangroves and swamps. It has several boardwalks that are wheelchair accessible. Although the beaches are beautiful, swimming is not recommended here as estuarine crocodiles live in the park's creeks and nearby coastal waters.

Top tracks and trails

Mossman Gorge: a 2.5km loop that crosses a suspension bridge over the river and leads through the rainforest to several riverside picnic spots. Along the way you'll find interpretation boards that provide information on rainforest plants and their uses by the Kuku Yalanji people.

Boardwalks: there are four wheelchair accessible boardwalks through the rainforest and mangroves in the Cape Tribulation section of the park, all of which include interpretation

Mossman Gorge. Image courtesy Tourism Queensland.

A Cassowary.

Footbridge over Mossman Gorge. Image courtesy Tourism Queensland.

boards and are a great way to explore the wet forests and swamps without getting your feet wet. The Dubuji and Kulki boardwalks lead out to beautiful Myall Beach.

Mt Sorrow Ridge Walk: a steep and difficult 7km return (allow six to seven hours) climb to a lookout over the coast.

Best picnic spots

Mossman Gorge has a number of good riverside picnic areas and there are picnic facilities at Jindalba, Dubuji and Kulki boardwalks in the Cape Tribulation section. All three sites have toilets and picnic tables. Dubuji has barbecue facilities.

Camping, caravanning and accommodation options

Camping is prohibited at Mossman Gorge, but you can camp at Noah Beach around 8km south of Cape Tribulation. The small sites are unsuitable for caravans or larger campervans. There is plenty of commercial accommodation available in Mossman and Cape Tribulation villages.

Contact information

For more information call QPWS on 13 13 04 or visit www.epa.qld.gov.au/parks_ and_forests.

Cape Tribulation. Image courtesy Tourism Queensland.

Eungella National Park

How to get there

Eungella National Park is around 80km west of Mackay. The road up the Clarke Range is very steep and not suitable for caravans. The Finch Hatton Gorge access road involves crossing several low-level causeways, so take care after rain.

When to go

The best time to visit is the cooler months between April and October. The best time of day to see platypus at Broken River is the early morning or late afternoon.

- January: 23–30°C
- July: 13–21°C

Drawing its name from an Aboriginal word meaning 'Land of the Clouds' Eungella's (pronounced *yun-galah*) mist-shrouded and forest-clad mountains contain Australia's longest and oldest stretch of sub-tropical rainforest, ranging over 51,700 hectares.

Split into two sections, above and below the ranges, both sections are well worth visiting. Finch Hatton Gorge, just a few minutes west of Pinnacle in the Pioneer Valley, is part of the lowlands section and features two delightfully icy swimming holes fed by waterfalls. The highland section is a rainforest-clad plateau, usually several degrees cooler than the coast, and has some fantastic short walks, most of which feature spectacular views. If you only

have time for one, make it the 10-minute Sky Window walk that leads to a stunning lookout over the valley below.

But the main reason most people come to Eungella is to see the platypus at Broken River. There are several viewing platforms strung out along the river near the picnic area, or you can simply find a comfortable rock and perch for as long as you like. Locals like to boast that it is one of the most reliable places 'on the planet' to see platypus in the wild, and they are probably right, as the river is home to dozens of the elusive and often hard-to-spot monotremes.

Top tracks and trails

Araluen Cascades Track: an easy 90-minute return walk from the Finch Hatton Gorge picnic area through lush rainforest to a lookout above Araluen Cascades, a great place to cool off with a swim.

Wheel of Fire Track: continue on from the Araluen Cascades Track to a large rock pool, also good for swimming. It will take around two hours return.

Rainforest Discovery Circuit: an easy 20-minute loop through the rainforest near the Broken River picnic area.

Crediton Creek Track: a lovely 6km one-way walk with riverside sections (watch for platypus), rainforest gullies and rocky ridges.

The Mackay Highlands Great Walk: a 56km, five-day challenging walk linking Eungella and

Homevale National Parks and passing through Crediton State Forest.

Best picnic spots

You'll be hard pressed to find a better view than that at the Sky Window near Eungella township. The picnic area has wheelchair-accessible toilets and picnic tables. There are picnic tables and barbecues at Broken River and a shady picnic area (no barbecues) at Finch Hatton Gorge.

Camping, caravanning and accommodation options

Fern Flat campground in the rainforest on the western side of the Broken River picnic area is walk-in only. For those who like a little more luxury, the Broken River Mountain Resort offers comfortable motel-style cabins within easy walking distance of platypus viewing areas, as well as a pool and licensed restaurant. Tel: (07) 4958-4000 or visit www.brokenrivermr.com.au.

Contact information

For more information call QPWS on 13 13 04 or visit www.epa.qld.gov.au/parks_and_forests.

Platypus at Broken River. Image courtesy Tourism Queensland.

Araluen Falls. Image courtesy Tourism Queensland.

8 Fraser Island, Great Sandy National Park

How to get there

Fraser Island is around 300km north of Brisbane and 15km off the coast of Hervey Bay and Maryborough. Access is via barge at Inskip Point on the northern end of Rainbow Beach and River Heads or ferry from Urangan Boat Harbour. All roads on the island are 4WD only. There are a number of tours available or you can self drive with 4WD hire available on the island and in nearby Hervey Bay.

When to go

Summer can be hot, wet and humid; winter is typically dry with very little rain.

- January: 22–32°C
- July: 9–23°C

The largest sand island in the world, 123km long and 22km wide, Fraser Island is a world heritage wilderness with towering rainforest, massive sandblows, beautiful freshwater lakes and continuous beach. It is the only place in the world where tall rainforests are found growing on sand dunes at elevations above 200m and has half the world's perched dune lakes (there are 40 on the island), lakes formed when organic matter, such as leaves, bark and dead plants, gradually builds up and hardens in depressions created by the wind.

One of the most popular sites is Lake McKenzie, with white sand and clear, blue water it offers fantastic swimming. Lake Wabby, at the advancing edge of the Hammerstone Sandblow, is the deepest lake on the island. Eli Creek is a crystal clear freshwater creek

Wanggoolba Creek. Image courtesy Kingfisher Bay Resort.

that flows right out to the beach and is a very popular place to swim as you can walk the boardwalk then float with the current to the beach. The wreck of the Maheno lies slowly deteriorating on the water's edge, about 10km north of Happy Valley. The trans-Tasman liner, bound for a Japanese wrecking yard, was driven ashore during a cyclone in 1935.

Waddy Point headland at the northern tip of Ocean Beach offers great views of beach and ocean and you can often see sea turtles, sharks and stingrays in the water below. Champagne Pools, where the surf crashes over a series of rock walls into a calm but bubbly rock pool below the headland, is another popular swimming spot.

The dingo population on Fraser island is regarded as the most pure strain of dingos remaining in eastern Australia. It is one of the best places to see humpback whales; they stop here on their trip south to Antarctica taking advantage of the calm waters.

Top tracks and trails

Fraser Island Great Walk: a 90km track that winds between Dilli Village and Happy Valley, passing iconic sites such as Lake McKenzie, Wanggoolba Creek, Lake Wabby and Central Station, as well as some of the islands most popular spots like the Valley of the Giants.

Central Station: there are several good short walks though the rainforest including the Wanggoolba Creek boardwalk along a creek with water so clear it is almost invisible.

Lake Wabby: you can walk across the sanddunes to Ocean Beach, but the shadeless

Aerial of Lake McKenzie. Image courtesy Kingfisher Bay Resort.

Eli Creek. Image courtesy Kingfisher Bay Resort.

white sands makes for a very hot walk in summer—go early in the morning, carry lots of water and allow around four hours return.

Central Lakes Scenic Drive: (30km, around two hours) meanders through tall open forest. Highlights include Pile Valley's impressive stand of tall, straight satinay trees, Lake McKenzie and Lake Wabby lookout for a view of Lake Wabby and Stonetool Sandblow. In peak periods (summer holidays and Easter) the road through Lake McKenzie can become very congested and parking may not be available. Plan to arrive at Lake McKenzie before 10.30am or after 2.30pm, otherwise there may be delays.

Best picnic spots

There are countless fantastic picnic spots scattered all over the island, but favourites include Central Station, Lake McKenzie and Champagne Pools.

Camping, caravanning and accommodation options

Fraser Island has eight campgrounds: Central Station, Dundubara and Waddy Point, Lake Boomanjin, Waddy Point beachfront, Ungowa, Lake Allom and Wathumba. Each has water and toilets and most have gas barbecues. Generators are not permitted. There are informal camping areas with no facilities behind the dunes on Eastern Beach and Western Beach offering quiet, wilderness experiences. There are also small, walk-in camping areas along the Fraser Island Great Walk set away from main campgrounds but they have few facilities. Dingos are a threat to young children. If you are camping with children under the age of 14 camp only in fenced campgrounds, available at Lake Boomanjin, Central Station, Dundubara, Waddy Point (top campground) and Dilli Village.

Kingfisher Bay Resort includes a 152-room, four-star hotel, 110 self-contained villas and a 180-bed Wilderness Lodge for backpackers and groups. The resort also offers a range of 4WD and guided eco-tours of the island and daily activities such as nature walks, bush-tucker talks and night-time animals spotting. For Kingfisher Bay resort visit www.kingfisherbay.com.au.

Contact information

For more information call QPWS on 13 13 04 or visit www.epa.qld.gov.au/parks_and_forests.

How to get there

Hinchinbrook Island is 8km east of Cardwell off the north Queensland coast, roughly halfway between Cairns and Townsville. Get there by water taxi from Cardwell and Dungeness (Lucinda) or via Hinchinbrook Island Ferries (also from Cardwell) which has scheduled services as well as day cruises on Sunday, Wednesday and Friday. Visit www.hinchinbrookferries.com.au. If you are staying at Hinchinbrook Island Wilderness Lodge the lodge can organise flight transfers from Cairns or Townsville.

When to go

Summer is very wet and humid. Heavy rain can fall between December and April. Winter is warm and sunny and much drier. Stinger season runs every year from October through to May. Swimming is not recommended during this time as Box Jellyfish and the Irukandji Jellyfish are prevalent in the waters and their stings can cause acute pain and serious illness. Box jellyfish can cause death in previously well humans in as little as three minutes.

- January: 23–32°C
- July: 14–25°C

A beautiful tropical island, Australia's largest island national park features lush rainforests, rocky headlands and beautiful sandy beaches. Much of the interior is mountainous—the highest peak Mt Bowen is 1121m high and usually shrouded in clouds, while lowlands are covered with extensive stands of mangroves.

With no development on the island, apart from a low-key resort at the northern tip, Hinchinbrook is truly an island wilderness. Surrounded by marine park waters, the fringing reefs and seagrass beds are home to a variety of marine life including dugong and green turtles, while saltwater crocodiles can be found in the inland rivers and coastal waters. Birdlife is prolific, particularly waders.

Top tracks and trails

The Thorsborne Trail: named after local naturalists Margaret and Arthur Thorsborne, this spectacular 32km trail along the east

The peaks of Hinchinbrook Island. Image courtesy Tourism Queensland.

coast of the island from Ramsay Bay to George Point will take at least three days and is for well-equipped and experienced hikers only. Only 40 walkers are allowed on the trail at any one time so you must book at least 12 months in advance during school holidays. (Tel: 13 13 04 or visit www.epa.qld.gov.au.)

Best picnic spots

Cape Richards on the very northern tip of the island is a superb place to watch the sun set.

Camping, caravanning and accommodation options

There are a number of bush camps on Hinchinbrook Island, but you'll need to book well in advance as numbers are limited. One of the most popular spots, Macushla (it can be directly accessed by ferry) is set amongst casuarina trees and overlooks Missionary Bay, Mt Bowen and Goold Island, although all campsites are superbly located. You can also camp at Goold Island, just a few kilometres north of Hinchinbrook Island (also accessible by ferry) on a long sheltered beach with views towards Dunk and the Family Group of Islands. It's a great, though remote, spot for oyster gathering, fishing and swimming. Facilities at both campgrounds include picnic tables and chairs, free gas barbecue, shelter shed, water tank and toilet.

At the northern end of the island, Hinchinbrook Island Wilderness Lodge offers high-end accommodation in beach cabins and treetop bungalows. Visit www.hinchinbrookresort.com.au.

Contact information

For more information call QPWS on 13 13 04 or visit www.epa.qld.gov.au/parks_and_forests.

Hikers at Ramsay Bay. Image courtesy Tourism Queensland.

How to get there

There are two entrances to the park. The Green Mountains entrance is 115km south of Brisbane via Canungra; or 70km from Surfers Paradise via Nerang and Canungra. Or you can enter via the Binna Burra section, which is 107km from Brisbane via Canungra and 55km from the Gold Coast. Both routes are fully sealed, but the road to Green Mountains is too steep and winding for caravans.

When to go

Summer is temperate, with the ranges being much cooler than the coast. Winter is more likely to be dry and sunny as most rain falls over the summer, although you can expect showers at any time of the year. Extreme winter temperatures can get below zero degrees Celsius.

- January: 17–26°C
- July: 8–17°C

Protecting one of the largest remaining tracts of subtropical rainforest in Australia, Lamington is part of the Scenic Rim, a chain of mountains stretching across the Queensland-New South Wales border with a spectacular landscape of cliffs, gorges and waterfalls and panoramic views.

Declared a national park in 1915 and part of the Gondwana Rainforests of Australia World Heritage Area, the park features stands of 15,000-year-old Antarctic beech trees and more than 160km of walking tracks.

Top tracks and trails

Treetops Canopy Walk: a 20m-high suspended walk amongst the rainforest canopy was the first of its kind to be built in Australia. It's at O'Reillys Guesthouse in the Green Mountain section of the park.

Bellbird Lookout: a 2km walk through rainforest to a natural lookout above a very high, steep cliff.

Border Track: this 22km track forms the backbone of most of the trails in the park and connects Binna Burra and Green Mountains. It's a difficult track but rewarding as it winds its way through rainforest and patches of Antarctic beech forest with lookouts along the way providing spectacular views of the Lamington area, Mt Warning and the Tweed Range.

Albert River Circuit: 20km loop with waterfalls, stunning temperate rainforest featuring Antarctic Beech and Coachwood and great views into northern New South Wales.

Box Forest Circuit: 11km (four-hour) walk featuring enormous 1500-year-old Brush Box trees, beautiful creek scenery, swimming holes and waterfalls, including Elabana Falls.

Coomera Circuit: 18km track to lots of waterfalls including Coomera, one of the most spectacular in the park.

Best picnic spots

The picnic area at Green Mountains has toilets, tables and electric coin-operated barbecues, but it gets very busy during holidays and weekends, so bring your own fuel stove and fold up chairs as a back up. There are also picnic facilities at the end of the Binna Burra road next to the main track entrance.

Camping, caravanning and accommodation options

You can camp in the Green Mountains section of Lamington National Park (facilities include drinking water, toilets and hot showers) and you can bush camp (walk-in only) in the park between February and November. All campsites must be booked and paid for three weeks in advance through the Green Mountains office or at www.epa.qld.gov.au. Binna Burra Lodge has resort accommodation as well as powered and unpowered caravan sites. Tel: 1800 074 260 or visit www.binnaburralodge.com.au.

O'Reilly's Guesthouse offers accommodation as well as restaurant and bar facilities that are open to day visitors. Tel: 1800 688 722 or visit www.oreillys.com.au.

Contact information

For more information call QPWS on 13 13 04 or visit www.epa.qld.gov.au/parks_and_forests.

Elabana Falls. Image courtesy Tourism Queensland.

Treetops Canopy Walk.

11 Lawn Hill (Boodjamulla) National Park

How to get there

Lawn Hill is 340km north-west of Mt Isa, 220km south-west of Burketown, or 425km north-west of Cloncurry. The Burketown route and the last 280km of the Mt Isa route are unsealed and become impassable after rain and are best negotiated with a four-wheel-drive.

When to go

Best time to visit Lawn Hill is during the cooler, dry season—April to early October. Daytime temperatures can be very hot and nights can be very cold.

- January: 24–36°C
- July: 12–28°C

Surrounded in every direction by grassy flatlands, the palm-filled lushness of Lawn Hill National Park in Queensland's western Gulf country comes as a bit of a surprise for most travellers. Once a tropical wetland region, the ancient sandstone and limestone has been gradually stripped away over millions of years leaving behind rugged escarpments, gorges and rocky outcrops with sheer red sandstone walls up to 60m high that drop into palm-filled creeks and permanent waterholes.

The vegetation is tropical—think water lilies, cabbage-tree palms and figs; the waters full of freshwater crocodiles and northern snapping turtles. Hire a canoe from the camping area and float for four kilometres on the calm green waters of the gorge, keeping an eye out for red-winged parrots, egrets, bitterns, kites and lazy freshwater crocodiles basking in the sun. Indari Falls is a great place to stop for a swim.

Also part of the park, Riversleigh World Heritage Site is one of the richest fossil sites in the world. The fossils here cover a mind-boggling period from 25 million to 10,000 years ago, and include the fossil remains of giant pythons, carnivorous kangaroos and marsupial lions. Public access to the World Heritage Area is restricted to Riversleigh's D Site about 75km from the park entrance. Read about the fossils in the information shelter then follow a self-guided interpretive trail, although it does take a bit of imagination to picture the giant marsupials and strange beasts described from the fragments of bones that are embedded in the limestone hillside.

Top tracks and trails

Island Stack: a 4km, one-hour walk that starts with a steep climb before opening up to a circular track that loops round the flat 'table-top' of a large island of rock in the heart of the gorge. This is the best walk for views. You can also add on a short half-hour walk to the Cascades, a delightful pandanus-fringed pool and shallow waterfall.

Explore Lawn Hill Gorge by canoe. Image courtesy Tourism Queensland.

Wild Dog Dreaming Walk: a two-hour walk along a semi-sheltered track to the lower gorge where you'll see plenty of crocs, several Aboriginal rock art sites and midden heaps.

Best picnic spots

There are picnic facilities at the campground at Lawn Hill Creek.

Camping, caravanning and accommodation options

In Lawn Hill National Park you can camp near Lawn Hill Creek (not suitable for caravans). Facilities include toilets and cold showers, and bookings are essential between Easter and October. Adels Grove is a privately-run campground 10km from the park entrance. Each camping/van site is provided with water, fireplace and barbecue plate, but no power. During June, July and August you'll need to book ahead. Visit www.adelsgrove.com.au. Camping is not allowed at Riversleigh.

Contact information

For more information call QPWS on 13 13 04 or visit www.epa.qld.gov.au/parks_and_forests.

Moreton Island National Park

How to get there

Moreton Island is 40km by ferry or barge from Brisbane. All roads on the island are four-wheel-drive only and all vehicles must have an access permit, available from www.epa.qld.gov.au or the barge operator. See the website for barge departure points.

When to go

Summer can be warm and humid, winter is temperate and drier.

- January: 17–25°C
- July: 9–15°C

The Lighthouse Track. Image courtesy Tourism Queensland.

The most natural of the large sand islands in Moreton Bay, most of the 38km-long Moreton Island is national park. Highlights are freshwater creeks and lakes, coastal heathlands, rocky headlands, paperbark swamps, an historic lighthouse and the ruins of coastal forts. Mt Tempest, the highest sand dune on the island, is the highest stable coastal sand dune in the southern hemisphere. Migrating wading birds flock to the island between September and April, nesting turtles occasionally come ashore in summer and watch for migrating humpback whales in late winter and spring.

A popular holiday spot, activities include sand boarding (the big sandhills reach up to 80m in height and speeds have been clocked up to 50km per hour), quad biking on the specially designed course in the dunes near Tangalooma resort, four-wheel driving and wreck snorkelling at Tangalooma, where 15 hulks were scuttled to form a small craft anchorage, and Curtin Artificial Reef (the scuttled wrecks of 19 vessels and one tram) home to giant Queensland gropers, tusk and parrotfish.

You can hand-feed wild dolphins at Tangalooma Wild Dolphin Resort each evening. The dolphins, varying in numbers from five to nine, swim into the shallow, well-lit area adjacent to the resort jetty to be hand fed their favourite fish.

The island is also a favourite with anglers and the famous 'Tailor Run' occurs from

Cape Moreton Lighthouse. Image courtesy Tourism Queensland.

August to December as the fish migrate north for breeding then run back down along the beaches.

Top tracks and trails

Mount Tempest lookout: it's a steep climb to the top of Mt Tempest, but the views are worth it. On a good day you'll get panoramic views of Moreton island, Moreton Bay and beyond to the Glass House Mountains on the mainland. Allow two hours return and take lots of water.

Rous Battery track: a 10km (one way) walk to the remnants of a World War II fort in the dunes and the only walk on the southern end of the island.

Best picnic spots

Unpack a picnic (BYO rug or chairs) near Queensland's first lighthouse, built in 1857 at Cape Moreton, where you might be lucky enough to see whales between June and November.

Dolphin feeding at Tangalooma Resort. Image courtesy Tourism Queensland.

Camping, caravanning and accommodation options

There are five campgrounds and four camping zones along the beach and most are accessible for off-road caravans and camper trailers (apart from The Wrecks, which is walk-in only and popular with school groups, and North Point). You will need to bring your own drinking water (some sites have untreated water) and a portable toilet in remote sites. Be prepared for busy holiday times, especially Christmas, New Year and Easter and you must obtain a camping permit before arriving on the island.

Tangalooma Wild Dolphin Resort has a range of beachfront hotel rooms, apartments and two-storey family villas. Tel: 1300 652 250, www.tangalooma.com.

Contact information

For more information call QPWS on 13 13 04 or visit www.epa.qld.gov.au/parks_and_forests.

One of Tangalooma's scuttled wrecks. Image courtesy Tourism Queensland.

How to get there

Noosa Heads is 139km north of Brisbane.

When to go

This is a great park to visit year round. Summer can be warm and humid, winter is temperate and drier, but it can be very crowded during the summer holiday season. Autumn, when the water is still warm enough to swim in but much less crowded, is a good time to go.

- January: 17–25°C
- July: 9–15°C

At the eastern end of Noosa's main street, this lovely national park is within a short stroll of the cafes and boutiques and includes the headland at Noosa Heads, parts of Lake Weyba (a large, shallow, saltwater lake in the Noosa River system), Emu Mountain and coastal lowlands extending south towards Coolum and some of the most picturesque coastline in south-east Queensland.

Most of the park is covered in open woodlands and low wallum heath, although there are small pockets of rainforest with hoop and kauri pines. Koalas are common in the park. Between June and November you can often see humpback whales (as well as turtles and dolphins) from Dolphin Point and Hell's Gates.

The waterways are a popular place for paddlers and anglers and the unpatrolled beaches offer some great surfing, although rips can make swimming dangerous on the surf beaches. The best swimming is at the patrolled Noosa Heads and Sunshine beaches.

There are more than 15km of walking tracks in the headland section of Noosa National Park. Note, however, that due to the popularity of the park, and its proximity to town, there have been some serious assaults in the park and the QPWS advises to always walk with a group or in sight of another group, to stay on marked walking tracks and walk in daylight hours only.

Top tracks and trails

Coastal Track: for beautiful coastal scenery you can't beat this three-hour walk that skirts the shoreline around the headland and provides access to several pretty beaches. Lookouts along the way provide spectacular views and the track ends on a high bluff at Hell's Gates.

Palm Grove Circuit: a 20-minute walk through rainforest with hoop pines and piccabeen palms.

Tanglewood Track: a sometimes difficult and relatively isolated three-hour walk meandering through rainforest and woodlands to Hell's Gates.

Alexandria Bay tracks: there are two sandy

View from the Coastal Track. Image courtesy Tourism Queensland.

tracks on the eastern side of the headland, both rated as fairly difficult and for fit walkers only. Both wind through open woodlands and heathland along a spectacular coastline that leads to Alexandria Bay.

Emu Mountain summit walk: a short walk to the summit with some steep sections but the panoramic view of the coast from the top is worth it. Look out for wildflowers in the heath.

Best picnic spots

There is a great picnic area overlooking Laguna Bay (just a short stroll from the centre of town) where you can see across the bay and along the coast from Noosa to Cooloola. Facilities include picnic tables, electric barbecues, drinking water and toilets. Toilets and tap water are also provided at Tea Tree Bay.

Camping, caravanning and accommodation options

Noosa National Park is a day use area only, but there are plenty of accommodation choices in and around Noosa.

Contact information

For more information call QPWS on 13 13 04 or visit www.epa.qld.gov.au/parks_and_forests.

Springbrook National Park

How to get there

The park is about 100km south of Brisbane. The steep, narrow road to Springbrook Plateau is not suitable for caravans.

When to go

At 900m above sea level, Springbrook Plateau can be quite cool even in summer and winter is more likely to be dry, although expect showers at any time of the year.

- January: 17–26°C
- July: 8–17°C

Natural Arch.

Part of the World Heritage-listed Gondwana Rainforests of Australia and the Scenic Rim (a chain of mountains stretching across the Queensland-New South Wales border that includes nearby Lamington National Park—see page 116) Springbrook National Park features a spectacular landscape of cliffs, gorges, cool rainforests, mountain streams, waterfalls and panoramic views. One of the most popular attractions is the Natural Arch, where a waterfall cuts through a rock bridge and the cave roof is home to thousands of glow-worms that light up after dark. They are present all year, but at their dimmest during the winter months.

Other wildlife found in the park includes pademelons (small rainforest wallabies), possums, sugar gliders, platypus and koalas. Birds to watch out for include the noisy yellow-tailed black cockatoo and elusive lyrebird.

There are also plenty of reptiles, including lace monitors, carpet pythons and countless frogs.

Top tracks and trails

Natural Arch: it's a fairly easy 30-minute stroll to the park's most popular attraction. There's quite a few steps, and walking in a clockwise direction is easiest.

Best of All Lookout: with a name like this how can you resist? It's an easy half-hour return walk through ancient Antarctic beech forest to a great view of northern New South Wales and Mount Warning, an extinct volcano.

Purling Brook Falls: this 4km loop is a popular walk to a stunning waterfall that plunges 100m to the valley below. If you want to get to the base of the falls follow the Warringa Pool track for a further 2km. Be careful of sheer cliffs and slippery rocks and keep an eye on your kids.

Rainforest walk. Image courtesy Tourism Queensland.

Twin Falls Circuit: this 90-minute loop is a good introduction to the park with rainforest, open forest and montane heath, waterfalls and scenic views.

Warrie Circuit: this 17km (five to six hours) walk features many waterfalls and a wide variety of vegetation—start the walk from Tallanbana picnic area or Canyon Lookout.

Best picnic spots

The most popular picnic area is at Natural Bridge, which has electric coin-operated barbecues. It can get very crowded though, so alternatives are The Settlement, Gwongorella and Goomoolahra, which all have sheltered picnic tables and barbecues as well as toilets with disabled access, or try Numinbah Forest Reserve and Bochow Park, a few kilometres to the north.

Camping, caravanning and accommodation options

You can camp at The Settlement, where the individual sites are large enough for camper trailers and campervans. It's a very new campground (the previous campground at Gwongorella near the top of Purling Brook Falls has closed) so until the vegetation grows it's a bit exposed with little shade. Toilets, drinking water and a cooking shelter with free electric barbecues are provided and you'll need to book well in advance during holiday periods.

Contact information

For more information call QPWS on 13 13 04 or visit www.epa.qld.gov.au/parks_and_forests.

How to get there

Tamborine Mountain is about 80km south of Brisbane via Beenleigh and Tamborine Village or via the Pacific Highway and the Oxenford-Tamborine Road. If travelling from the south, the steep, narrow roads from Nerang and Canungra are unsuitable for buses, trailers or caravans.

When to go

Tamborine Mountain is a good year round destination. Summer is temperate, with the ranges being much cooler than the coast.

- January: 17–26°C
- July: 8–17°C

Queensland's first national park was established at Witches Falls in 1908 and since then additional reserves of subtropical rainforest and open forest on the Tamborine plateau and surrounding foothills have been added, making up what is now known as Tamborine National Park.

It's an island of rainforest surrounded by urban development—according to the QPWS, the Tamborine Mountain escarpment contains 85 per cent of all fauna species and 65 per cent of all flora species in the Gold Coast City area.

There are 22km of graded walking tracks, with most walks taking less than half a day and almost all walks accessible from the township,

Rainforest Drive Tamborine National Park. Image courtesy Tourism Queensland.

which makes it a very popular park with day trippers and picnickers. Most of the walks are also either wheelchair accessible or graded as easy, so it's great for kids and families with strollers.

Palm Grove, Witches Falls and The Knoll have spectacular views, and Zamia Grove has ancient cycads, relics of plants which flourished 150 million years ago, and there are a number of lovely waterfalls and rock pools throughout the park.

Top tracks and trails

Cedar Creek Falls: an easy 30-minute stroll to a lookout with views of waterfalls, cascades and rock pools. The track to the lookout is suitable for strollers and assisted wheelchair access, but not the section from the lookout to the rock pools.

Palm Grove Rainforest Circuit: a one-hour walk that winds through Piccabeen palm groves and rainforest with strangler figs.

Curtis Falls: a 30-minute walk through rainforest (there are some steep steps) to a large pool at the base of Curtis Falls. In winter you may hear the call of the lyrebird, which often mimics the calls of other birds and even the urban noises around it, such as car alarms!

Sandy Creek Circuit: a one-hour walk with scenic views, rainforest and tall trees, and a cliff-edge section.

Witches Falls Circuit: a 3km moderate walk that zigzags down the steep mountainside through open forest with banksia trees and into rainforest with huge strangler figs, past seasonal lagoons to Witches Falls, which flow only after rain.

Best picnic spots

There are picnic facilities at the start of almost all of the walking tracks. Good spots include the top of the Cedar Creek Falls track where there are tables and wheelchair-accessible toilets in a large grassy area surrounded by tall eucalypt forest and at the start of the Witches Falls track on Main Western Road. The grassy area has electric barbecues, picnic tables and toilets.

Camping, caravanning and accommodation options

There is no camping within the national park, but there are plenty of caravan parks and accommodation to suit all budgets in nearby Mount Tamborine village and on the Gold Coast.

Contact information

For more information call QPWS on 13 13 04 or visit www.epa.qld.gov.au/parks_and_forests.

How to get there

Undara is 275km south-west of Cairns on sealed roads.

When to go

Undara is 2,500 feet above sea level and enjoys low humidity with warmer days and cooler evenings, but the best time to go is between April and November.

- January: 21–33°C
- July: 10–26°C

The Undara Lava Tubes in the heart of the Savannah Gulf Country are part of the longest lava flow from a single volcanic crater on Earth. These lava tubes, which extend more than 160km, were formed around 190,000 years ago, when a large volcano erupted violently, spewing molten lava over the surrounding landscape. The lava, which has been estimated at 233 cubic kilometres or enough to fill Sydney Harbour in just six days, flowed rapidly down a dry riverbed. The top outer layer cooled and formed a crust while the molten

The Kalkani Crater. Image courtesy Tourism Queensland.

lava below drained outwards leaving behind a series of hollow tubes. There are 68 separate sections of lava tube that have been identified from more than 300 lava tube roof collapses, and more than 164 volcanoes in the area.

Undara Volcanic National Park is a 'closed' national park, which means you can only explore the lava tubes on a guided tour (high carbon dioxide levels make the lava tube area dangerous for visitors without an experienced guide) and no camping is allowed. Undara Experience has several guided tours available.

Top tracks and trails

Full-day trip: includes a walk around the rim of Kalkani crater where you can get the best view of the collapsed line of the lava tubes and guided tours inside several of the tubes where you'll learn about the geology of the caves and surrounding countryside as well as the local plant and animal life. You'll need a moderate fitness level as there are some rough tracks and some climbing.

Two-hour tours: include trips inside two tubes, but do not have time to visit the crater and are mainly on boardwalks.

Scenic flights: for those strapped for time, there are 15- and 30-minute scenic helicopter flights above the volcanic province, following the lava tube line and around dormant craters.

Kalkani Crater Rim Walk: this is one walk you can do without a guide. The start of the track is 17km from the lodge. Allow around 90 minutes to walk around the rim.

Best picnic spots

There are toilets and picnic tables at Kalkani. Otherwise, a favourite picnic spot is atop the volcanic remnant. The Undara Experience Sunset wildlife tour, a two-hour tour, begins with an animal-spotting drive through the sparse woodland visitors can tuck into fresh fruit and cheese while sipping some orange juice and bubbly as they watch the sun set over the golden savannah plain. It includes a visit to Barker's Cave which is home to 40,000 micro bats after dark.

Camping, caravanning and accommodation options

The Undara Experience is set on what was originally Rosella Plains Station, a cattle station owned and run by the Collins family (the first white settlers in the district) since 1862. It incorporates a range of accommodation options, including camp and caravan sites. Call the lodge for more details: 1800 990 992, www.undara.com.au.

Contact information

For more information call QPWS on 13 13 04 or visit www.epa.qld.gov.au/parks_and_forests.

Inside the lava tubes at Undara. Image courtesy Tourism Queensland.

Whitsunday Islands National Park

How to get there

The bulk of the islands are clustered off the coast near Airlie Beach and Shute Harbour, midway between Mackay and Townsville and are accessible by private boat or commercial tours. Commercial boats will drop off and collect campers. Tel: 1800 801 252 or www. whitsundaytourism.com for details.

When to go

The best time to visit is between April and October. Swimming is not recommended between October and May as Box Jellyfish and the Irukandji Jellyfish are prevalent in the waters and their stings can cause acute pain and serious illness. Box jellyfish can cause death in previously well humans in as little as three minutes.

- January: 22–31°C
- July: 11–24°C

The Whitsundays are picture-postcard perfect: think swaying palm trees and white sandy beaches, uninhabited islands and warm azure waters teeming with tropical fish and coral.

Discovered by Captain Cook on Whit Sunday in 1770, the 74 Whitsunday islands are essentially the drowned volcanic peaks of a submerged range. Part of the Great Barrier Reef World Heritage Area the Whitsunday Islands National Park protects most of the hilly islands, the largest of which are Whitsunday and Hook islands.

Whitehaven Beach on Whitsunday Island is world-renowned for its pure, white, silica sands and crystal-clear waters and the Whitsunday reefs have good coral—visibility is usually best at the northern sides of the outer islands. From May to September the Whitsundays are an important calving ground for migrating humpback whales.

The Whitsundays are also the premier sailing destination in Australia as the large number of sheltered bays and coves make it an ideal place for bareboat sailing charters—hiring a boat without a skipper or crew. You don't need a boat licence and you'll receive the necessary training before you set off.

Top tracks and trails

Whitsunday Island: you can walk through woodland from Tongue Bay to a lookout for a fantastic view over Hill Inlet and Whitehaven Beach. A 1km track connects Dugong and Sawmill Beaches on the western side of the island.

Hook Island: a short walk leads to a rock art site at Nara Inlet

Lindeman Island: the 9km walk to Mt Oldfield gives a magnificent view over the islands.

South Molle Island: it's just a bit over 6km to walk the island end to end. The climb to the highest point on the island, Mt Jefferys (194m), provides great views.

Snorkelling off Hook Island. Image courtesy Tourism Queensland.

Best picnic spots

You really can't beat Whitehaven Beach—it really is as gorgeous as the tourist brochures say it is. Go early or late in the day to avoid the day trippers.

Camping, caravanning and accommodation options

There are 33 campsites scattered amongst various Whitsunday Islands including Whitsunday, Hook, Cid and Henning islands, ranging in size from 60 people at Whitehaven Beach to Planton and Denman islands, where you will share the island with just three others. Facilities vary but are limited to toilets and picnic tables and you must be self-sufficient with fresh water and have a fuel stove for cooking. You'll need insect repellent and you must take all your rubbish with you back to the mainland. See www.epa.qld.gov.au for details of each of the sites—bookings are essential.

Daydream, Long, Lindeman, Brampton, Hayman, South Molle and Hamilton islands all have medium-to-large scale resorts. The wilderness resort on Hook Island is more low key.

Contact information

For more information call QPWS on 13 1304 or visit www.epa.qld.gov.au/parks_and_forests.

Hill Inlet and Whitehaven Beach. Image courtesy Tourism Queensland.

18
Glass House Mountains National Park

The 16 eroded volcanic plugs known collectively as the Glass House Mountains, approximately 75km north of Brisbane, were named by Captain Cook, who thought the jagged rock peaks resembled the glass furnaces of his native Yorkshire. Rising dramatically from the valley floor below, Aboriginal people gathered here for ceremonies and trading and there are a number of protected ceremonial sites. Drive up to the Glass House Mountains Lookout for great views. Follow one of several good bushwalking tracks, some involving challenging climbs to summits. There are camping facilities (tent and caravan sites) at Coochin Creek 9km east of Beerwah.

Glass House Mountains. Image courtesy Tourism Queensland.

19
Jardine River National Park

Jardine River National Park is 400,000ha of true wilderness at the remote northern tip of Cape York Peninsula, 900km north of Cairns, accessible only in the dry season (June to November) and definitely four-wheel-drive only. The national park protects much of the catchment of the Jardine River, the largest perennial stream in Queensland, and is bounded by the headwaters of the Jardine River to the south and the mangroves of Jacky Jacky Creek and the Escape River in the north. The park's western boundary follows the historic telegraph line installed in 1887. Estuarine crocodiles live in rivers and waterholes in this park, and along the entire coastline and offshore islands. Highlights include Eliot Falls and Fruit Bat Falls. You can camp beside the Jardine River or at Captain Billy Landing, Ussher Point or Eliot Falls. Only Eliot Falls has facilities (picnic tables, fireplaces and toilets) so you must be self-sufficient; take drinking water, a fuel stove and a screened tent or nets for protection against insects at night.

Fruit Bat Falls, Jardine River National Park. Image courtesy Tourism Queensland.

20
Lakefield National Park

Another park accessible only during the dry season and only by 4WD, Lakefield, 300km north-west of Cairns, is Queensland's second largest park and features large rivers, spectacular wetlands, mangroves and mudflats. Rivers become a series of waterholes in the dry season but the wet season transforms the park into a vast inaccessible wetland, home to waterbirds, barramundi and estuarine and freshwater crocodiles. Visit the restored Old Laura Homestead or the site of the former Breeza Homestead where horses were bred for the Palmer River goldfields. The Red and White Lily Lagoons, 8km north of Lakefield ranger station, have spectacular displays of red lotus lilies and white lilies. There are a number of remote campsites in the park near rivers and waterholes but you must be totally self sufficient with food, water and fuel, including a fuel stove.

Ant hills, Lakefield National Park. Image courtesy Tourism Queensland.

21 Lark Quarry Conservation Park

The world's only known site of a dinosaur stampede where 95 million years ago a large meat-eating dinosaur startled and chased a horde of much smaller dinosaurs on the muddy shores of a lake. The footprints made in the mud have been fossilised. Entry to the park is free but a fee applies if you want to view the trackways. Lark Quarry is 110km or 90 minutes south-west of Winton along the Jundah Road and is a day use area only.

Dinosaur footprint at Lark Quarry. Image courtesy Tourism Queensland.

22

Magnetic Island National Park

Just over half this large island surrounded by marine park waters and fringing reefs 8km north-east from Townsville is national park. Features include rocky granite headlands dotted with hoop pines, sandy bays and pockets of rainforest. WWII coastal forts are listed on the Queensland Heritage Register. There are some lovely short walks and many of the beaches offer superb swimming and snorkelling during the winter months (marine stingers are prevalent in the water from November to May). There are regular passenger and car ferry services from Townsville—the trip to the Nelly Bay Marina on the island takes about 30 minutes. No camping.

23

Millstream Falls National Park

Forget the highest, Millstream Falls, 3km from the small town of Ravenshoe in the Atherton Tablelands west of Cairns, are the widest falls in Australia. The falls, which spill over an old basalt lava flow, are best seen during the wet season when they are at their most spectacular. It's a great place for a picnic, particularly after rain or very early in the dry season when water flows are still fairly high.

24

Mon Repos Conservation Park

14km east of Bundaberg, Mon Repos is the rookery for the largest number of nesting loggerhead turtles on mainland eastern Australia. Every year, between November and March, sea turtle come ashore to lay their eggs. Eight weeks later, the newly hatched turtles return to the sea. The best time to see turtles laying eggs is after dark from mid-November to February. Hatchlings usually leave their nests at night from mid-January until late March. Best time to go is January, when you might be lucky enough to see both adults and hatchlings. Between 6pm and 6am, public access to Mon Repos beach is restricted and turtle viewing is by guided ranger tour only; they operate nightly from November to late March, excluding 24, 25 and 31 December. For bookings call (07) 4153-8888.

Hatchling turtle, Mon Repos. Image courtesy Tourism Queensland.

Glass House Mountains. Image courtesy Tourism Queensland.

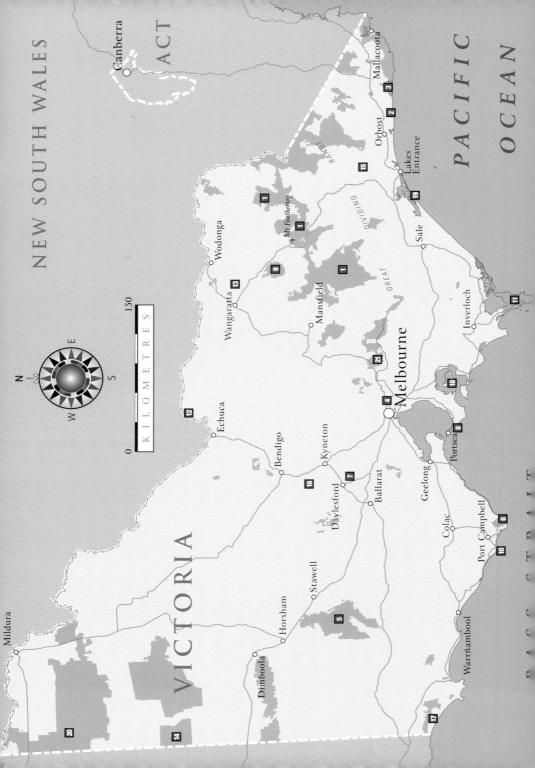

Victoria

Bordered by the Murray River in the north and the rugged coastline of the Southern Ocean and Bass Strait in the south, the tail end of the Great Dividing Range runs across the eastern half of Victoria. In the west of the state you'll find the vast volcanic plain of the western districts and the much drier Mallee and Wimmera area that borders South Australia.

With well over 200 national parks there's something for everyone in the mainland's smallest state, from beautiful garden parks to snow-capped mountain wilderness, heritage sites, wildlife sanctuaries, marine reserves and long stretches of wild windswept beaches, including some of the county's most iconic landscapes. Facilities range from basic walk-in campsites to luxury safari-style wilderness retreats, cabins with wheelchair access and historic lighthouse accommodation. Parks with caravan sites are almost always unpowered.

Not all parks charge entry fees, although many do, and some parks require campers to obtain camping permits. You can get these at local park visitor centres or at the campground, where sites are allocated on a first-come, first-served basis. You'll need to book a site at many of the popular parks (including most of those featured in this book) during peak holiday periods and some, such as Wilsons Promontory and Cape Conran even work on a ballot system. Annual parks passes and multi-day parks passes area available from Parks Victoria, and are particularly good value if you intend spending a lot of time in the alpine parks or the popular coastal parks near Melbourne. You can buy a park pass at major national park visitor centres, or the Parks Victoria Information Centre on 13 1963. Visit www.parkweb.vic.gov.au for more information.

1 Alpine National Park

How to get there

The Great Alpine Road, one of Australia's great mountain drives, cuts through the heart of the national park, as does the currently unsealed Bogong High Plains Road (due to be sealed by the end of 2009) which closes during winter. The Great Alpine Road is fully sealed and is open all year, although you will need to carry snow chains in winter. Falls Creek is 385km north-east of Melbourne, Dinner Plain is 391km.

When to go

Summer temperatures are generally around 10°C cooler than the surrounding plains, but conditions may change without warning, so always be prepared with warm and waterproof clothing. Expect lots of snow and ice in winter.

- January: 10–21°C
- July: -1–4°C

Alpine National Park is Victoria's largest national park. With adjoining national parks in New South Wales and the ACT, it forms a protected area that covers almost all of Australia's high country. Extensive snowfields are the main winter attraction; spring and summer bring stunning wildflower displays and opportunities for bushwalks, four-wheel driving, trout fishing and horse riding.

Like many winter skiing areas, during the summer the ski runs make for some great mountain biking. There are bike tracks around the Horse Hill Chairlift on Mount Buller of varying difficulty, from easy terrain to the 'Abominable Downhill' track that crosses Chalet Creek and is one of the most difficult in the country. During peak holiday times in summer and over Easter, chairlifts are available to lift mountain bikers at Falls Creek and Mount Hotham.

Falls Creek is the largest ski and boarding resort, with good cross-country skiing terrain on the Bogong High Plains and is also home to some of Australia's steepest and deepest

Bogong High Plains.

slopes at Mt McKay. Special tours include a skidoo transfer to the slopes for a 40-minute night Kassbohrer ride and snow bike riding every Wednesday and Saturday nights during winter. Visit www.fallscreek.com.au.

Mt Buller has the most chairlifts of all the Victorian ski resorts with the capacity to lift 40,000 skiers per hour. It also has 80km of resort trails suitable for skiers and snow boarders as well as snow tubing, tobogganing and cross-country trails. See www.mtbuller. com.au.

Hotham is known as the 'powder capital' and holds the record for the highest annual snowfall of any Victorian resort over the past decade. Hotham offers 320 hectares of ski area, including 35km of tree-lined cross-country trails and a network of 13 lifts—the longest run is 2.5km long. Visit www.mthotham.com.au.

Kayaking at Rocky Valley Lake near Falls Creek. Image courtesy Tourism Victoria.

Falls Creek is Victoria's largest ski and boarding resort. Image courtesy Tourism Victoria.

Top tracks and trails

There are literally hundreds of good walking trails that crisscross this national park. See www.parkweb.vic.gov.au for more.

Wallace Hut to Cope Hut Trail: this 6km trail is an easy loop that visits two of Victoria's best-known cattlemen's huts on your way to one of the highest peaks on the Bogong High Plains. Wallace Hut was built by the Wallace brothers in 1889 from slabs of snow gum and old bits of kerosene tins. It is the oldest of the high country cattleman's huts and is surrounded by beautiful gums, some of the few in the area that were miraculously left unscathed by the 2003 and 2006 fires.

Falls Creek: there is a network of walking trails around the village, including the 10km Aqueduct Trail that traces the ridgeline above the tiny township. Go right once you trek up the hill from the town centre and you can follow the waterway trail out to Wishing Well for some fantastic views back to the village and across the valley and distant peaks, or head left to Rocky Valley Lake, a man-made dam full of trout and a great spot for a picnic or paddle.

Mt Bogong via Staircase Spur Trail: a steep four-hour walk to the summit of Mt Bogong, Victoria's tallest mountain.

Mt Feathertop via Razorback Trail: another demanding four-hour walk from Mt Hotham to the summit of Mt Feathertop, the state's second highest mountain, following the sharp, craggy spine of the ridge above the treeline.

Australian Alps Walking Track: a 650km (10-week) trek across the Australian Alps from Walhalla (Gippsland, Victoria) to the outskirts of Canberra. It can be broken into smaller, multi day sections. See www.australianalps.deh.gov.au/parks/walktrack/index.html.

Best picnic spots

There are plenty of fabulous spots to unfold a picnic blanket in the high country. The best view though, is from the top of Mt McKay, Australia's highest driveable spot at 1842m above sea level, where you can gaze out over the treeless Bogong High Plains to see almost all of Victoria's highest peaks. It's a superb spot to watch the sun set.

Camping, caravanning and accommodation options

There are a number of good bush camping spots throughout the park, but you will need to be self sufficient, carry drinking water and be prepared for all weather conditions, even in summer. There are good spots on the Howqua River near Mt Buller, on JB Plain near the village of Dinner Plain, Pretty Valley Hut. Anglers Rest near Omeo is a beautiful setting beside the Mitta Mitta River. There are also several good camping spots just off the Bogong High Plains Road. There is also a range of accommodation available year-round at the ski resorts.

Contact information

Parks Victoria, Tel: 13 1963 or www.parkweb.vic.gov.au.

2 Cape Conran Coastal Park

How to get there

Cape Conran Coastal Park is 420km east of Melbourne, via the Princes Hwy (turn off at Cabbage Tree Creek) or via the towns of Orbost and Marlo.

When to go

The Gippsland area of enjoys a year-round temperate climate, with mild summers and relatively warm winters.

- January: 14–24°C
- July: 5–15°C

Near Marlo in East Gippsland this Coastal Park features heathlands, rivers, wild, windswept ocean beaches, banksia woodlands brimming with nectar-feeding birds and a range of accommodation options from basic camping to luxury permanent safari tents.

While the beautiful beaches are the main drawcard, the park is also a popular spot for scuba diving, particularly around West Cape Beach and Salmon Rocks, while rock pinnacles and rock pools also provide plenty of interest at low tide for snorkellers.

Because Cape Conran is a coastal park, rather than a national park, you can bring your dogs with you as long as they stay on a leash, although be careful of ticks which are common in coastal areas of East Gippsland.

Boardwalk on Cape Conran Nature Trail.

Top tracks and trails

Cape Conran Nature Trail: a very pleasant 90-minute walk from East Cape across to West Cape along boardwalks, beaches and through banksia forest.

Heathland Walk: this 90-minute loop walk starts (and ends) near the rangers office and is a favourite with birdwatchers and wildflower lovers.

Beach walks: pick a beach, any beach and you can walk for hours. Good places to start are West Cape Beach (seven kilometres later you'll end up at Point Ricardo) or East Cape where you can walk up the beach to the Yeerung River, around 90 minutes one way.

Dock Inlet: a 14km, five-hour return walk from Yeerung River leads to a landlocked fresh-water lake in the sand dunes.

Yeerung Gorge: if you have a 4WD take the East Yeerung Track (or walk from the bridge,

West Cape.

four hours return) to a gorge with deep, dark rock holes.

Best picnic spots

Yeerung River has picnic facilities and is also a popular swimming and paddling spot and there are picnic tables at nearby Yeerung Beach at the mouth of the river. The best beachside picnic area is Sailors Grave on the north side of East Cape, where facilities include gas barbecues and toilets.

Camping, caravanning and accommodation options

You can camp at Banksia Bluff Camp and East Cape Beach. Both campgrounds have large shady unpowered sites, basic toilet facilities and cold showers and are only a minute's stroll to the beach.

There are also seven self-contained timber cabins, each sleeping up to eight, which are ideal for families, although there is not much privacy between sleeping areas. One cabin is wheelchair accessible. You will need to bring pillows, sleeping gear and towels.

More upmarket are the five new wilderness retreats; raised, hard-floored safari-style tents with double bed, small fridge, reading lights and a large verandah. The retreats are fairly close together, so for maximum privacy ask for number 5 when booking. Bedding and linen is supplied, and there is a (small) communal kitchen and shower block nearby. See www.conran.net.au for more details.

Contact Information

Contact: during peak holiday periods a ballot system is used to allocate cabins and campsites. Contact the manager's office for further information on (03) 5154-8438. For general information contact Parks Victoria, Tel: 13 1963 or www.parkweb.vic.gov.au.

How to get there

Croajingolong is around 450km east of Melbourne and 500km south of Sydney via the Princes Highway. Most of the access roads are unsealed and many are not suitable for caravans. The nearest sizable town is Mallacoota, at the northern end of the park.

When to go

The Gippsland area enjoys a year-round temperate climate, with mild summers and relatively warm winters.

- January: 14–24°C
- July: 5–15°C

Extending for 100km along the wilderness coast of Victoria's East Gippsland, Croajingolong National Park is a Unesco World Biosphere Reserve and features remote beaches, tall forests, wildflower-strewn heathlands, rainforest, estuaries, granite peaks and sand dune wilderness.

The tranquil waters of the Mallacoota inlet and the Thurra and Mueller rivers are popular with paddlers and anglers, and there are a number of sheltered swimming spots.

Point Hicks was the first part of Australia's east coast sighted by Captain Cook in 1770 and was named after his lieutenant aboard the *Endeavour*. Tours of the 1890, 38m-high lighthouse are on Friday, Saturday, Sunday and Monday at 1pm. It's a long and winding 162 steps to the top but the views are wonderful.

Top tracks and trails

Point Hicks: unless you're staying at the lighthouse you'll have to trek up the hill from the gate, but the views are worth it. It will take around 90 minutes return, but allow extra time once you're there to continue on for 45 minutes or so to either the viewing platform overlooking the wreck of the *SS Saros*, or down to the remnants of the old jetty and on to West Beach. Keep an eye out for sea eagles.

Dunes Walk: starting at the Thurra River campground, this two-hour return walk takes you through banksia forest and up through a narrow gap to some of the tallest dunes in the Sandpatch Wilderness Area. Once at the dunes there is no shelter and it is very hot, so avoid walking in the middle of the day and take adequate water and good sunglasses. (Be warned, the dunes all look the same, so don't lose your bearings because it is easy to become lost and disorientated.)

Best picnic spots

If the weather is kind, unpack a picnic near the lookout at Genoa Peak, 490m above sea level. Otherwise, most of the camping areas have day use areas and there are many lovely secluded spots in and around Mallacoota Inlet.

Camping, caravanning and accommodation options

Wingan Inlet camping area has secluded campsites set in a tall bloodwood forest near the shores of the inlet. Other good spots to camp in the park include the Peachtree Creek camping area on the banks of the Cann River, Mueller River camping area, perfect for launching canoes or kayaks, and Shipwreck Creek camping area above rocky headlands at the mouth of Shipwreck Creek. If you're after easy boat launching access, camp at Tamboon Inlet. Thurra River camping area has 46 campsites scattered between the river and the ocean beach (bookings essential for the Christmas and Easter holidays). It's also the starting point for several of the most popular walks. You will need to bring in all your drinking water.

You can also stay in one of the two lighthouse keepers cottages at Point Hicks, both of which sleep eight. Linen is supplied, but you'll need to bring your own food.

Enquiries and bookings for the Thurra and Mueller campgrounds should be made at the Point Hicks Lightstation office. Tel: (03) 5158-4268.

Contact information

Contact Parks Victoria on Tel: 13 19 63 or visit www.parkweb.vic.gov.au.

Point Hicks lighthouse.

4 Dandenong Ranges

How to get there

The national park is approximately 35km east of Melbourne via Belgrave, Emerald and Olinda. For a novel way to get there catch a ride on Puffing Billy, a century-old steam train running on its original mountain track from Belgrave to Gembrook on the edge of the park. Trains operate daily; for timetables visit www.puffingbilly.com.au.

When to go

Summer is mild and winter is frosty, with the occasional dusting of snow in the Dandenongs, especially in the upper reaches.

- January: 13–23°C
- July: 3–8°C

An hour or so to the east of the city rise the Dandenong Ranges, where lush fern-filled gullies, forests of mountain ash (one of the tallest trees in the world) and more than 300km of walking tracks, along with a host of good barbecue and picnic areas, are just some of the many features of the park that attract Melbournians to the area every weekend.

It's a good place to spot the elusive lyrebird in the wild, at the very least you'll hear its song. The Superb Lyrebird is thought to have the loudest bird call in the world, although it is a master of mimicry and its call can often take the form of those of other birds or even human-made noises such as chainsaws and car alarms.

Another highlight is the William Ricketts Sanctuary, where almost 100 kiln-fired clay sculptures of Aboriginal figures are set among rocks, fern trees and Mountain ash. William Rickets bought the four-acre bush block on Mount Dandenong in 1930s and called it Potter's Sanctuary. Word soon spread about the extraordinary sculptures that began to adorn the property, and in the 1960s the Victorian Government heard about his work and bought the property, which is managed by Parks Victoria. William Ricketts lived on at the Sanctuary into his nineties and continued to create his sculptures until his death in 1993.

Another spectacular public garden, also managed by Parks Victoria, the National Rhododendron Gardens, is host to 15,000 rhododendrons, 12,000 azaleas, 3000 camellias and 250,000 daffodils. In spring and autumn it is clothed in colour and perfume.

Top tracks and trails

Hardy Gully Nature Walk: a lovely, 45-minute loop from Grants Picnic Ground winds through remnant cool temperate rainforest.

Margaret Lester Forest Walk: this 300m walk into the forest is great for those with limited mobility.

Olinda Creek Walking Track: a two-hour walk with some steep sections follows the course of Olinda Creek (for the most part) from Silvan Reservoir Park in the east to Mt Evelyn in the west.

1000 Steps and Kokoda Trail: a steep five-kilometre walk from the Fern Tree Gully picnic area to One Tree Hill with 1000 steps. Along the way there are plaques depicting the lives of the men who fought and died on the Kokoda Trail in Papua New Guinea during World War II.

Horse trails: there are a number of designated horse riding trails throughout the park. See www.parkweb.vic.gov.au for details.

Best picnic spots

There are electric and/or gas barbecues at Fern Tree Gully and in Grants, Sherbrooke, O'Donohue and One Tree Hill picnic grounds.

Camping, caravanning and accommodation options

The national park is a day use area only. However, the area is a favourite weekend escape for Melbournians and many historic cottages in the villages have been transformed into romantic B&Bs.

Contact information

Contact Parks Victoria on Tel: 13 1963 or visit www.parkweb.vic.gov.au.

The ranges offer great cycling trails. Images courtesy Tourism Victoria.

How to get there

The park is accessible from Halls Gap (266km north-west of Melbourne)—turn left off the Western Highway at Stawell. The southern area of the Grampians National Park is accessible from Dunkeld, north-east of Hamilton.

When to go

Summers are dry and warm, most rain falls during winter when temperatures can get very chilly. Expect higher summer temperatures in the north west.

- January: 13–29°C
- July: 4–12°C

Rising rather abruptly from the western Victorian plains, the wild and rugged Grampian Range is one of the most popular places in Victoria for a weekend escape from the city. The 167,000-hectare park is made up of four spectacular tilted sandstone ridges, rising gently on the western side and falling abruptly away in ragged overhangs and rocky bluffs on the eastern side. The photographic ridges are crisscrossed with walking trails, lookouts, and clear streams cascading down some of the state's largest waterfalls and provide good places for rock climbing, abseiling and other adventure activities. In spring, vast areas are blanketed in wildflowers.

A highlight is the collection of Aboriginal rock art sites—approximately 60 rock art sites, containing more than 4000 different motifs have been identified in the park to date. The Brambuk Aboriginal Living Cultural Centre, adjacent to the Grampians National Park Visitor Centre, provides a good overview of the area's Aboriginal history and accessible rock art sites.

Top tracks and trails

Mackenzie Falls: there are more than 50 marked walking trails in the Grampians National Park, but if you only have time for a short one, choose the half-hour descent to Mackenzie Falls; 265 steps later you'll emerge at a beautiful waterhole at the foot of the falls.

Wonderland Walk: one of the most popular walks in the park is this five-hour loop from Halls Gap around the spectacular Pinnacle Lookout. Highlights include the high-walled Grand Canyon, the sandstone rock face named 'Elephant Hide' and the Venus Bath Rock Pools.

Mt Abrupt Trail: a steep 90-minute climb to the top of Mt Abrupt (Mt Murdadjoog, 827m), one of the park's finest lookouts.

Best picnic spots

There are a host of good picnic areas scattered through out the parks, but favourites include the picnic area above Mackenzie Falls which

has a kiosk and wheelchair accessible toilets and Ngamadjidj Rock Art Shelter.

Camping, caravanning and accommodation options

There are five main camping areas in the park, all with toilets, fireplaces and picnic tables, but you'll need to bring your own drinking water. The large camping ground at the base of Mount Stapylton in the northern Grampians offers good walking opportunities; the Old Mill site is near the MacKenzie Falls; Borough Huts is by Fyans Creek near the Wonderland Ranges in the central area; Jimmy Creek is on the Wannon River in the south-east and Buandik, a forested area on Billimina Creek, is near a number of aboriginal sites in the south-west of the park. All areas get busy at Easter, long weekends and during summer holidays. You can also bush camp in other areas of the park.

Contact information

Contact Parks Victoria on Tel: 13 1963 or visit www.parkweb.vic.gov.au. The Halls Gap Visitor Information Centre is on the Grampians Road, Halls Gap. Tel: 1800 065 599 or visit www.visitgrampians.com.au.

Rock overhang known as The Balconies. Image courtesy Tourism Victoria.

6 Great Otway National Park

How to get there

Lorne is 140km south-west of Melbourne via the Great Ocean Road. Cape Otway is a further 68km west along the coast.

When to go

Summers are dry and warm, most rain falls during winter when temperatures can get very chilly.

- January: 14–21°C
- July: 4–13°C

This huge park covers much of the hinterland north of the cliff-hugging Great Ocean Road and includes the tall forests and steep slopes of the Otway Ranges as well as the rugged, largely inaccessible coastline around Cape Otway and west to Princetown. Highlights include beautiful waterfalls, giant mountain ash gums, fern gullies and many coastal and rainforest walking tracks. Melba Gully, one of the wettest places in the state with an annual rainfall over 2000mm, is a dense rainforest of myrtle beech, blackwood and tree ferns with an understorey of low ferns and mosses. The 'Big Tree' is more than 300 years old. In holiday periods there are guided night walks to see glow worms.

Cape Otway Lighthouse, one of the best preserved groups of historic lighthouse buildings in Australia, has guided tours each day at 9.30am. Keep your eyes open on the drive in as you will often see koalas crossing the road or asleep in the trees beside the road.

Dogs are allowed in the Otway Forest Park sections.

Top tracks and trails

Triplet Falls: a 2km boardwalk to a beautiful waterfall, set amongst tall mountain ash, blackwoods, myrtle beech and high ferns.

Stevensons Falls: another great rainforest track to a waterfall begins at the campground, follows the river and ends at a viewing platform at the base of Stevenson's Falls.

Maits Rest Rainforest Trail: a 30-minute boardwalk stroll through beautiful rainforest where giant myrtle beeches tower above a delicate understorey of tree ferns, lichens and moss.

Madsens Track Nature Walk: another delightful half-hour walk that gives a good introduction to the features of the Otway forest.

Otway Fly: get close-up views of the rainforest on the elevated boardwalk 25m above the ground, with a 47m lookout tower. Open daily and fees apply. Visit www.otwayfly.com.

Erskine Falls: just a few minutes drive from the centre of Lorne, these falls are the highest drop in the Otways. There is a short walk though the rainforest past the falls.

Best picnic spots

You're spoilt for choice with dozens of great picnic spots. Pick of the bunch include Triplet Falls and cool and shady Blanket Leaf picnic area, not far from Cora Lyn Cascades.

Camping, caravanning and accommodation options

The Wye River Reserve, 15km south of Lorne, has unpowered caravan sites and the Allenvale Mill Site is a basic but secluded walk-in camping area beside the George River on Allenvale Road 2km south-west of Lorne. There is also a large camping area beside the river at Stevensons Falls which is suitable for caravans.

At Blanket Bay near Cape Otway campsites are on the edge of a good swimming beach but get very busy during school holidays and operate on a ballot system during peak times. Other good camping spots in the park include the mouth of the Aire River, behind the sand dunes at Johanna Beach and on the river bank at Dandos (both have room for caravans), and at Lake Elizabeth.

You can stay in the lighthouse keeper's cottage at Cape Otway Lightstation. For details visit www.lightstation.com.

Contact information

Contact Parks Victoria on Tel: 13 1963 or visit www.parkweb.vic.gov.au.

Magnificent forest of the Otway Ranges. Image courtesy Tourism Victoria.

How to get there

Hepburn Regional Park is on the outskirts of Daylesford, an 80-minute drive from Melbourne. To get there take the Calder Highway from the city to Woodend or Kyneton and head east to Daylesford and Hepburn Springs from there.

When to go

Summers are temperate, most rain falls during winter when temperatures can get very cool.

- January: 10–25°C
- July: 3–10°C

With the highest concentration of mineral springs in the country, the area around Daylesford and Hepburn Springs is the undisputed capital of spa country.

Although first discovered by goldminers in the 1850s, it was the early Swiss-Italian settlers, with their long heritage of 'taking the waters' in Europe, who recognised the value of the springs and sought to have the Hepburn area preserved in a reserve. In 1895, Hepburn Springs bathhouse was opened and people have been travelling to Hepburn and Daylesford to partake of the healing waters ever since.

They say that the sulphate purifies your liver; that the calcium is good for your bones; the bicarbonate balances the pH in your bloodstream; the magnesium is good for your kidneys; the silica will help strengthen your bones; the sodium helps prevent stomach disorders; the iron will help carry oxygen to your brain and that your mind and muscles will thank you for the potassium.

Of course, the best way to get all this goodness is to drink it and there are a number of springs (with lovely old-fashioned hand-operated pumps) in the Hepburn Mineral Springs Reserve (adjacent the regional park) where you can fill up as many containers as you can carry, for free.

Springs aside, other features of this park include relics of the gold mining era, the Blowhole—an artificial diversion tunnel on Sailors Creek built by gold miners in the early 1870s—and the extinct volcanic crater of Mount Franklin.

Because this park is classified as a regional park, rather than a national park, dogs are permitted in the park but must be kept on a leash at all times.

Top tracks and trails

Argyle Spring Track: you can taste the water from four natural springs on this easy 1.5km track in Hepburn Mineral Springs Reserve. Some smell strongly of sulphur, others taste quite metallic and all are quite effervescent. Naturally, the best tasting springs are those furthest from the car park.

Tipperary Walking Track: a 16km walk that takes you past the remains of water races used by gold miners in the last century, through native bush and stands of European trees and past mineral springs in Hepburn Regional Park. It runs from Lake Daylesford to the Hepburn Mineral Springs Reserve, following Sailors Creek and Spring Creek through foothill forest for most of the way. The 16km track takes five to six hours and is quite easy walking. There are also shorter sections between Lake Daylesford and Bryces Flat on both sides of Sailors Creek.

Mt Franklin Crater: you can drive to the summit of this extinct volcano, where there is a pleasant walk along the rim.

Best picnic spots

There are several picnic areas in the park. Most have wood barbecues and electric barbecues are available at Hepburn Mineral Springs Reserve and at Sailors Falls.

Camping, caravanning and accommodation options

There is a camping and (unpowered) caravan area at Mount Franklin in Hepburn Regional Park with basic facilities.

Contact information

Contact Parks Victoria on Tel: 13 1963 or visit www.parkweb.vic.gov.au.

Taste the water at Hepburn Springs.

Mount Franklin. Image courtesy Tourism Victoria.

Mornington Peninsula National Park

How to get there

The national park is about 90km south of Melbourne.

When to go

Summer is mild, winter is more likely to be wet.

- January: 14–23°C
- July: 8–12°C

The Mornington Peninsula is one long beach—a 100km boot-shaped peninsula jutting into the ocean on the eastern edge of Port Phillip Bay, just 80km south of Melbourne with more than 260km of coastline. The Mornington Peninsula National Park, with its windswept dunes and steep cliffs, stretches along the peninsula's Bass Strait foreshore (the foot of the boot) from Portsea to Cape Shanck.

Colonies of seals and bottle-nosed dolphins cruise and frolic in the bay and beyond the windswept dunes the rolling hills are home to grey kangaroos, southern brown bandicoots, echidnas, native rats, mice, reptiles, bats and many forest and ocean birds.

This 2600-hectare park includes the basalt cliffs of Cape Schanck and the 150-year-old lighthouse, which is open for tours daily, the former quarantine station and military fort at Point Nepean; spectacular and rugged surf beaches and Greens Bush native bushland area, a great place to see kangaroos.

Top tracks and trails

Fort Nepean Walk: an easy 90-minute one-way walk to the tip of the peninsula. The walk passes Cheviot Beach, where Prime Minister Harold Holt disappeared in 1967, and The Rip, a treacherous strip of water between Point Nepean and Point Lonsdale that has claimed many ships. Once at Fort Nepean there are a number of self-guided heritage walks around the historic military fortress and you can download free audio guides (podcasts) from www.parkweb.vic.gov.au/1podcasts.cfm. Bicycles are also available for hire here and entry fees apply to Point Nepean.

Bushrangers Bay Trail: the 6km track starts at the historic 1859 Cape Schanck Lighthouse and offers sweeping views of the wild coastline and at the point of Bushrangers Bay, an impressive spire called Elephant Rock.

Two Bays Trail: the Peninsula's longest continuous track connecting Port Phillip to Cape Schanck: the 26km walk will take around 10 hours to complete.

Coppins Track: from Sorrento Ocean Beach this 4km trail winds along the cliff tops to Diamond Bay.

Best picnic spots

Fingal picnic area is around 2km north of Cape Schanck and has electric barbecues, toilets and tables, and there is a nice walk that leads to Fingal Beach. There are also picnic facilities near the lighthouse and there is a boardwalk that goes down to the beach and rock platforms as well as lookouts over Pulpit Rock. There are wheelchair accessible facilities at Sorrento Ocean Beach, which is patrolled by surf lifesavers (as is Portsea Ocean Beach) during summer.

Camping, caravanning and accommodation options

No camping is allowed in Mornington Peninsula National Park although you can pitch a tent on one of the many stunning foreshore reserves all along the coasts of the Mornington Peninsula that offer beautiful settings with bay views. They are generally open only during summer periods and are very popular so early bookings are recommended. You'll find reserves at Dromana, Rosebud, Rye, Sorrento, Balnarring Point Leo and Shoreham.

You can also stay in the lighthouse keepers cottages at Cape Schanck. To book, call 0500 527 891 or visit www.austpacinns.com.au.

Contact information

Contact Parks Victoria on Tel: 13 1963 or visit www.parkweb.vic.gov.au.

The Mornington Peninsula offers great surfing opportunities. Image courtesy Tourism Victoria.

Mount Buffalo National Park

How to get there

Mount Buffalo is about 320km north-east of Melbourne via the Hume Freeway and Great Alpine Road. Snow chains must be carried in winter.

When to go

Summer temperatures are generally around 10°C cooler than the surrounding plains, but conditions may change without warning, so always be prepared with warm and waterproof clothing. Expect lots of snow and ice in winter.

- January: 10–21°C
- July: -1–4°C

Named in 1824 by explorers Hume and Hovell, who thought the granite mountain looked like a buffalo, this alpine national park was first declared in 1898, making it one of the first two national parks in Victoria (Wilsons Promontory was also declared a national park in 1898—see page 170).

Features include fantastically shaped granite boulders and cliffs, waterfalls, alpine lakes and snow gum woodlands. In summer there is a huge range of walks as well as canoeing, swimming, horseriding, bike riding, abseiling, rock climbing and hang gliding. In winter it is a popular tobogganing, downhill and cross-country skiing area.

Mt Buffalo ski fields. Image courtesy Tourism Victoria.

It has a wealth of wildlife, from the peregrine falcons that soar on the thermals, to crimson rosellas and bogong moths that shelter in the rock crevices, to kangaroos, wallabies, possums, echidnas and wombats. In summer wildflowers are abundant.

Top tracks and trails

The Horn Trail: a 30-minute steep climb to a magnificent lookout at the highest point on Mt Buffalo.

Gorge Heritage Walk: an easy one-hour walk around the top of the Buffalo Gorge, with towering granite cliffs, tumbling waterfalls and views over the surrounding countryside.

View Point Nature Walk: a 4km-return walk from just below the Lake Catani dam wall that leads to the view point lookout. The entire walk is at or above 1250m and a Parks Victoria leaflet provides information about various sub-alpine plants and features along the way.

The Cathedral.

The Big Walk: living up to its name, this 11km (one way) walk is the longest on the mountain and climbs the plateau from the park entrance to the Gorge Day Visitor Area. There are side tracks to Rollasons Falls and lookouts along the way.

Mount McLeod Track: you'll need at least six hours for this 16km return walk to North Buffalo Plateau, one of the most remote sections of the park. It begins at the Reservoir picnic area.

Best picnic spots

There are picnic facilities at the Gorge, where there are several spectacular lookouts below the chalet that have sweeping views over the cliffs and across the mountains, all the way to Mount Kosciuszko, and you can watch, with either trepidation or envy, abseilers and hang gliders launch themselves over the cliff edges. There are also picnic facilities at Lake Catani

and Rollason Falls, just off the winding road up the mountain, The Horn and The Reservoir.

Camping, caravanning and accommodation options

Lake Catani at Mount Buffalo is set amongst the snow gums, and is open from the beginning of November until the end of April and has 49 unpowered sites suitable for car camping and small caravans or camper trailers. You will need to bring in your own drinking water. Bookings are essential during peak holiday periods.

Mt Buffalo Chalet, a grand old guesthouse built in 1910 at the Gorge is, at the time of writing, closed. To check for reopening details visit www.mtbuffaloresort.com.au.

Contact information

Contact Parks Victoria on Tel: 13 19 63 or visit www.parkweb.vic.gov.au.

Port Campbell National Park

How to get there

Port Campbell National Park is 285km west of Melbourne via the Great Ocean Road.

When to go

Summers are dry and warm, most rain falls during winter when temperatures can get quite cool.

- January: 14–21°C
- July: 4–13°C

Top of any list of great Australian drives is Great Ocean Road. Built between 1919 and 1932, the cliff-hugging road was hewn from the rock by 3000 returned World War I soldiers using picks, crowbars and shovels, who dedicated the 14-year project as a memorial to their colleagues who died in the war.

The most photographed section of Great Ocean Road is in Port Campbell National Park and includes the Twelve Apostles rock formations (there are actually only eight), the result of wind and wave erosion that carved the towers out of the surrounding cliffs. The cliffs rise to nearly 70m in some places and the highest Apostle is around 50m from base to tip. Other attractions include Loch Ard Gorge, the site of a tragic shipwreck in 1878 that left just two survivors, and London Bridge, which dramatically lost one of its arches in

1990 stranding two startled sightseers on the newly formed tower.

Some of Australia's best but least-known dive sites are located along the Great Ocean Road with giant kelp forests, abundant fish and underwater caves. Local dive operators run trips out to some of the best spots, including shipwrecks.

One of the best ways to really see the rugged coastline is on a scenic helicopter flight. There are several helicopter charter companies who offer joy flights over the Twelve Apostles.

The Great Ocean Road is very popular during holiday periods and summer weekends, so if you can, try and visit on a weekday or during winter time.

Top tracks and trails

Great Ocean Walk: is a 91km (eight day) coastal walk linking Apollo Bay to the Glenample Homestead, near Port Campbell and includes many of the prime attractions of the Great Ocean Road. It passes through the dense mountain forests and spectacular coastal margin of the Otway Ranges and Otway Plain through the Otway and Port Campbell National Parks, coastal reserves and road reserves. Highlights include all the coastal formations (Bay of Martyrs, Loch Ard Gorge, Twelve Apostles and London Bridge) as well as Maits Rest rainforest boardwalk, giant mountain ash gums, fern gullies and rugged, inaccessible beaches and the historic 150-year-old Cape Otway Lighthouse (see the Great Otway National Park section on page 160 for more information). Many of the beaches along the walk are exposed to tides, rips and reefs and are not patrolled. The safest time to walk along them is during low tide. Check tide times before setting off.

Best picnic spots

Bring a picnic rug to spread on one of the beaches as there are few picnic facilities available at lookout areas aside from some picnic tables at Point Sturgess on the outskirts of Port Campbell.

Camping, caravanning and accommodation options

There is no camping in the park, but there is a commercial campground and caravan park in Port Campbell and a wide range of accommodation options to suit all budgets along the Great Ocean Road. Visit www.greatoceanroad.org.au.

Contact information

Contact Parks Victoria on Tel: 13 19 63 or visit www.parkweb.vic.gov.au. The Great Ocean Road Visitor Information Centre is at Apollo Bay. Tel: 13 28 42, www.greatoceanroad.org.au.

Dramatic cliffs at Port Campbell. Image courtesy Tourism Victoria.

Wilsons Promontory National Park

How to get there

Wilsons Promontory is 200km south-east of Melbourne via the South Gippsland Highway, around a three-hour drive.

When to go

During summer, from Melbourne Cup weekend through to Easter, is when most people head to the Prom, which also means that's when it's at its most crowded. Go in late spring for masses of wildflowers in full bloom and milder daytime temperatures make for more pleasant bushwalking, or go in winter and you'll have the place almost to yourself. Just be sure to have lots of warm woollies for cold nights.

- January: 14–24°C
- July: 5–15°C

Known simply as The Prom to locals, Wilsons Promontory is a wild and rugged knob of land hanging like a fishhook-shaped pendant off the southern-most tip of mainland Australia, surrounded by sea on three sides. Its granite headlands, undeveloped beaches, rivers, walking trails and wildlife make it one of Victoria's most well-loved national parks.

Wilsons Prom is crisscrossed by a network of trails, ranging from short 300m tracks to beautiful beaches to long overnight hikes. Must-see spots include: Squeaky Beach, a beautiful arc of white sand flanked by large granite boulders and famous for its squeaky sand; Whisky Beach; the panoramic views from the summit of Mount Oberon and the historic 1859 lighthouse.

Catch a movie at the outdoor cinema in Tidal River, which operates during the main summer and Easter holidays, and on weekends and Wednesdays until Easter. Shuttle buses also operate for walkers between Tidal River and Mt Oberon during the holiday season.

Top tracks and trails

Lilly Pilly Gully: two-hour loop through stringy bark and tea tree forest to a boardwalk through a lush and ferny rainforest.

Squeaky, Picnic and Whisky Beaches: a two-hour walk across three beaches, best done at low tide.

Mount Oberon Summit: a fairly strenuous one-hour walk to the summit of Mt Oberon, where the jaw-dropping views make the steep slog worth it.

Vereker Lookout: a one-hour climb through a silent banksia forest to a picnic area amongst fantastically-shaped granite formations.

Lighthouse Walk: a 19km fairly challenging one-way walk to the remote Wilsons Promontory lighthouse, built in 1859.

Whisky Bay. Image courtesy Parks Victoria.

Best picnic spots

Head to Norman Beach for free gas barbecues and safe swimming. Norman Lookout and Whisky Bay are both great spots to watch the sunset.

Camping, caravanning and accommodation options

Tidal River has 484 camping and caravan sites, including some powered caravan sites. Facilities include toilets, hot showers, laundry facilities and some gas barbecues, as well as a general store and cafe. Other accommodation options at Tidal River include huts that sleep between four and six, ensuite cabins sleeping up to six people and luxury 'wilderness retreats' each with ensuite and private deck. You can also stay in the lighthouse, but you'll need to be able to carry all your food and gear on the long hike in, and carry all your rubbish out. There are also 11 hike-in campsites on many of the overnight wilderness walks.

Contact information

Campsites and accommodation are allocated on a ballot system during the peak summer holiday season (19 December–26 January), usually held in the preceding June. For more information call Parks Victoria on 1800 350 552 or visit www.parkweb.vic.gov.au.

In brief . . .

12 Barmah State Park

On the floodplain of the Murray River between Tocumwal, Deniliquin and Echuca, the Barmah Forest is the largest red gum forest in the world and has more than 180 Aboriginal sacred sites. The area is frequently flooded and the resulting wetlands are home to almost 900 species of wildlife. You can camp at the Barmah Lakes area and at several spots along the river.

Barmah State Forest. Image courtesy Tourism Victoria.

13 Beechworth Historic Park

One of the best preserved gold towns in Victoria Beechworth has more than 30 buildings classified by the National Trust, including the courthouse where bushranger Ned Kelly stood trial. Outside the town a number of significant goldmining sites are incorporated in sections of the Historic Park. The 20-minute, 5km Gorge Scenic Drive begins at the Golden Horseshoe Monument and continues past the National Trust Powder Magazine that once stored gunpowder and gelignite used in deep alluvial and quartz mining, and along the Spring Creek goldfields. There are two historic bridges, some beautiful lookouts over the hills and valleys and a number of short walks. Woolshed Falls are a highlight. The well-marked track follows the creek and shows how dramatically the miners changed the course of the original creek and the methods they used to find the elusive gold —in 1853 there were more than 8000 miners along this small section of creek.

Beechworth is 270km north-east of Melbourne. Woolshed Falls is a day-use area only.

14
Big Desert Wilderness

Victoria's first declared wilderness area, the inhospitable terrain of the Big Desert Wilderness has been left largely untouched by Europeans. More than 50 species of lizards and snakes and 93 species of birds have been recorded in the park including the extremely rare western whipbird. There are campsites at Big Billy Bore, the Springs, Moonlight Tank and Broken Bucket Reserve along the Nhill-Murrayville Road. You must carry your own drinking water and the park is best avoided during the middle of summer when high temperatures make bushwalking unsafe. There are no tracks into the park and you must walk in from the Nhill-Murrayville Road (a rough, dry-weather road only), separated from the park by a 5km strip of public land.

Woolshed Falls, near Beechworth.

15 Buchan Caves Reserve

Buchan Caves Reserve, near the township of Buchan 360km north-east of Melbourne, offers guided tours of the richly decorated Royal Cave and Fairy Cave several times daily. Both caves are lit and have walkways, and they feature extensive limestone stalactites and stalagmites. Tours to 'wild' unlit caves can be arranged for small groups. You can also book tours of some of the other caves that have been opened, including the less accessible Murrindal Caves, just north of Buchan. The reserve has a swimming pool and playground, 49 powered (plus more unpowered) campsites, as well as cabins and luxury safari-style permanent tents (bookings essential, Tel: 13 1963).

16 Castlemaine Diggings National Heritage Park

Australia's first National Heritage Park, gold was discovered in the Castlemain Diggings area in 1851. Highlights include the 22m Garfield Water Wheel, Spring Gully and Eureka Reef, ruins of an old Welsh Village and other ruined house sites and the mineral springs at Vaughan, which has a camp ground. The heritage park is near Castlemaine, around 120km north-west of Melbourne.

Discovery Bay. Image courtesy Tourism Victoria.

17

Discovery Bay Marine National Park and Lower Glenelg National Park

A dramatic 50km-long sweep of ocean beach backed by huge dunes and coastal lakes. Attractions include mainland Australia's largest breeding colony of fur seals at Cape Bridgewater, blowholes, a sand-petrified forest and the highest coastal cliffs in Victoria, 130m above sea level. The Bridgewater Lakes, 16km west of Portland, are popular for picnics, swimming, boating, water skiing and surf-fishing. You can camp (tents sites only) at Lake Monibeong.

Cape Bridgewater Seal Walk is a moderate two-hour return walk with striking views across Cape Bridgewater, once a volcanic island that is now joined to the mainland. The viewing platform at the end of the trail looks out over rock platforms and on to a colony of about 650 Australian fur seals. You can continue through a petrified forest—the limestone remains of huge trees that once covered the sea cliff to the blowholes.

The park is adjacent to Lower Glenelg National Park, where the Glenelg River has carved a spectacular 15km-long gorge that in some sections is up to 50m deep through limestone as well as some extraordinary caves including the richly decorated Princess Margaret Rose Cave. There are a number of camping sites spread out along the river and caravan sites at Princess Margaret Rose Cave and Pritchards.

Both parks are in south-west Victoria near the SA border, about 420km from Melbourne and 490km from Adelaide.

18

French Island National Park

Accessible by a 10-minute passenger ferry ride from Stony Point, French Island in Western Port south-east of Melbourne is home to Victoria's largest population of koalas. The island is also home to a large population of the long-nosed potoroo and the waterbirds, including sea eagles and waders can often be seen in and around the wetlands, mangroves and salt marshes. You can camp at Fairhaven on the west coast. For ferry information and bookings Tel: (03) 9585-5730.

19
Gippsland Lakes Coastal Park

A narrow coastal reserve covering a portion of the Ninety Mile Beach from Seaspray to Lakes Entrance with lakes, wetlands, fishing and boating opportunities. The park also includes Lake Reeve, several islands and the Boole Poole Peninsula. There are 20 large free camping areas between Golden Beach and Seaspray on Ninety Mile Beach. Sites are located behind the dune, 50m to 100m from the beach and are perfect for fishing, swimming or walking. The western section of the park is accessible by road via Seaspray, around 240km east of Melbourne.

Gippsland Lakes. Image courtesy Tourism Victoria.

Murray-Sunset National Park

Named for its spectacular sunsets and one of the few remaining semi-arid regions in the world where the environment is relatively untouched this is the state's second largest national park. A highlight is the Pink Lakes, which turn pink during late summer when a red pigment, carotene, is secreted from the algae. The best time to see them is early or late in the day. The lakes evaporate over summer leaving concentrated salt crusts over black mud. The park is in north-west Victoria, about 550km from Melbourne and 400km from Adelaide and while some tracks are okay for conventional vehicles 4WD is recommended. More information at www.parkweb.vic.gov.au.

Yarra Ranges

The Yarra Ranges and nearby township of Marysville was devastated by the tragic Black Saturday bushfires in February 2009, which destroyed much of the tall forests and several towns, including Marysville. The forest is slowly regenerating, and locals are committed to rebuilding their communities. Lake Mountain is Australia's premier cross-country ski resort and is one of the southernmost sub-alpine areas of the Australian continent. Its highest point is 1530 metres and for several months of the year, Lake Mountain plateau (undulating between 1330 metres and 1490 metres) is blanketed in snow. There are 40km of well-marked ski trails through snow gum woodland, ranging from trails suitable for the first-time skier to the most advanced, which become popular walking tracks and challenging mountain bike rides in spring and summer. Entry fees apply during winter at Mount Donna Buang and Lake Mountain. Also worth seeing is the Rainforest Gallery at Mount Donna Buang, a treetop observation platform and rainforest walkway.

Yarra Ranges rainforest. Image courtesy Tourism Victoria.

Western Australia

Australia's largest state, Western Australia, is both vast and varied. Almost nine per cent of the state is protected by national park, conservation area or marine reserves, with everything from ancient rocks and dry deserts to spectacular coastlines, one of the world's great coral reefs and the breathtakingly wild gorges of the Kimberley, a place so remote that some of it still remains unexplored. Even one of the state's most well known natural wonders, Purnululu (the Bungle Bungles) was only discovered by Europeans less than 30 years ago. You may have to travel a long way between parks, but that's part of the attraction of travelling in Western Australia—the outback is never far away.

Not all parks have entry fees, although some of the more popular parks charge camping fees on top of park entry fees. Given the isolation of many of these parks, you will need to be well prepared with good maps and drinking water. Be mindful of fire bans and carry a fuel stove. Not all campsites allow the use of generators and many have four-wheel-drive access only. Some campsites are closed during the summer wet season.

A range of park passes are available from the offices of the Department of Environment and Conservation, the online Nature Base Shop (www.naturebase.net) and at local state tourist centres, as well as entry points to parks or rangers within the parks. Be aware that park passes do not include camping; separate fees apply.

For more information about Western Australia's national parks visit the website www.naturebase.net.

How to get there

Cape Le Grand National Park is 50km south-east of Esperance by sealed road.

When to go

Winter can be cold and wet, although when the sun shines it's delightful and the beaches are uncrowded. The best time for wildflowers is early spring and the park can be very busy during summer months.

- January: 15–25°C
- July: 8–17°C

Wide, white sandy beaches punctuated by rocky headlands are just some of the features of this beautiful coastal park near Esperance.

Named by French explorer Bruni D'Entrecasteaux in 1792, the area was also visited by Matthew Flinders, who sheltered from a storm in the cove he subsequently called Lucky Bay in 1802. Wild and windswept, the surrounding sand plains that cover much of the park are home to dense thickets of banksia, some as tall as three to four metres. In the south-west corner of the park, which is accessed by sealed roads, there is a striking chain of rocky granite peaks honeycombed with caves and tunnels and some great bay-to-bay walking trails along the clifftops, where sea eagles soar above carpets of brightly coloured banksias and other wild flowers in full bloom during late winter and early spring.

Oak-leaf dryandra.

Kangaroos are common near the camping areas and can often be seen lazing in the sun on the beaches. Keep an eye out for honey-possums and southern brown bandicoots after dark.

Top tracks and trails

Coastal Trail: a fantastic 15km (one-way) coastal walk from Le Grand Beach to Rossiter Bay along the edge of Cape Le Grand. It can be broken up into shorter sections: Le Grand Beach to Hellfire Bay is hard going (allow three hours), as is the next section to Thistle Cove (two hours). Thistle Cove to Lucky Bay, also called the Le Grand Heritage Trail, is a medium walk (allow around 45 minutes each way if doing the circuit from the car park) with a bit of rock hopping but very scenic and well worth doing. The final section from Lucky Bay to Rossiter Bay will take around three hours and is rated as medium.

Lucky Bay.

Frenchman Peak: a two-hour (3km) hard trek up the 'gentle' east slope of the peak to the summit that provides great views. It's not recommended in wet or windy weather.

Best picnic spots

Favourite picnic spots are Lucky Bay, where there are free gas barbecues and a spectacular view over the beach and surrounding coastline, and Thistle Cove, where a lone picnic table has been bolted into the rocky cliff on the headland.

Camping, caravanning and accommodation options

There are two beachside camp grounds in the park and both feature solar-powered hot showers as well as septic toilets. Lucky Bay has a boat ramp and large (unpowered) caravan sites with a great view overlooking the beach, although it is really just one big open area, so

Le Grand Beach.

if you prefer individual sites with privacy head instead to Le Grand Beach where sites are tucked behind the dune and well spaced from each other, although a bit small for those with big caravans or motorhomes. Both areas have a very good camp kitchen.

Contact information

WA Department of Environment and Conservation (DEC) on (08) 9334-0333 or visit www.naturebase.net.

How to get there

The park stretches for 130km from Black Point (35km east of Augusta) to Long Point (10km west of Walpole) extending inland for between five and 20km. Most roads within the park (except the road to Windy Harbour, Salmon Beach, and Broke Inlet) are 4WD only and can be very sandy, so lower your tyre pressure and carry a carry a compressor to re-inflate them. Beware of fallen trees blocking roads.

When to go

Winter can be very wet and some roads may close after rain; the best time to visit is between September and April. The Fisherman track to Broke Inlet Mouth is closed June to November.

- January: 14–23°C
- July: 8–16°C

Wild and untouched, D'Entrecasteaux (pronounced *don-truh-cast-oh*, with the stress on the *oh*) is a park for four-wheel-drivers, as most of the park is inaccessible by conventional vehicles. It's long and narrow with stands of karri and jarrah and forests of eucalypt in the inland section, wildflowers in spring, beautiful inland lakes, rivers and wetlands, vast sand dunes (Yeagarup Dune is an impressive mobile dune 10km long), long, white sandy beaches

Parrot Bush.

flanked by imposing cliffs almost 100m high and hexagonal basalt columns (west of Black Point) that originated from a volcanic lava flow 135 million years ago.

Named in honour of French explorer Bruni D'Entrecasteaux, who charted the coastline on a scientific expedition in 1792, the park is popular with anglers who come here to fish from the rocks, beaches and river banks and with off-roaders who like to tackle the sand dunes and sandy tracks. If you want a rugged and remote coastal park where you can get away from it all, then this is the one for you.

Top tracks and trails

Clifftop Walk: an easy 1.3km walk with great views of the 85m high cliffs and Southern Ocean from Point D'Entrecasteaux to Tookulup.

Coastal Survivors Walk: a 2.8km coastal

View from Salmon Beach.

walk from Point D'Entrecasteaux to Windy Harbour via Cathedral Rock.

Mount Chudalup: a steep climb to the summit, but worth it for the views. Allow around an hour for the return walk.

Best picnic spots

The picnic site at Salmon Beach has great views of the cliffs and coastline looking west.

Camping, caravanning and accommodation options

There are several campsites scattered throughout the park but you'll need a 4WD to access the coastal ones, apart from the commercial caravan park (unpowered sites only) at Windy Harbour (Tel: (08) 9776-7203). Inland, there is a basic campground at Snottygobble Loop (named after the tree, not those kids in the back seat!) and beneath the peppermints at Crystal Springs that are both accessible to 2WD vehicles. For those with a 4WD, you can camp beside the lake or near the sand dunes at Yeagarup, on the beach at Black Point or at Lake Jasper in the north-western section of the park, or at Coodamurrup Beach, Fish Creek or Madalay Beach in the southern section. The Banksia Camp Lodge is a roomy shelter containing four bedrooms and a common area that is designed to accommodate 12 people comfortably, but it is first-in, best-dressed, so carry a tent. There is a three-night limit at the lodge.

Contact information

WA Department of Environment and Conservation (DEC) on (08) 9334-0333 or visit www.naturebase.net.

How to get there

Fitzgerald River National Park is 180km north-east of Albany. Best access to Point Ann in the western section of the park is via Bremer Bay; from the east, best access is via Hopetoun or the Hamersley Drive from the South Coast Highway. All roads within the park are unsealed and unsuitable for caravans, buses or large motorhomes.

When to go

The winter months between June and October is the best time for whale watching; for wildflowers visit in spring, peak flowering time is August to November.

- January: 15–25°C
- July: 7–18°C

Fitzgerald River National Park is one of the most diverse botanical regions in the world. A UNESCO Biosphere Reserve, more than 1800 beautiful and bizarre species of flowering plants thrive here, nearly 20 per cent of the Western Australia's plant species. You can't miss the brightly-coloured Royal hakea that towers above the surrounding plains and if you're here during the right time of year (spring) it won't take you long to find the pretty Quaalup bell, which is not found anywhere else.

Other highlights of this large tract of coastal wilderness include deserted beaches with 4WD access, inland lakes and rivers, spongolite cliffs full of sea sponge fossils and whale watching at Point Ann, just one of two places in Australia (the other is Head of Bight in South Australia), where many southern right whales come to calve in the calm waters of the bay. There are two whale watching platforms that extend out from the headlands over the sea and offer great opportunities for whale watching between June and October.

Top tracks and trails

Hamersley Drive: scenic unsealed drive bisecting the eastern section of the park. Allow at least an hour for the 57km drive, longer if you like photographing wildflowers along the way.

East Mount Barren: allow two to three hours for the climb to the summit, but the views are worth it.

Point Ann Heritage Trail: an easy 45-minutes stroll around the headlands with sweeping coastal views.

Best picnic spots

You can't beat Point Ann as the perfect picnic spot, especially if there are whales at play in the bay. Facilities include a brand new shelter with tables and gas barbecues and a knockout view.

Camping, caravanning and accommodation options

There are several good campsites spread

Point Ann.

throughout the park. Favourites include St Mary Inlet, a sheltered site behind the sand dunes near Point Ann, where on a good day, you'll be able to see whales just beyond the breakers and Hamersley Inlet, a lovely lakeside camping spot amongst the paperbarks and a great place to watch the sunset over the water. If you have a four-wheel-drive you can camp at Point Charles and Quoin Head. All campgrounds have toilets and gas barbecues, but no drinking water is supplied anywhere in the park, so make sure you bring your own.

Bremer Bay Beaches Resort offers good caravan sites (and spa cabins) within easy walking distance of beautiful beaches and a short drive from the national park. For details, contact Wellstead Road, Bremer Bay. Tel: (08) 9837-4290.

Contact information

WA Department of Environment and Conservation (DEC) on (08) 9334-0333 or visit www.naturebase.net.

Hamersley Inlet, Fitzgerald River National Park. Image courtesy Bill McKinnon.

Geikie Gorge National Park

How to get there

Geikie Gorge National Park is 20km from the settlement at Fitzroy Crossing and 280km from Derby. Access is by good unsealed road from Fitzroy Crossing.

When to go

Roads are impassable from November to April. The dry 'winter' season, May to October, is the best time for travelling.

- January: 24–37°C
- July: 11–33°C

Kayaking through Geikie Gorge.

The annual flood waters of the Fitzroy River have carved a 30m deep gorge through the limestone at the junction of the Oscar and Geikie Ranges in the southern Kimberley. During the wet season, the Fitzroy River rages through this narrow gorge at a height of around 16 or 17m, flooding the national park.

In the dry, between April and November, the river is a quiet stream strung out beneath the towering cliffs where you can trace the mark of the eons of floods on the pocked cliff faces, creamy grey below the high water mark; rich, rusty red above. Freshwater crocodiles sun bake on the banks and small turtles float in the shallows. Birdlife is prolific, particularly in the early morning and late afternoon.

The reef is Devonian, so unlike modern reefs (which are built by corals) this reef was formed from algae and a group of now extinct lime-secreting organisms. This is the same reef that forms Windjana Gorge on the Gibb River Road (see page 219) around 150km to the north-west, resurfacing here near Fitzroy Crossing. Here, the river is much higher and you can take a one-hour cruise with national park rangers, or a five-hour cruise with local Aboriginal guides, to learn about the ecology, geology and history of the gorge.

The traditional Aboriginal owners, the Bunaba, call the gorge *Darngku*, and according to Dreaming stories, a blind elder, having left his tribe to go travelling, drowned in the gorge. Before he sank to the bottom, he sighed and sneezed and, according to legend,

Sunset reflections at the gorge.

you can still hear his sighs when the gorge is quiet.

During the dry season boats, kayaks and canoes are allowed access to Geikie Gorge after 4.30pm, just in time to see the creamy walls of the gorge glow a deep but vibrant red in the late afternoon light. You must notify rangers before launching your boat.

Top tracks and trails

Geikie Gorge Reef Walk: a pleasant 3km walk along the base of one of the gorge walls. It's best in the early morning and late afternoon. Carry lots of water.

River walk: the 20-minute river walk is along the banks of the Fitzroy River to the Sandbar, a popular fishing and swimming place. Keep an eye out for freshwater crocodiles.

Best picnic spots

There is a nice grassed picnic area adjacent to the information centre. Facilities include toilets, water and gas barbecues and the area is wheelchair accessible.

Camping, caravanning and accommodation options

Geikie Gorge is a day-use area only so camping is not allowed, although there is a very good commercial campground with a large, shady grass camping area at nearby Fitzroy Crossing, as well as plenty of caravan sites.

Contact information

WA Department of Environment and Conservation (DEC) on (08) 9334-0333 or visit www.naturebase.net.

How to get there

Kalbarri is 577km north of Perth.

When to go

Summer is normally dry and warm. Almost all the region's scarce rain falls during the winter months. Wildflower season is July-November.

- January: 22–39°C
- July: 11–27°C

Coastal cliffs at Red Bluff.

Magnificent red and white banded gorges, formed by the Murchison River as it makes its way to the Indian Ocean, sea cliffs and vast, rolling sand plains are just some of the spectacular scenery in this national park.

The park is split into two sections; the coastal section is on the southern outskirts of the town of Kalbarri; the river section is to the north-east of the township.

Along the coast, wind and wave erosion has exposed the layers of the coastal cliffs that rise more than 100m above the ocean. From Red Bluff extensive views south overlook colourful coastal limestone and sandstone ledges, which look their best in the late afternoon as they glow in the setting sun. There are scenic lookouts signposted off the main road at Mushroom Rock, Rainbow Valley, Pot Alley and Eagle Gorge.

The most famous, and most photographed, of all sights in the national park is the Natures Window, around 26km north-east of the town. It's part of a wider area of the park known simply as The Loop, a short cliff-top walking trail above a loop of the Murchison River that has several lookouts along the way that give different perspectives on the river's switchback course. The star attraction, Nature's Window, is a natural rock arch which perfectly frames the upstream view and has become a must-have photo for almost all of the travellers who come here and sit at its edge. 11km down the road, the gorge known as the Z-bend is another star attraction, where the River has cut a Z-shaped gorge deep into the rock.

Top tracks and trails

Mushroom Rock Nature Trail: a leisurely two-hour return walk between the scenic lookouts along the cliff top near Red Bluff. It is not suitable for young children as most of the cliff edges are unfenced.

The Coastal Trail: this 8km one-way walk also takes in the views from many of the sea cliffs, but you'll need to arrange to be dropped off at Eagle Gorge and picked up at Natural Bridge.

Around The Loop: a six-hour return walk from the Nature's Window. It's not marked but easy to follow, but keep the river on your right once you get past the first river bend east of the window.

Canoe safaris: Kalbarri Adventure Tours run full day bushwalking and canoeing trips exploring the area between the Loop and Z-Bend, which includes a 6km paddle along the river through the gorges. You'll need to be reasonably fit and agile, but it's a stunning day's adventure. Tel: (08) 9937-1677 or visit www.kalbarritours.com.au.

Best picnic spots

There is a picnic shelter with barbecues, and toilets, at the Natures Window car park area.

Camping, caravanning and accommodation options

There are no camping facilities within the national park, but there is a range of accommodation to suit all budgets in Kalbarri. A favourite with caravanners is pet-friendly Murchison Park Caravan Park, which has shady sites opposite the beach in the heart of town. It's very popular during school holidays however, so you'll need to book. Contact 29 Grey Street, Kalbarri. Tel: 1300 851 555.

Contact information

WA Department of Environment and Conservation (DEC) on (08) 9334-0333 or visit www.naturebase.net.

The Z-Bend.

Leeuwin-Naturaliste National Park

How to get there

The park is south of the town of Margaret River, which is roughly halfway between the two capes. It is 274km south of Perth on the Bussell Highway.

When to go

Summer is normally dry and warm, although tempered by sea breezes. Almost all the region's rain falls during the winter months.

- January: 14–25°C
- July: 7–16°C

Strung out along the coastline that juts into the sea off the south-west corner of Western Australia, this national park is crowned in the north by Cape Naturaliste and Cape Leeuwin in the south and features stunning coastal views, sea cliffs and rocky headlands. It is also home to some of the best surfing breaks in the country, an extensive network of caves and vast forests of karri, one of the world's tallest trees.

Cape Leeuwin, 10 minutes drive south of Augusta, is the most south-westerly tip of Australia and the lighthouse here has watched over the point where the Indian and Southern oceans meet since 1895. It's open daily between 8.45am and 5pm and has regular tours of the lighthouse. In the north, Cape Naturaliste lighthouse is also open every day for tours. Both spots are great whale watching vantage points during the winter months when both humpback and southern right whales often cruise past.

Many of the limestone caves are open for tours. Calgardup and Giants Cave are both unlit self-guided caves. The floor of the two main caverns in Calgardup Cave is covered in water, which throws up beautiful reflections— there are elevated viewing platforms. Giants Cave is a unique 'walk through' cave that you can enter on one side and reappear out of another opening. Elevated platforms and marked paths are provided along its 800m length. Jewel Cave just north of Augusta is home to one of the longest straw stalactites to be found in any tourist cave. Inside Lake Cave near Margaret River is a stunning pristine chamber with a tranquil lake reflecting the delicate formations. Mammoth Cave houses the ancient fossil remains of numerous extinct animals. Ngilgi Cave, just north of Yallingup, offers a stunning display of stalactite, stalagmite, helicitite and shawl formations plus an interpretative area detailing the cave's rich history.

Top tracks and trails

Cape to Cape: a 140km walk between Cape Naturaliste and Cape Leeuwin with breathtaking coastal scenery and wildflowers from August to November. Between June and December, you can also spot migrating

whales. You can join the track at popular spots such as Sugarloaf Rock, Canal Rocks near Yallingup, Injidup Point and Hamelin Bay.

Boranup Karri Forest Drive: Take a detour off Caves Road for a short (gravel) drive that winds beneath the towering pale-barked trees. There is a short walk here that leads to a lookout over the karri forest and the coast.

Meekadarabee Falls: an easy (wheelchair accessible) 40-minute walk from the historic Ellensbrook Homestead to Meekadarabee Falls.

Best picnic spots

A favourite picnic spot is underneath the karri trees in Boranup Forest, but there are also picnic facilities at most of the scenic lookouts and at both capes.

Camping, caravanning and accommodation options

Conto and Boranup campground both have toilets, barbecues, tables, water and individual sites in the bush. The Point Road campground, at the northern end of Boranup Drive, is four-wheel-drive only.

Contact information

WA Department of Environment and Conservation (DEC) on (08) 9334-0333 or visit www.naturebase.net.

Cape Leeuwin. Image courtesy Bill McKinnon.

How to get there

Access is via the 4WD-only Gibb River Road and Kalumburu track and then the rough 240km track to Mitchell Falls. You'll bounce your way across miles of corrugations and through thick red bulldust with several creek crossings, but the trip through the changing landscape of Livistonia Palms up to the Mitchell Plateau with its gorge walks, clear swimming holes and magnificent waterfalls is well worth it. Allow at least two days travelling time from Kununurra.

When to go

Roads are impassable November to April. The dry 'winter' season, May to October is the best time for travelling.

- January: 24–37°C
- July: 11–33°C

Less than 25,000 people live in the remote north-western corner of Australia known as the Kimberley, an area bigger than Germany. It is a rough and rugged, but breathtakingly beautiful place, with jagged mountain ranges, spectacular gorges, beautiful waterfalls, serene billabongs, ancient rock art galleries and wild uninhabited wilderness. The oldest rocks in the Kimberley were formed approximately 2000 million years ago, and there has been so little geological activity in the area since

Swimming hole at Little Mertens Falls. Image courtesy Bill McKinnon.

that the landscape has remained relatively unchanged, making it some of most ancient land on earth.

One of the most remote national parks in the Kimberley is Mitchell River; access is by four-wheel-drive only and is two days of rugged and very rough driving from Kununurra. The Mitchell River, which flows into the Admiralty Gulf to the north, has carved a number of deep gorges with stunning waterfalls through the Mitchell Plateau.

Highlights are the three-tiered Mitchell Falls and crystal clear Surveyors Pool as well as the extensive stands of *Livistonia* fan palms. Saltwater crocodiles inhabit the area, so not all of the beautiful pools below the falls are for swimming, although you can swim at

Gibb River Road. Image courtesy Bill McKinnon.

Little Mertens Falls, which is an easy 500m walk from the campground. During the dry season you can also take a scenic helicopter flight over the plateau and falls. The office is at the campground.

Top tracks and trails

Mitchell Falls: the four-to-six-hour walk to Mitchell Falls is a moderate to difficult trek from the camping area across rough and rocky country, skirting several dangerous cliffs and passing by Little Mertens Falls and Big Mertens Falls along the way. Beware of snakes, wear stout boots, and carry more water than you'll think you need.

The Aunuayu walk: is a moderate, 8km walk to Surveyors Pool from the Surveyors Pool car park.

Best picnic spots

Apart from the campground near Little Mertens Falls there are few formal picnic facilities, but plenty of gorgeous spots to choose from.

Camping, caravanning and accommodation options

Mitchell Falls and King Edward River have basic bush camps, although a few have fireplaces and toilets. There is a shady camping area with toilets at the start of the Punamii-Unpuu (Mitchell Falls Track).

Contact information

WA Department of Environment and Conservation (DEC) on (08) 9334-0333 or visit www.naturebase.net.

How to get there

The Pinnacle Desert is 17km from Cervantes or around 245km (three hours drive) north of Perth.

When to go

If you really want to see these fantastic rock towers at their best you need to be here at sunset or sunrise, when they glow in the softer light; temperatures are less severe and you don't have to share the view with busloads of day trippers.

Summer is normally dry and warm. Almost all the region's scarce rain falls during the winter months. Best wildflower season is September and October.

- January: 17–30°C
- July: 10–19°C

Thousands of huge limestone pillars rise out of a stark landscape of yellow sand in the area known as the Pinnacles Desert deep inside Nambung National Park. In places they reach up to three-and-a-half-metres tall. Some are jagged, sharp-edged columns, rising to a point; others squat and rounded like a gravestone, some are little more than triangular-shaped boulders emerging from the dunes. All of them are totally surreal.

The towers were formed as seashells were compacted and dissolved inside the surrounding dune system, which in turn eroded away leaving the crazy spikes that exist today. However, while the pinnacles themselves may be hundreds of thousands of years old, they have, according to the Department of Environment and Conservation, been exposed only relatively recently. 'Aboriginal artefacts at least 6000 years old have been found in the Pinnacles Desert despite no recent evidence of Aboriginal occupation. This tends to suggest that the Pinnacles were exposed about 6000 years ago and then covered up by shifting sands, before being exposed again in the last few hundred years', says the Department's literature on the park. And it's still happening. The predominantly southerly winds are uncovering pinnacles in the northern part of the Pinnacles Desert and covering those in the south, which means that over time, the cycle will most likely repeat itself and the limestone spires that you can see today will be covered again by other sand drifts.

During spring the area is blanketed in wildflowers, and you'll often see kangaroos and emus, white-tailed black-cockatoos, lizards and carpet pythons. Sandgropers, (large burrowing insects that have inspired the nickname for residents of Western Australia) can often be found in the dunes— follow their tell-tale raised 'trails' that crisscross the sand.

A Sandgroper.

The Pinnacles Desert.

Top tracks and trails

Pinnacles Lookout: you can drive around the park on a one-way loop to a lookout platform, but it is unsealed (and not suitable for caravans or buses). Navigating the narrow track can be tricky, as the countless paint scrapes on the sides of the pinnacles beside the road indicate. There are no walking trails as such, but you can spend hours wandering around the stone towers when the weather is kind. If walking, be careful of extreme summer temperatures and carry plenty of drinking water.

Best picnic spots

There are tables and toilets at Kangaroo Point and great views to Thirsty Point and the beaches of Cervantes. Hangover Bay, which also has barbecues, is a beautiful white sandy beach that is good for swimming, snorkelling and windsurfing. If you're lucky you may see dolphins and sea lions.

Camping, caravanning and accommodation options

There are no camping facilities within the national park. There is a full range of accommodation options in Cervantes.

Contact information

WA Department of Environment and Conservation (DEC) on (08) 9334-0333 or visit www.naturebase.net.

Cut leaf wattle.

The surreal spires known as The Pinnacles in Nambung National Park.

Ningaloo Marine Park

How to get there

Ningaloo Marine Park is north of Coral Bay, which is 1133km north of Perth; Exmouth is a further 137km north.

When to go

Coral Bay and Exmouth are dry and warm almost all year—perfect beach weather. Whale shark season is between April and early July.

- January: 21–36°C
- July: 12–30°C

Coral Bay.

Ningaloo Reef, which stretches almost 300km from the Exmouth Gulf around the North-West Cape and south to Red Bluff on the Western Australia coral coast 1200km or so north of Perth, is the main attraction of this marine park. It is the largest fringing coral reef in Australia and is every bit as magnificent as Queensland's Great Barrier Reef, with the added advantage that it is one of the few places in the world where you can actually walk out straight from the beach to the coral. The reef protects a shallow, brilliant white sandy lagoon of clear tropical waters, full of colourful fish and a wealth of marine life, including humpback whales, tiger sharks, dolphins, dugongs, giant manta rays and the amazing whale shark.

Despite their fierce sounding name, these massive but harmless fish are truly the gentle giants of the deep; they can measure up to 18m in length with an adult whale shark weighing in at more than 15 tonnes with a mouth more than a metre wide. Ningaloo Reef is the only place in the world where they are known to visit on an annual basis (between April and early July) in large numbers, so close to the coast.

There are a number of tours that operate from both Coral Bay and Exmouth that allow you to get in the water and swim with these magnificent fish—and because they swim close to the surface, all you need is a snorkel and fins, although you do have to be pretty fit. Despite their massive bulk, whale sharks are fast swimmers and the day involves lots of clambering in and out of the boat and sprint-like swims to keep up.

Other highlights include the Coral Bay foreshore, which is great for novice snorkellers

Whale Shark. Image courtesy Steve Gibson.

as the coral begins just metres from the shore (but be aware of boats in the water), and the mass coral spawning, a three-day event that begins a week or so after the full moon during March and April when the coral release millions of bright pink egg and sperm bundles, which float to the surface of the water, creating a floating slick of coral spawn each night.

In winter this area is also a great place to see humpback whales on their annual migration to and from warmer waters.

Top tracks and trails

Turquoise Bay Drift Snorkel: let the current carry you north over the coral for several hundred metres. It's great fun, but not suitable for weak swimmers as currents can be strong. Turquoise Bay is 65km south of Exmouth.

Best picnic spots

The foreshore area at Coral Bay has good picnic facilities.

Camping, caravanning and accommodation options

There are several beachside camping and caravanning areas in neighbouring Cape Range National Park (see page 214). There are also commercial caravan parks and a full range of accommodation choices in Coral Bay and Exmouth.

Contact information

WA Department of Environment and Conservation (DEC) on (08) 9334-0333 or visit www.naturebase.net.

Purnululu National Park (Bungle Bungles)

How to get there

The turn-off to the park is 250km south of Kununurra or 109km north of Halls Creek via a sealed road. The final 55km from the main road into the park is 4WD only and is narrow and rough; watch out for large oncoming tourist buses.

When to go

Roads are impassable during the wet season and the park is open only between April and September. Days are very hot as heat radiates from the rocks, and nights often hover around the zero mark, so be prepared with the appropriate gear.

- January: 24–37°C
- July: 11–33°C

The domes of the park as seen from the air.

The World Heritage-listed 45,000-hectare Bungle Bungle Range, with its huge expanse of striking banded domes, sandstone cliffs and towers, is one of Australia's most recent discoveries, found by Europeans less than 30 years ago. Twenty million years of weathering has produced the eroded sandstone towers, the dark bands formed by cyanobacteria, (single cell photosynthetic organisms), winding horizontally around the domes, contrasting with the lighter sandstone.

Ground access to the domes is still difficult: although it is only 55km from the main road into the park, it is 4WD only and takes a couple of hours, so many visitors opt for a scenic flight (available from Kununurra and Halls Creek) which is well worth doing even if you are intending to visit the park at ground level, as the vast outcrop of distinctive beehive-shaped towers really are best seen from the air. Most flights also fly over Lake Argyle, the body of water created by the Ord River Scheme, one of the world's largest man-made bodies of water and the huge open cut Argyle Diamond mine.

From the surrounding flat plains the sandstone domes rise up sharply to heights of more than 57m, and the deep cracks, crevices and gorges are home to more than 130 species of birds, the most common being rainbow bee-eaters and colourful budgerigars, as well as wallabies and euro and fan palms that cling to the rock walls.

Top tracks and trails

Cathedral Gorge: the most popular walk in the park is the one-hour easy walk into a huge natural amphitheatre.

Mini Palms Gorge: there's a lot of rock hopping and clamouring over boulders on this walk through a narrow gorge full of Livistona Palms. Allow around three hours return.

Echidna Chasm: a 2km walk through a narrow gorge similar to the Mini Palms Gorge that eventually leads to a metre-wide gap that is so deep it gets very little sunlight except at midday.

Picaninny Creek and Gorge: technically a challenging 30km two-day hike but you don't have to go all the way, although the deeper you go, the better it gets.

Best picnic spots

Watch the setting sun paint the escarpment red from the sunset lookout near Kurrajong Camp.

Camping, caravanning and accommodation options

The park has two public campgrounds. Kurrajong Camp is 7km north of the visitor centre. The Walardi campground is 12km

Cathedral Gorge.

south of the visitor centre, and closer to the beehive domes and Cathedral Gorge, but it is also close to the helicopter landing pad and more frequented by tour groups, which means it can get noisy. Both sites have pit toilets and bore water, but you will need to boil it before drinking.

Contact information

WA Department of Environment and Conservation (DEC) on (08) 9334-0333 or visit www.naturebase.net.

Shark Bay Marine Park and Hamelin Pool Nature Reserve

How to get there

This park, and its key attraction, Monkey Mia, is 856km north of Perth and 23km north-east of Denham.

When to go

The best time to visit is between June and October, when winds are generally lightest and the temperature is in the mid-20s. Temperatures can be extremely hot in the summer months.

- January: 21–37°C
- July: 9–21°C

Part of the Shark Bay World Heritage Area, Shark Bay Marine Park has the largest area of seagrass and the largest number of species ever recorded in one place on the planet.

For most visitors though, Shark Bay is synonymous with Monkey Mia, one of Western Australia's most popular destinations. Around 400 bottlenose dolphins live in the waters near Monkey Mia, and most mornings, several dolphins drift into the shallows to be handfed by scores of eager tourists, as they have been since 1964, when a woman from one of the nearby fishing camps befriended the dolphins and began regularly feeding them.

The dolphins are wild, and they come and go as they please. The Department of Environment and Conservation (DEC), insists they are not reliant upon humans for their complete diet. At the beach they are fed up to three times per day under the guidance of DEC officers, receiving a maximum of 2kg of fish per day—their average daily intake is between 8 and 15kg, so they remain self sufficient. The dolphins are not fed after 1pm.

According to staff at the resort, dolphins have visited every day (except for four) in the last five years. It is one of the few places in Australia where dolphins visit daily, not seasonally, and unlike most dolphin encounters it costs nothing.

But the dolphins are not the only attraction of this world-heritage listed marine park. It's also home to turtles, whales, prawns, scallops, sea snakes, fish and sharks, together with a unique mix of tropical and temperate fish species and the vast underwater meadows of seagrass. You can often see dugongs and marine turtles in the bay—indeed the bay is home to the world's largest population of dugongs, nature's only vegetarian sea mammal. They feed only on seagrass, and Shark Bay's massive expanse of seagrass mean it is home to about 10 per cent of the world's dugong population (around 10,000). It's also one of the country's top dive spots, with underwater gardens of both soft and hard corals and colourful sponges.

Stromatolites at Hamelin Pool.

Shell Beach.

Hamelin Pool Marine Nature Reserve is adjacent to Shark Bay Marine Reserve, and is one of only two places in the world with living marine stromatolites, or 'living fossils'. Much more interesting than they look (they look rather like rocky lumps strewn untidily around the beach) they are actually built by microscopic living organisms, up to 3000 million individuals per square metre, that use sediment and other organic material to build stromatolites up to 1.5m high—up to 10 million times their size. Because they grow very slowly, a metre-high stromatolite could be about 2000 years old. They are able to survive here because Hamelin Pool's water is twice as saline as normal sea water.

A few kilometres down the road (roughly half-way between Monkey Mia and Hamelin Pool) is the remarkable Shell Beach made up of millions of tiny coquina shells—one of only two such beaches in the world. It stretches for approximately 110km and is between seven and 10m deep.

Top tracks and trails

The Wulibidi Yaninyina Trail: a 2km loop from Monkey Mia through coastal sand plains and along the beach. Some deep sand patches can be hard going and the walk is best just after sunrise or just before sunset. There is a bird hide and lookout around half way.

Hamelin Pool boardwalk: behind the tearooms at the Hamelin Pool Telegraph Station a track leads to a wooden boardwalk out over a large patch of stromatolites. It includes information boards about the formation and growth of the stromatolites.

Best picnic spots

There are picnic facilities at Monkey Mia, Hamelin Pool and Shell Beach.

Camping, caravanning and accommodation options

All overnight visitors to Monkey Mia must stay at Monkey Mia Dolphin Resort, which has a range of accommodation from beachfront motel-style units to backpacker dorms and powered caravan sites, some of them beachfront. Facilities include a swimming pool, hot tub and tennis court, internet café, digital photo lab, BBQs, mini-mart and laundries. The resort also has two restaurants, a café and two bars. Tel: 1800 653 611 or visit www.monkeymia.com.au.

You can also camp at the Hamelin Pool Telegraph Station which is next door to the marine reserve and only a few minutes walk from the stromatolites. Facilities include powered caravan sites, a tearoom and a somewhat dusty telegraph station museum.

Contact information

WA Department of Environment and Conservation (DEC) on (08) 9334-0333 or visit www.naturebase.net.

How to get there

Stirling Range National Park is around an hour's drive (around 100km) north-east of Albany.

When to go

The best time to go is October to December, when the stunning wildflower show is at its best. Winter time can be cold and wet, but be prepared for sudden changes in weather at any time.

- January: 13–26°C
- July: 6–14°C

Scarlet Banksia.

One of few truly rugged mountain ranges in the west, the Stirling Range is one of the few areas in Western Australia that is high enough, and cold enough, to get dustings of snow in winter, sometimes as much as five centimetres on the highest peaks. Around 100km north-east of Albany, the 65km-long range rises abruptly from the surrounding farmland, dominating the landscape long before you actually reach them. Called *Koi Kyeunu-ruff* (mist moving around the mountains) by the Noongar, they are famous for spectacular cloud formations that cling to the granite peaks like a gauzy veil, even when the rest of the sky is clear and blue.

It's one of the world's most important areas for wildflowers, with an astonishing 1,500 species (many of which grow nowhere else) packed within its boundaries; more species occur in the Stirling Range than in the entire British Isles and 87 plant species found here occur nowhere else on earth, although unlike other areas in Western Australia that are famous for their carpets of springtime wildflowers that stretch from horizon to horizon, the Stirling Range blooms in patches, hidden behind the prickly scrub that lines the road. Follow any of the paths that lead off the road and within a few metres you'll stumble across thickets of exquisite ground-hugging flowers and stands of flowering trees, like the brilliant red domed scarlet banksia nodding in the breeze, masses of orchids (38 per cent of all known Western

The Stirling Range.

Australian orchids are found here), the white starlike flowers of the southern cross, spiky yellow dryandra, fluffy pink pompom-ish pixie mops and the famous red mountain bells.

Top tracks and trails

The Stirling Range Road: a very scenic unsealed road that cuts through the heart of the range for 42km, linking up with the sealed Chester Pass Road. Drive west to east (from Red Gum Pass Road north of Mount Barker) for the best mountain views.

Bluff Knoll: the park's most popular attraction and highest peak. There's a boardwalk at the top of the winding road that leads out towards the 6km track that climbs up to the summit, 1095m above sea level. It's a tough four-hour return hike to the top.

Talyuberlup Peak: a demanding three-hour walk (3km) with quite a lot of rock hopping and scrambling over rock ledges.

Best picnic spots

There are picnic tables at White Gum Flat, Mount Magog and Talyuberlup Peak, all of which are easily accessed from the Stirling Range Road and feature a wide variety of wildflowers in season.

Camping, caravanning and accommodation options

You can camp at Moingup Springs, just off the Chester Pass Road in the heart of the national park. Facilities include gas barbecues. Stirling Range Retreat on the boundary of the park opposite the Bluff Knoll turnoff has caravan sites and a camping area as well as self-contained cabins: www.stirlingrange.com.au.

Contact information

WA Department of Environment and Conservation (DEC) on (08) 9334-0333 or visit www.naturebase.net.

How to get there

The park surrounds the towns of Walpole, Nornalup and Peaceful Bay, approximately 420km south of Perth. The Valley of the Giants Tree Top Walk is on the South Coast Highway between Walpole and Denmark.

When to go

Any time is a good time to visit this park, although it can be wet in winter and the wildflowers are at their best during spring.

- January: 13–26°C
- July: 7–16°C

Best known for the huge buttressed red tingle trees which are unique to the Walpole area and forests of towering karri trees, the most famous attraction of this coastal park is the Valley of the Giants Tree Top Walk, a 600m-long wheelchair-accessible steel walkway elevated 40m above the forest floor that winds through the canopy of the tingle trees. It's open every day except Christmas Day from 9am (last entry 4.15pm) with extended opening hours from 8am (last entry 5.15pm) 26 Dec–26 Jan.

Many visitors to the park don't see beyond the Valley of the Giants, however, which means they miss out on some stunning coastal

Valley of the Giants Tree Top Walk.

scenery and waterways, particularly Nonralup Inlet (Coalmine Beach is a great spot for swimming, canoeing, windsurfing and sailing) and Conspicuous Cliffs, one of the few places on the south coast accessible to 2WD, where you can often see whales in season (May to November) and there is a great lookout over the beach and coastal headlands. Another top spot is Circular Pool on the Frankland River in the northern section of the park, a delightful pool surrounded by forest that is a popular place for canoeing and catching marron in season (mid-Jan to mid-Feb, see www.fish. wa.gov.au for licence and season details).

Top tracks and trails

Ancient Empire Walk: part of the Valley of the Giants walk, a boardwalk winds through a grove of ancient tingle trees.
Circular Pool: wheelchair accessible, there are a number of viewing platforms that provide lookouts over the river, pool and forest as well as a boardwalk around the pool below.
Delaney Walk: a 10km return walk from Hilltop Lookout through karri and red tingle forest to Coalmine Beach. There's a lot of uphill on the way back.

Best picnic spots

Circular Pool is one of the park's most popular picnic spots, especially in summer, as is the Giants Picnic area among the giant tingle trees

not far from the Valley of the Giants treetop walk. There are gas barbecues at Coalmine Beach where you can picnic on the grass and swim in the inlet in summer, and the Channels (alongside the channel between Walpole and Nornalup inlets). Sandy Beach, also on Nornalup Inlet, is another good picnic spot where you can swim in summer, but you'll need to bring your own wood.

Camping, caravanning and accommodation options

There are no designated campsites in Walpole-Nornalup National Park, but you can camp in bordering D'Entrecasteuax National Park at Crystal Springs (see page 184) and there is a very good, if a little rustic, caravan park at Peaceful Bay that offers large grassy powered sites just behind the beach, Tel: (08) 9840-8060. There is also a caravan park at Coalmine Beach, Tel: 1800 670 026.

Contact information

WA Department of Environment and Conservation (DEC) on (08) 9334-0333 or visit www.naturebase.net. For information on the Valley of the Giants Tree Top Walk call (08) 9840-8263.

In brief...

14
Cape Range National Park

Bordering Ningaloo Marine Park near Exmouth (1200km north of Perth) is the Cape Range National Park. The Cape Range is the only elevated limestone range on the north-western coast of Western Australia. The weathered limestone range has plateaus of up to 314m high, and forms the spine of the peninsula that stretches up towards North West Cape. It is around ten million years old, and lies just half an hour south of Exmouth and it's a good way to access Ningaloo Reef (see page 202). Take a scenic drive along Shothole Canyon Road (not suitable for caravans) to a picnic area at the end of the canyon. You can camp at one of several beachside camping areas or live it up in one of the luxury safari tents at Sal Salis. www.salsalis.com.au.

Goongarrie homestead.

15
Gloucester National Park

Home of The Gloucester Tree, Western Australia's most famous karri tree. This 60m-high giant tree towers above the forest near Pemberton. It was once a fire lookout. Today, you can climb to a cabin in its upper branches for sensational views of the surrounding karri forest.

16
Goongarrie National Park

A former pastoral station set amongst arid plains and mulga 90km north of Kalgoorlie, Goongarrie offers a fascinating glimpse into remote station life. You can camp at the old homestead or shearers quarters—neither has power but both have woodchip heaters for hot showers and well-equipped kitchens; the homestead is particularly ideal for groups.

Shothole Canyon, Cape Range National Park.

17
John Forrest National Park

On the northern edge of The Hills Forest just east of Perth, this park was Western Australia's first national park, established in 1898. Highlights include views of the Swan coastal plain, walking trails, quiet pools and waterfalls. Follow the old railway track from the main picnic area to Hovea Falls, or wander north-west to National Park Falls. Just past the falls is Western Australia's only 'true' railway tunnel, The Swan View Tunnel built in 1893 and a major feature on the John Forrest Heritage Trail, a 10km trail through the park.

18
Karijini National Park

Formerly called Hamersley Range National Park this is the second largest national park in Western Australia. The park is famous for its gorges, many of the sheer-sided chasms are up to 100m deep. Highlights include Dales Gorge, where a stream with pools, waterfalls, and ferns contrast with the red, terraced cliffs and Oxer Lookout at the junction of Weano, Red, Hancock and Joffre Gorges, where tiers of banded rock tower over a pool at the bottom of the gorge. There are a number of walks exploring the many gorges and swimming holes, but most of them are rated as difficult and involve following narrow paths and clinging to rock ledges and splashing through near-freezing water. You can camp or stay at the new Karijini Eco Retreat, safari-style hard-floored tents with ensuites, visit www.karijiniecoretreat.com.au. The park is 310km from Roebourne or 1400km north-west of Perth.

Rocky outcrops at Mirima (Hidden Valley) National Park.

Windjana Gorge.

19 Mirima (Hidden Valley) National Park

If you can't get to Purnululu National Park this tiny park, just two kilometres from Kununurra, will give you a taste of what the Bungle Bungles are like, albeit on a much smaller scale. The area abounds in wildlife with lots of lizards, birds and rock wallabies as well as very photogenic boab trees that grow on the rock faces. There are three very good short walks (400–800m) that lead to lookouts with view over Kununurra. Day use only.

20 Tunnel Creek National Park

Tunnel Creek flows through a tunnel beneath the Napier Range forming Western Australia's oldest cave system. It was made famous in the 19th century by an Aboriginal leader known as Jandamarra who used the 750m-long tunnel-like cave as a hideout. You can walk 750m through the tunnel. Take a torch and shoes that you don't mind getting wet. It's a day use area only and is 115km from Fitzroy Crossing, 180km from Derby.

21 Windjana Gorge National Park

The same ancient reef that forms Tunnel Creek (above) and Geikie Gorge (page 190) has been eroded by the Lennard River to create a wide, 100m-high gorge that cuts through the limestone of the Napier Range exposing countless fossils. You can take a self-guided 7km return walk along the length of the gorge beside the river where you can see freshwater crocodiles sunning themselves beside the rock pools. There's basic camping but you'll need to bring your own drinking water. Windjana Gorge is 150km from Fitzroy Crossing (via unsealed road) and 145km north-east of Derby on the Gibb River Road.

South Australia

Australia's driest state with the largest proportion of semi-desert, South Australia has some of the most inhospitable landscapes in the country. It also has some of the most fertile—Australia's longest river, The Murray, spills into the ocean in the east of the state; the peninsulas and islands provide a rugged and beautiful coastline and to the west, the spectacular cliffs of the Great Australian Bight trace the path of the longest, straightest road in the world across the Nullarbor Plain.

Most parks with facilities charge an entry fee, as well as a camping fee. Twelve-month multi-park passes are available and cover unlimited entry to all parks except Kangaroo Island and the desert parks. For travellers there is a two-month holiday pass. You can also buy a camping option that entitles you to camp for periods of up to five nights at a time in any one place in any park that has designated camping.

The Kangaroo Island pass provides 12-month entry into the islands parks and guided tours at most of Kangaroo Island's popular nature-based tourist attractions such as Seal Bay and the lighthouses of Flinders Chase National Park.

If heading into the South Australian outback you will need to purchase a Desert Parks Pass for access and camping (where permitted) for a period of 12 months. Parks covered include Simpson Desert Conservation Park, Simpson Desert Regional Reserve, Innamincka Regional Reserve, Coongie Lakes National Park, Lake Eyre National Park, Witjira National Park, Tallaringa Conservation Park, Wabma Kadarbu Mound Springs Conservation Park (camping not permitted) and Strzelecki Regional Reserve. At the time of going to print these cost $107 ($67 to renew) but are good value as they include a useful information pack and excellent detailed maps.

You can buy passes at various Department of Environment and Heritage (DEH) and National Parks Offices through the state. For Desert Parks Passes call the desert parks hotline 1800 816 078 or visit www.parks.sa.gov.au.

How to get there

Coffin Bay is 50km west of Port Lincoln, which is 650km south-west of Adelaide.

When to go

Temperatures are moderate most of the year. Summer is usually much drier than the winter months.

- January: 15–25°C
- July: 8–16°C

One of the best kept beach secrets in the country is the Eyre Peninsula, the triangle of land jutting into the sea between Adelaide and the Great Australian Bight. It is the outback gone coastal; where vast, undulating wheat fields tumble into the sea over towering, knife-edged limestone cliffs. In this beautiful and sometimes remote region you'll find beach after beach, visited only by the occasional fisherman, screeching seagulls and very few of the madding coastal crowds you find along the rest of the Australian coast.

Coffin Bay National Park is on the western side of the Peninsula, about 40km from Port Lincoln and is great for 4WDs. You can drive the length of the peninsula to Point Sir Isaac, but be warned, the sand can trap even the most experienced four-wheel driver. Lower your tyre pressures and carry a compressor

to re-inflate them—you will need to do this several times during the trip. It's only 55km from the ranger station but it will take around three hours each way. Much of the road is actually on the beach, so you need to check the tide chart before you set off.

Fishing is one of the park's most popular pastimes and around Coffin Bay you'll get whiting, trevally, salmon, garfish, tommy ruff, flathead and snapper. Good beach fishing spots include Seven Mile Beach, Black Springs, Sensation Beach and Almonta Beach.

Top tracks and trails

Yangie Bay: there is a short climb to Yangie Lookout with views overlooking Yangie Bay and Marble Range or you can extend it with the 40-minute Kallara Nature Walk, via Yangie Lookout or the 5km Yangie Island Trail that leads to a close up view of Yangie Island from the adjoining beach. Or walk between the vegetated dunes that come out on the expansive Long Beach, a 10km one-way walk from the Yangie Bay campground.

Black Springs Well: follow the coast around the headland overlooking sheltered Port Douglas. 40 minutes return.

Black Rocks: a two-hour return walk to the rugged coastline of Avoid Bay with views overlooking Lake Damascus.

Boarding House Bay: an eight-hour, 23km

return walk through coastal heathlands, samphire flats and mallee woodlands to Boarding House Bay, a rugged coastline of cliffs, beaches and offshore reefs.

Best picnic spots

Pick a beach, any beach and lay out the picnic rug. The best spots with facilities are Black Springs and Yangie Bay.

Camping, caravanning and accommodation options

The most popular campground is at Yangie Bay, a sheltered bay surrounded by dense shrub. All other campsites in the park are four-wheel-drive only and most have no facilities. Sensation Beach is quite exposed, while Big Yangie, Black Springs, Morgans Landing and The Pool near Point Sir Isaac all offer more sheltered beachside campsites.

Campsites are right on the edge of the beach and you could have the place to yourself.

Contact information

For more information visit www.parks.sa.gov.au.

Fresh oyster. Image courtesy Mark Bean.

Coffin Bay track.

Coorong National Park

How to get there

The Coorong National Park is about two hours drive from Adelaide and extends 130km south east from the mouth of the River Murray near Goolwa. Best road access is via the Princes Highway, or via boat from Goolwa.

When to go

Summer temperatures are much higher away from the coast. Winter is generally wetter than summer.

- January: 12–24°C
- July: 5–16°C

A long, narrow stretch of windswept beach flanked by coastal dunes, lagoons and wetlands extending 145km south-east from the mouth of the Murray River are among the highlights of this 50,000ha park. Home to an enormous variety of birds, animals and fish including many species of migratory birds, the area was made famous by the 1976 movie made from Colin Thiele's children's novel, *Storm Boy* (1963), about a young boy who befriends a pelican. Pelicans are abundant in the park. Indeed, the largest breeding colony of the Australian Pelican (*Pelicanus conspicillatus)* is at Jack's Point Observatory.

The Coorong is also rich in archaeological sites with many Aboriginal middens and burial

The Coorong is popular with paddlers. Image courtesy South Australia Tourism Commission.

sites scattered through the park's dunes, indicating that the area has been home to Aboriginal people for many thousands of years.

Bird watching, fishing and boating aside, the Coorong is also a popular 4WD destination, and you can drive along the stunning narrow ribbon of sand called the Younghusband Peninsula for 150km from the Granites near Kingston SE to the mouth of the Murray River. Separated from the mainland by a chain of salt-water lagoons, huge flocks of waterbirds, gorgeous beaches and tough dunes make this a great drive, but you need to be wary of wind and tide conditions and the route should not be attempted in winter.

The Murray River, Australia's longest, seeps rather than spills into the sea at the Murray Mouth on Hindmarsh Island. There is a lookout platform and you can walk along the beach, although at the time of going to press

Boardwalk over the dunes. Image courtesy South Australia Tourism Commission.

the area is being dredged due to low water flows to prevent its closure.

Top tracks and trails

Nakun Kungun Trek: from Salt Creek to 42 Mile Crossing via Chinaman's Well is the best walk in the Coorong. The 27km trail winds its way through several different types of vegetation, passing ephemeral lakes and areas rich in wildlife and will take around 48 hours. You can camp along Loop Road and at 42 Mile Crossing.

Godfrey's Landing Walk: you'll need a boat to access the 90-minute walk trail from Coorong Lagoon through the sand dunes of the Younghusband Peninsula to the Southern Ocean.

Best picnic spots

There are picnic tables at most of the campsites but the best is the picnic shelter at 42 Mile Crossing where you can walk across the dunes to the wild and windswept Southern Ocean Beach. Salt Creek and Parnka Point, which has great views up and down the lagoon, are other favourite picnic spots.

Camping, caravanning and accommodation options

There are campsites at 28 Mile Crossing, 32 Mile Crossing, 42 Mile Crossing, Barker Knoll, Godfreys Landing, overlooking the Coorong lagoon at Long Point, Loop Road, Mark Point, Old Coorong Road, Parnka Point (and Tea Tree Crossing. Facilities are pretty much limited to toilets and picnic tables only. 42 Mile Crossing, Parnka Point, Long Point and Mark Point are suitable for caravans but do not have power.

Contact information

For more information visit www.parks.sa.gov.au.

Flinders Chase National Park

How to get there

Flinders Chase is approximately 110km west of Kingscote.

You can fly to Kangaroo Island or take your car across on the ferry. Air South (www.airsouth.com.au) and REX (www.regionalexpress.com.au) both have several flights daily between Adelaide and Kingscote. Kangaroo Island Sealink operates vehicle and passenger ferries between Cape Jervis on the Fleurieu Peninsula and Penneshaw. Tel: 13 13 01 or visit www.sealink.com.au.

When to go

The weather is relatively mild during both summer and winter, although ocean breezes can be cold so good windproof clothing is essential.

- January: 14–24°C
- July: 9–15°C

Flinders Chase National Park, which covers most of the western end of Kangaroo Island, is one of Australia's largest reserve areas and contains many of the island's most popular attractions and a wealth of wildlife.

At Cape du Couedic on the south-western tip of the island the rocks below the lighthouse are home to a colony of New Zealand fur seals, wallowing in the sun or frolicking in the surf under the dramatic rock arc of Admirals Arch.

Nearby is another island must-see, a cluster of huge weather-sculptured granite boulders perched on a granite dome that swoops 75m to the sea, appropriately called Remarkable Rocks.

Other highlights include Cape Borda, with its unusually-shaped lighthouse 155m above sea level. Guided tours are available. Four kilometres to the east is Scotts Cove lookout, where you can see the spectacular cliffs of Cape Torrens and Cape Forbin. At Rocky River you can see koalas and walk the Platypus Waterholes Walkway. Wherever you are, keep your eyes peeled for koalas in the tree tops beside the road, dawdling echidnas crossing in front of your car, and of course, the hundreds of wallabies and kangaroos that are ubiquitous on the island. If you can't spot wildlife here you just aren't trying.

Top tracks and trails

Breakneck River Trail: this 6km trail follows the river valley to a small beach and coastal lagoon surrounded by cliffs.

Cape du Couedic walk: a 40-minute loop taking in the east and west sides of the cape with views from the cliff-top lookout of Remarkable Rocks and the southern coastline. The walk joins the Admirals Arch Walk.

The Platypus Waterholes walk: this lovely little walk has part-disabled access to waterholes of the Rocky River with boardwalks,

Remarkable Rocks.

lookouts and viewing platforms where, if you are lucky, you may see platypus.

Snake Lagoon walk: follows a ridgeline through mallee woodland, before reaching Rocky River crossing to the river mouth (two hours).

Weirs Cove trail: a 3km walk linking the Cape du Couedic Lighthouse to the landing site at Weirs Cove, taking in spectacular coastal views along the bay.

Best picnic spots

There are good picnic facilities near the Flinders Chase Visitor Centre and there is a picnic shelter at Cape Borda Lightstation.

Camping, caravanning and accommodation options

The best camping in Flinders Chase is at Rocky River near the Visitor Centre. Facilities include showers, gas barbecues and (unpowered) caravan sites. You can bush camp at Snake Lagoon, Harveys Return and West Bay.

Accommodation is also available in the lighthouse keeper's cottages at Cape Borda and Cape de Couedic. Call (08) 8559-7235 or email kiparksaccom@saugov.sa.gov.au.

Contact information

For more information visit www.parks.sa.gov. au and www.tourkangarooisland.com.au.

4 Flinders Ranges National Park

How to get there

Wilpena Pound is 443km north of Adelaide, via Quorn and Hawker.

When to go

The Flinders is fairly dry all year, with most chance of rain falling during the summer months. The best time to visit is in spring, when the ragged hills and valley floors are carpeted in wildflowers.

Yellow footed rock wallaby. Image courtesy South Australia Tourism Commission.

- January: 20–34°C
- July: 3–16°C

The Flinders Ranges in central South Australia is an astonishing landscape of deeply weathered mountain peaks, deep gorges, dry riverbeds and vast arid stony plains that erupt into colour when they become carpeted by wildflowers in spring. The craggy ranges are the eroded stumps of mountains that are more than 600 million years old and were, according to the geologists who are drawn to the geological riches of the area, once higher than the Himalaya.

The park's star attraction, Wilpena Pound, is a crater-like pile of rock that covers 83 square kilometres and rises sharply from the surrounding flat plains. The wooded interior—accessible through just one gorge—is 11km long and 8km across. The best way to really see the distinctive shape is on a scenic flight

from Wilpena Pound Resort. Other highlights include Brachina Gorge, a refuge for the rare yellow-footed rock-wallaby as well as many species of birds and reptiles, and Chambers Gorge, a huge red rock gorge and waterhole with a gallery of Aboriginal engravings. The 10km access track east into the gorge is rough and rocky, but fine for 2WD vehicles except after rain. A short walking track leads into the gorge to the engraving site.

While the Flinders is remote and rugged, main roads are accessible to conventional sedans, but many side tracks are 4WD only.

Top tracks and trails

Hills Homestead Walk: an easy two-hour walk along Wilpena Creek to a restored 1914 homestead. You can also walk to Wangara Lookout from Hills Homestead for breathtaking views of Wilpena Pound at the lookout. A shuttle bus service is provided to shorten the walk.

Blinman Pools Walk: a pretty five-hour walk

Wilpena Pound. Image courtesy South Australia Tourism Commission.

through a rocky creek bed to the Blinman Pools where there are cascading waterfalls, majestic river red gums and wedge-tailed eagles.

St Mary Peak Trek: a challenging long walk (nine hours, 21.5km) to the highest peak in Flinders Ranges.

Brachina Gorge Geological Tour: is a 20km self-guided driving trail that passes through 130 million years of earth history. The trail is best travelled from east to west, from the Brachina Gorge/Blinman Road junction.

Morlana Scenic drive: 28km unsealed road connecting the Wilpena and Leigh Creek Roads, this is one of the best drives through the Flinders Ranges. You will see stunning scenery featuring the southern wall of Wilpena Pound, Black Gap Lookout, red Range, Elder Range. It is especially colourful during spring and late afternoon. Signposted drive entrances are 24km north of Hawker on the Wilpena Road, and 42km north of Hawker on the Leigh Creek Road.

Best picnic spots

There are a number of good picnic spots scattered throughout the park. A favourite is Bunyeroo Lookout for its stunning views across the ranges.

Camping, caravanning and accommodation options

You can camp at Bunyeroo and Brachina gorges and Aroona Valley, although facilities are limited to toilets and firepits and you will need to bring your own water.

Wilpena Pound Resort has 30 powered caravan sites or you can stay in one of the motel-style units at the resort. For details visit www.wilpenapound.com.au.

Contact information

For more information visit www.parks.sa.gov.au.

Brachina Gorge. Image courtesy South Australia Tourism Commission.

Gawler Ranges National

How to get there

Gawler Ranges National Park is approximately 350km (as the crow flies; around 560km by road) north-west of Adelaide, at the top of the Eyre Peninsula. Closest town is Wudinna (40km south of the park).

When to go

The Gawler Ranges are dry most of the year. The best times to visit are in spring, winter and autumn, when daytime temperatures are less severe.

- January: 20–34°C
- July: 3–19°C

One of Australia's youngest national parks (it was declared in 2002), the Gawler Range is one of Australia's oldest mountain ranges, a mind boggling 1500 million years old. Originally more than three times their current height, they have been eroded through the millennia to become a small ridge of weathered hills that rarely rise more than 450m (the highest is Nukey Bluff at 465m). Rough, rugged and remote, the battered ranges were formed by massive volcanic activity that spewed more than 3700 cubic kilometres out of the earth in one huge eruption, leaving behind a dramatic landscape of rock formations, including one of the largest examples of volcanic rhyolite (commonly known as organ pipe formations) in the world.

It's a relatively unknown and unvisited area, eclipsed and overshadowed by the bigger tourist attractions and resorts of the Flinders Ranges, which, if like to have your wilderness pretty much to yourself, is rather a good thing. Most tracks within the park are four-wheel drive only.

Wildlife is plentiful, particularly kangaroos, wallabies, wombats and emus, and the park is also home to about 21 rare and threatened species including the yellow-footed rock-wallaby, central long-eared bat, sandhill dunnart, mallee fowl, Major Mitchell cockatoo, honey myrtle, and the locally endemic crimson mallee.

Top tracks and trails

Kolay Mirica Falls: a short walk into a gorge-like chasm of rhyolite organ pipe shaped rock formations. The waterfall only runs after rain.

Waulkinna Hill: there are no marked walking trails but a scramble up this hill gives great views over the surrounding area.

Organ Pipes: a short walk to one of the most visited attractions in the park, the Organ Pipes, a very photogenic outcrop of rhyolite formations.

Sturts Track: 4WD track around the dry salt lake, Lake Sturt. The track is closed during the fire ban season (usually 1 November to 31 March).

Best picnic spots

There are no formal picnic facilities in the park,

but head to Kolay Mirica Falls where you can perch on the rocks in the shade. Another good spot is Old Paney Homestead. Lake Sturt is a great place to watch the sunset.

Camping, caravanning and accommodation options

There are several good, reasonably shady, campgrounds with views to red rocky outcrops although you will need a four-wheel-drive to access all of them and there are no facilities. For those that like a touch of luxury you can join a three-day guided tour of the park with Gawler Ranges Safaris, where accommodation is at Kangaluna Camp—three permanent safari tents encircling a large dining area and kitchen on the edge of the national park. Each of the 'tents' is raised up above the ground with a carpeted floor, has two bedrooms, is solar powered and has an ensuite. Call 1800 243 343 or visit www.gawlerrangessafaris.com.

Contact Information

Contact: for more information visit www.parks.sa.gov.au.

The Organ Pips. Image courtesy Bill McKinnon.

Lake Sturt.

How to get there

Innamincka is 1065km north of Adelaide and you will need a four-wheel drive to navigate the final 460-km long Strzelecki Track from Lyndhurst, north of Leigh Creek at the northern end of the Flinders Ranges. The actual 'track' was originally blazed by Harry Redford, a cattle thief droving 1000 stolen cattle over untracked country from central Queensland to Adelaide. Redford was eventually caught, but the jury was so impressed with his heroic efforts in establishing a new stock route they declined to convict him.

When to go

Summer can be extremely hot. The best time to travel is during the winter months when days are dry and warm but nights can be freezing.

- January: 21–45°C
- July: 4–19°C

Surrounded by desert and gibber plains, Innamincka is a tiny outback settlement that is pretty much just a general store, petrol station and pub on the banks of Cooper Creek, most famous as the place where ill-fated explorers Burke and Wills died. Unfortunately, the tragic death of the two explorers has unjustly given this beautiful watercourse a bad reputation. Sure it's remote, but far from being bleak and inhospitable, Cooper Creek (often mistakenly called Cooper's Creek) is a beautiful oasis in the midst of harsh and stony desert country.

One of Australia's last unspoiled inland waterways, the Cooper is a wide, clean river that attracts a wealth of birdlife to its almost constant water supply. At sunrise and sunset the reflections of the river gums shimmer while hundreds of cockies screech and pelicans drift by feeding on fish. Cooper Creek is one of the few carp-free rivers in Australia and it is popular with anglers who often pull in good bream, catfish and yellowbelly. It is also perfect for paddling and you can hire canoes and kayaks at the Innamincka Hotel.

Wills' grave is about 25km west of the town, a memorial to Burke is along the creek to the east and the famous 'Dig' tree where supplies were left for the explorers is 55km from town.

Top tracks and trails

The extreme conditions of the outback deserts are not conducive to bushwalking and there are few marked trails to follow. If you are stepping out, walking along a creek or between two dunes is best and will provide more wildlife and flora-spotting opportunities. Make sure you take water and do not loose your bearings.

Cooper Creek. Image courtesy Bill McKinnon.

Best picnic spots

Most of the campsites are also ideal places to set up for a picnic lunch or sunset sundowner, although you'll need to be self sufficient with your own chairs and tables, as there are no picnic facilities within the park. A favourite spot is Cullyamurra Waterhole, a great place for swimming, bird watching or simply admiring the view.

Camping, caravanning and accommodation options

Cooper Creek is a beautiful place to camp and there are good camping sites on the south side of Cooper Creek in the Innamincka Town Common, including Policemans Waterhole, Ski Beach, King's Site, Minkie Waterhole and Will's Grave. There are also camp sites west of the township and at Cullyamurra Waterhole. Avoid camping under river red gums as they can drop large branches without warning, even on still days.

Contact information

You will need to have a valid Desert Parks Pass to visit this park. For more information visit www.parks.sa.gov.au or call 1800 816 078.

How to get there

Innes National Park is on the southern tip of the Yorke Peninsula, approximately 300km west of Adelaide.

When to go

Temperatures are moderate most of the year. Summer is usually much drier than the winter months, although winter is a great time for salmon fishing.

- January: 15–25°C
- July: 8–16°C

On the southern tip of the Yorke Peninsula, this park offers great coastal scenery, from the rugged cliffs of Ethel Beach to the wide, sweeping expanse of West Cape and the beautiful protected sandy bays of Dolphin and Shell Beaches.

More than 40 shipwrecks lay off the coast of the Yorke Peninsula, many off the coast of Innes National Park. The park's most famous wreck is *The Ethel,* wrecked in 1904 during a storm. You can still see traces of the wreck at Ethel Beach.

One of the best surfing spots in South Australia, the waters are also popular with snorkellers and divers who enjoy exploring the sea life around the jetties and off-shore reefs as well as some of the many shipwrecks dating from 1849 to 1982. Browns Beach is one of South Australia's best salmon fishing areas and the sheltered coves of Dolphin and Shell beaches and the Fisherman's Village end of Pondalowie Bay are great spots for swimming.

Whale watch from the cliff tops for Southern Right Whales during the winter at Stenhouse Bay and Cape Spencer and explore the historic ruins of Inneston mining village. There are three lighthouses in the park and other highlights include 3000-year-old living stromatolites around the edges of the salt lakes and The Gap, an impressive wind and rain-eroded cutting in a 60m vertical cliff face.

Top tracks and trails

Thomson-Pfitzner Plaster interpretative trail: the park has an extensive network of coastal bushwalking trails, but one of the best is this three-hour trail that follows an old wooden horse-drawn rail line. It is a loop from Inneston Village.

Barkers Rock Walking Trail: a good 5km walk for coastal views.

Browns Beach to Gym Beach: a three-hour walk past high sand dunes between Browns Beach and Gym Beach.

Royston Head: a two-hour return walk with panoramic coastal views of offshore reefs and islands.

Best picnic spots

There are barbecue facilities at Stenhouse Bay and Pondalowie campground.

Camping, caravanning and accommodation options

There are a number of good camping spots including caravan sites at Stenhouse Bay; and Pondalowie, which also has showers, flushing toilets and barbecues with easy access to the Fisherman's Village boat ramp and Pondalowie Bay as well as several beachside camping spots. Jolly's Beach and Cable Bay are much quieter with very basic facilites (Jolly's Beach has no facilities at all), and at Surfers Camp a boardwalk through the sand dunes runs to the popular surf break and viewing platform of Pondalowie Bay. Generator use is only permitted in Pondalowie West and Stenhouse Bay campgrounds. It's a popular park with families, but no bookings are taken and campsites are allocated on a first-in basis. You can also stay in heritage accommodation within the park: five lodges are available at old Inneston township and there's a cute cottage, Shepherds Hut, at Shell Beach. BYO bedding. Phone (08) 8854-3200.

Contact information

For more information visit www.parks.sa.gov.au.

Cape Spencer. Image courtesy South Australia Tourism Commission.

Surfing at Chinamans Hat. Image courtesy South Australia Tourism Commission.

Lake Eyre National Park

How to get there

There are two access tracks to Lake Eyre National Park. One turns off the Oodnadatta Track approximately 7km south-east of William Creek and runs to Halligan Bay (64km). The second runs 94km north from Marree to Level Post Bay via Muloorina Station. Both tracks cross pastoral properties and are 4WD only. Make sure you have reserves of fuel, water and food. There are no public access tracks into Elliot Price Conservation Park.

When to go

Summer can be extremely hot and makes travel in this area a very dangerous proposition. The best time to travel is during the winter months when days are dry and warm but nights can be freezing.

- January: 21–45°C
- July: 4–19°C

Lake Eyre National Park is about as remote as it gets! It's a stark, largely inaccessible, inhospitable wilderness where a vehicle breakdown can quickly develop into a life-threatening situation, sometimes with tragic results. That said, it is an incredibly beautiful place that will linger in your imagination for many years.

Most of the time, the 'lake' is a vast, shimmering plain of bright, white salt. The

Pelicans. Image courtesy South Australia Tourism Commission.

lake fills with water, on average, around once every eight years, when it becomes a breeding ground for masses of waterbirds that have flown thousands of kilometres to the newly arrived body of water.

Before you visit the park, have a beer at William Creek (population 10) which is inside the boundaries of Anna Creek, the largest cattle station in the world at over 30,000 square kilometres. The tiny township was first built to service the Overland Telegraph and the railway, but now all you'll find is a character-filled pub built of corrugated iron, a caravan park with new cabins and a general store. You can also take scenic flights over nearby Lake Eyre during the winter months.

Full or not, the lake is a great place to camp for a few days. You must be self sufficient with gas stoves and plenty of

Salt crust. Image courtesy South Australia Tourism Commission.

Lake Eyre in flood. Image courtesy South Australia Tourism Commission.

water—and if something does go wrong, under no circumstances should you leave your vehicle; people have perished out here walking to help after a breakdown. Although the lakebed looks firm and safe to drive on, it is only a thin crust that covers quicksand-like mud, so always keep to the track. Sign in and out at the William Creek pub before you go and when you return.

Top tracks and trails

Walking is definitely not recommended in this park due to the extreme remoteness and inhospitable climate.

Best picnic spots

Self sufficiency is the key here—there are countless great vantage points around the lake, but no structured picnic areas or facilities.

Camping, caravanning and accommodation options

There are no designated camping spots within the park and no facilities. But if you don't mind bush camping, and are totally self-sufficient with food and water, Halligan Bay is a great spot with endless views over the salt pan and desert plains. You can camp at the William Creek Hotel, which also has very basic rooms (tel: (08) 8670-7880) and across the road at the William Creek Caravan Park.

Contact information

You will need to have a valid Desert Parks Pass to visit this park. For more information visit www.parks.sa.gov.au or call 1800 816 078.

Lincoln National Park

How to get there

Lincoln National Park is 15km south of Port Lincoln, which is 650km south-west of Adelaide. Access to Memory Cove Wilderness Area is limited and is locked; the key is available from the Port Lincoln Visitor Information Centre, 3 Adelaide Place, Port Lincoln.

When to go

Temperatures are moderate most of the year. Summer is usually much drier than the winter months.

- January: 15–25°C
- July: 8–16°C

A rugged peninsula with vast expanses of coastal mallee, spectacular ocean cliffs and extensive sand dunes, sandy beaches and sheltered camping sites are just some of the highlights of this beautiful national park on the southern tip of the Eyre Peninsula.

Access to the park's northern section including Cape Donington is fine for conventional vehicles, but most of the side tracks are four-wheel-drive only.

The track in the rugged southern section of the park is largely along the cliff edges to the Sleaford sand dunes, an endless sea of towering white sand dunes leading to beaches pounded by enormous waves, although the final dune section should only be attempted by experienced four-wheel-drivers. Make sure you lower your tyre pressure before driving on the sand.

The more sheltered, northern section of the park has a string of pretty bays and calm beaches. Pick of the crop is Memory Cove, a pretty beach protected by two headlands that was named by Matthew Flinders as a reminder of the tragic accident which took the lives of eight of his crewmen in 1802, but you will need to get a gate key from the Visitors Centre in Port Lincoln before you go.

Top tracks and trails

The Investigator Trail: a 93km long-distance coastal loop trail which takes its name from the *Investigator*, the ship commanded by Matthew Flinders while surveying the rugged coastline of Lower Eyre Peninsula in 1802. The trail is easy to walk and well marked and can also be broken up into smaller sections.

Stamford Hill: an energetic 45-minute walk up Stamford Hill provides spectacular views of Boston Bay, Port Lincoln and across the national park. A monument commemorating Matthew Flinders voyage of discovery is at the top.

Donington Loop: a two-hour walk around the tip of the Donington Peninsula with great views of offshore islands, granite outcrops and sandy beaches. You can often see Australian sea

Take a drive along the dramatic coastline. Image courtesy Bill McKinnon.

lions and New Zealand fur seals on Donington Island near the lighthouse.

Best picnic spots

There are picnic facilities at Stamford Hill, September Beach and Memory Cove.

Camping, caravanning and accommodation options

There is a variety of beachside camping. The most popular is Memory Cove, but you will need to book at Port Lincoln Visitor Information Centre and it is four-wheel-drive access only. Other good campsites include Fishermans Point, Surfleet Cove, Taylor's Landing and September Beach (each with toilet facilities) and beach-side bush camping at Carcase Rock, MacLaren Point, Spalding Cove and Woodcutters Beach. Best campgrounds for caravans are at September Beach or Surfleet Cove, although neither have power.

You can also stay at historic Donington Cottage overlooking Spalding Cove. Contact Port Lincoln Visitor Information Centre for bookings on (08) 8683-3544 or 1300 788 378.

Contact information

For more information visit www.parks.sa.gov.au or the Port Lincoln Visitor Information Centre, tel: (08) 8683-3544 or 1300 788 378.

Nullarbor National Park and Regional Reserve

How to get there

Nullarbor National Park stretches for 185km from Border Village, on the WA/SA border east to Nullarbor Roadhouse, 1070km west of Adelaide.

When to go

Summer can be extremely hot. The best time to travel is during the winter months when days are dry and warm but nights can be freezing.

- January: 10–40°C
- July: 4–25°C

Watch out for wildlife. Image courtesy South Australia Tourism Commission.

At the head of the Great Australian Bight and part of the immense, treeless Nullarbor Plain, this park contains the world's largest semi-arid karst (cave) landscape. It is rich in Aboriginal culture and has the largest population of the southern hairy-nosed wombat. The 80m-high Nullarbor cliffs, which stretch for 200km, provide spectacular views of the Southern Ocean coastline.

At Head of Bight, the dip in the coastline 20km east of Nullarbor Roadhouse, there is a whale viewing platform where, during the whale season between June and October, you can see up to 100 Southern Right Whales and their calves lolling in the water at the foot of the cliffs beneath. The whales come here each year during winter, escaping from the freezing Antarctic waters to give birth and it's one of the best whale watching places in the world.

The lands surrounding the highway east of Nullarbor Roadhouse until almost as far as Nundroo, 145km to the east, are owned by the Anangu people. The Yalata Roadhouse, the best on the Nullarbor, also has an Aboriginal art gallery where paintings, carvings and other work by local artists is sold at a fraction of the price you'd find in city galleries. From Yalata, the scenery begins to subtly change, with more trees and homesteads along the way as you head towards the Eyre Peninsula.

Beneath the Nullarbor Plain lies an extensive network of limestone caves, including Australia's (and one of the world's) longest underwater caves, Cocklebiddy Cave. The object of numerous cave diving expeditions over

Whale watching at Head of Bight. Image courtesy South Australia Tourism Commission.

the years and several world record attempts, the entrance chamber is more than 300m-long and leads to a 180m-long lake. The cave then consists of a single, straight tunnel more than six kilometres long, of which more than 90 per cent is underwater. The Nullarbor is unique as it is the only desert region with extensive caves that contain large quantities of water. Most of the Nullarbor caves are difficult or dangerous to locate and enter, and the cave environment and inhabitants are extremely fragile and can easily be damaged or destroyed; these caves are considered the sole preserve of expert cavers and can be explored only through organised caving expeditions.

Top tracks and trails

Bunda Cliffs: there are six cliff-top lookouts, the first is signposted just east of Border Village.

Best picnic spots

There are a number of rest areas to stop at along the way.

Camping, caravanning and accommodation options

No camping is permitted in Nullarbor National Park. There are designated camping areas at road houses or bush camping at rest areas. Note that limited water supplies are available between Norseman and Ceduna so be sure to stock up before crossing the Nullarbor.

Contact information

For more information visit www.parks.sa.gov.au or www.nullarbornet.com.au.

Bunda Cliffs. Image courtesy South Australia Tourism Commission.

Seal Bay Conservation Park

How to get there

Seal Bay is approximately 60km west of Kingscote.

You can fly to Kangaroo Island or take your car across on the ferry. Air South (www.airsouth.com.au) and REX (www.regionalexpress.com.au) both have several flights daily between Adelaide and Kingscote. Kangaroo Island Sealink operates vehicle and passenger ferries between Cape Jervis on the Fleurieu Peninsula and Penneshaw. Tel: 13 1301 or visit www.sealink.com.au.

When to go

The weather is relatively mild during both summer and winter, although ocean breezes can be cold so good windproof clothing is essential. The best time to see the sea lions is in the late afternoon.

- January: 14–24°C
- July: 9–15°C

There is no better place to come face to face with a host of wild animals than Kangaroo Island. Close to half of Australia's third largest island is either natural bushland or national park, and you won't be on the island for very long before you come across some of the 4000 thousand penguins, 6000 fur seals, 700 rare Australian sea lions, 5000 koalas, 15,000 kangaroos, 254 species of birdlife and somewhere in between 500,000 and one million tammar wallabies that call the island home.

One of the most popular spots on the island for wildlife watching is the mis-named Seal Bay, a long, windswept beach where around 700 Australian sea lions haul out of the water to rest after spending three days or so hunting for food out at sea. It's the only place in Australia where you can get this close to the sea lions, all other colonies are perched amongst inaccessible rocky headlands, and you can join a 45-minute ranger-led tour of the beach, walking just metres away from the huge, sleepy animals.

Other animals you may see in the park include echidnas and southern right whales during the migration season between June and October, as well as sea eagles and other sea birds.

Also part of the same park, the area known as Little Sahara seven kilometres to the west is an area of massive razor-backed inland sand dunes. It's a tough climb up, but it only takes seconds to slide down on a well-waxed board and is almost too much fun. Just resist the urge to squeal or you'll end up with a mouthful of sand. Sand boards and toboggans are available for hire from the Vivonne Bay General Store through KI Outdoor Action. Tel: (08) 8559-4296.

Top tracks and trails

Boardwalk: if you don't want to join a guided tour of the beach at Seal Bay, there is a self-guided 800m wheelchair-accessible boardwalk with good viewing of the sea lions, although it does not allow you to get onto the sand or as close to the sea lions as the guided tour.

Best picnic spots

Picnic facilities and toilets are available at the Bales Bay, 3km from the Seal Bay Visitor Centre. There's a lookout here with great views of Cape Gantheaume and the wilderness area.

Camping, caravanning and accommodation options

Seal Bay is a day use area only. Camping and accommodation are available in nearby Vivonne Bay and in neighbouring Cape Gantheaume Wilderness Area you can camp at Murray's Lagoon or D'Estrees Bay.

Contact information

For more information visit www.parks.sa.gov.au and www.tourkangarooisland.com.au.

Seal Bay.

Australian sea lion.

12 Simpson Desert

How to get there

Most people access the park via Birdsville in Queensland, 1688km west of Brisbane (the park is 79km west of Birdsville) or via Dalhousie, 990km south-east of Alice Springs, although you can also access the park via the Birdsville Track.

When to go

Summer is extremely hot and the park is closed from December 1 to March 15. During the winter months days are dry and warm but nights can be freezing.

- January: 21–45°C
- July: 4–19°C

The Simpson Desert is one of the last frontiers of the outback, a sea of parallel red sand ridges some 300–500km across, covering a total area of 170,000 square kilometres that extends across the corners of South Australia, Queensland and the Northern Territory. It is protected in South Australia by the Simpson Desert Regional Reserve and the adjoining Simpson Desert Conservation Park and Witjira National Park to the west, as well as Simpson Desert National Park in Queensland.

It was the last of the Australian deserts to be explored by Europeans. Ted Colson was the first European to cross its expanse of red dunes, on camel, in 1936; the first vehicle crossed it in 1962. Now, it's top of the list for serious four-wheel drivers, and while thousands of people cross the Simpson each year, it is still not a trip to be taken lightly. You'll need to be self sufficient, carry good maps, make sure your vehicle is in tip-top condition, carry enough water for several days and basic spares.

Although one of the driest areas in Australia, the Simpson has a surprising amount of vegetation, ranging from spinifex and salt bush, gidgee and mulga and exquisite carpets of wildflowers after rain. Wildlife you will see includes red kangaroos, dingoes, small marsupials such as dunnarts and a vast range of birds and reptiles, including large lizards, such as perenties and the dangerous western brown snakes.

Top tracks and trails

Crossing the Simpson: travelling west to east across the desert, from Dalhousie hot springs to Birdsville, is easier than travelling east west, as prevailing winds have shaped the dunes with a more gentle slope in this direction. Be alert for oncoming vehicles on dune crests. Use a UHF CB radio to scan frequencies to detect oncoming vehicle convoys and fly a bright flag high on whip aerials or a pole to alert others of your approach. This is not a summer-time trip, temperatures can exceed 50°C. Total length: 650km, allow three days.

Best picnic spots

Anywhere where you can find some shade. Dalhousie Hot Springs at the beginning of the crossing in neighbouring Witjira National Park is a welcome oasis and a great swimming spot.

Camping, caravanning and accommodation options

There are no designated campsites as such, but you can camp anywhere near the track. The best places are in the lee of the dunes and towards the salt lakes in the central region where there is more shade from gidgee and mulga trees. You will need to be totally self sufficient with water, food and extra fuel and carry all rubbish out with you. Caravans and trailers are not recommended.

Contact information

You will need to have a valid Desert Parks Pass to visit this park. For more information visit www.parks.sa.gov.au or call 1800 816 078. For information on the Queensland sections of the park visit www.epa.qld.gov.au/parks_and_forests or call QPWS Birdsville on (07) 4656-3249 or (07) 4656-3272.

Make your own camp in the Simpson Desert. Image courtesy Bill McKinnon.

Desert dunes in the setting sun. Image courtesy Bill McKinnon.

Desert tracks and dune driving can be challenging. Image courtesy Bill McKinnon.

13
Cleland Conservation Park

This popular day-use park conserves an area of natural bushland on the Adelaide Hills (12km from Adelaide) and includes the family-friendly Cleland Wildlife Park, the viewing platform of Mt Lofty Summit and scenic Waterfall Gully. The wildlife park is open 9.30am to 5pm daily.

Feeding the wildlife at Cleland Wildlife Farm. Image courtesy South Australian Tourism Commission.

14
Coongie Lakes National Park

Coongie Lakes National Park, north of Innamincka is listed as a Ramsar Wetland of International Importance, comprising channels, waterholes, lakes, shallow floodplains and swamps that attract an enormous amount of waterbirds. Unlike most outback lakes, Coongie Lakes contain water most of the time, although the surrounding ephemeral wetlands fill only after rain, which can mean that access to the park is often cut. The area is an important spiritual site for the Aboriginal people who inhabited the area as well as significant for the European history relating to early exploration and pastoralism. There are a number of superb lakeside camping areas. No generators or campfires are permitted, so carry a fuel stove. Four-wheel-drive access only. You will need to have a valid Desert Parks Pass to visit here.

15
Lake Torrens National Park

A stark wilderness to the west of the Flinders Ranges, this vast 250km-long ephemeral salt lake has filled with water only once in the past 150 years, although passing rain storms will provide a small amount of water and when this happens birds seem to materialise from nowhere. There are no facilities and access to the lake is by either of two tracks, both of which are on private pastoral properties and you must get permission from the pastoralists to use the road or to camp beisde it. The two tracks are the Leigh Creek to Lyndhurst to Farina Ruins to Andamooka via Mulgaria Station track (permit required)—to use this track you must get permission from Mulgaria Station (08) 8675-8313—and Roxby Downs to Andamooka to Lake Torrens—to use the track you must get permission from Andamooka Station (08) 8671-0754.

Cooling off in Coongie Lakes. Image courtesy Bill McKinnon.

Alligator Gorge, Mt Remarkable National Park. Image courtesy South Australian Tourism Commission.

16
Mount Remarkable National Park

The 16,000ha park in the southern Flinders Ranges is where South Australia's arid north and wetter southern regions overlap. It features pretty valleys and dramatic mountain scenery. Highlights include Mount Remarkable summit (960m), rugged ridges, sheer rock faces and Alligator Gorge. There are unpowered caravan sites at Mambray Creek campground, with flushing toilets, solar heated showers, water supply, firewood (in season), rubbish disposal and communal fireplaces. Facilities provided are suitable for disabled access and it is very busy during Easter, April and September school holidays and long weekends so you'll need to book. There are a number of good bushwalks, including the 90-minute loop walk through 'the narrows' in spectacular Alligator Gorge and the longer four-hour, 9km Alligator Gorge Ring Route which follows Alligator Creek upstream beyond the Terraces. The Hidden Gorge walk is a beautiful seven-hour (18km) slightly more challenging walk and the climb to the summit of Mt Remarkable will take around five hours.

17
Naracoorte Caves National Park

South Australia's only World Heritage Site, these 26 caves have acted as pitfall traps, collecting animals for at least 500,000 years, preserving countless fossils and the bones of Megafauna such as *Thylacoleo carnifex* (marsupial lion), thylacine, zygomaturus and sthenurine kangaroos. A number of guided cave tours are available, including some adventure caving tours, and there is a caravan park and café as well as a large area for tents. The caves are 10km south of Naracoorte, which is 335km south-east of Adelaide.

The Fossill Cave, Naracoorte.
Image courtesy South Australian Tourism Commission.

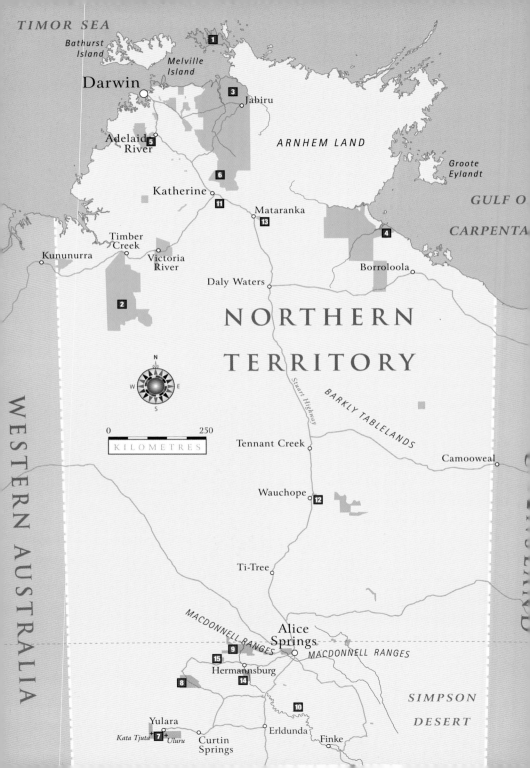

Northern Territory

The Northern Territory is Australia's last wild frontier, home to less than one per cent of Australia's total population. It is a place of extremes, from the harsh red centre to the steamy jungle-like tropical forests of the Top End and the World-Heritage Listed wilderness of Kakadu National Park.

Vast tracts of the land are Aboriginal land, including the remote and wild Arnhem Land in the north-east, and you may need permits to travel across them. Many communities are also alcohol free—please respect their wishes by not taking alcohol into their communities or consuming it on their land. Many aboriginals do not like to be photographed and in some areas it is an offence to photograph sacred sites.

Most national parks are free to enter, although camping fees apply and vary depending on the level of facilities offered. Some parks are very well developed, with hot showers and free gas barbecues; others offer little more than a bush clearing and pit toilets. Not all supply drinking water, so you will need to be prepared to be self sufficient and carry out all rubbish with you. Some parks are extremely remote and can only be accessed by a high clearance four-wheel drive during the dry season, May to October. Always check local road and track conditions with rangers or police before travelling. Be aware that conditions can change rapidly after rain, when flash flooding can close roads for several days.

The Territory Parks Alive program offers free walks and talks at many of the more popular parks from May to October. Contact the Parks and Wildlife Service of the Northern Territory for more information on (08) 8999-4555 or visit www.nt.gov.au/nreta.

Garig Gunak Barlu National Park

How to get there

The park is around 570km (by road) north-east of Darwin. The road into to the Cobourg Peninsula and Garig Gunak Barlu National Park is marked on the maps as a 4WD track, but it pleasantly easy, although there are a couple of creek crossings that can get tricky after rain. Caravans are not permitted and the last fuel stop is at Jabiru. Check tide times for crossings of the East Alligator River (Cahills Crossing).

When to go

The dry season is early May to late October. Roads are closed and impassable during the wet season. Be aware that creek levels rise quickly after rain, which may cause road closures no matter what time of year.

- January: 24–33°C
- July: 18–32°C

This wild and remote national park on Arnhem Land's Cobourg Peninsula is the only area in the Northern Territory which contains adjoining land and marine park areas; it's a place of pristine beaches carpeted in sea shells where turtles come up to lay their eggs and the world's largest remaining wild herd of banteng roam in the monsoon forests behind the hide tide mark. Even better, only 20 permits to enter the park are issued at any one time, so you know you've got the place pretty much to yourselves. You'll need to arrange permits well in advance and they are expensive (around $230 at the time of publication) so plan to spend at least three or four days here.

Most people make the long trek to get here purely to go fishing. As well as barramundi the tropical waters yield huge queenfish, trevally, saratoga, Spanish mackerel, longtail tuna, threadfin salmon, mangrove jack, marlin and sailfish and reef dwellers such as black jewfish, coral trout, red emperor and golden snapper.

One of the parks highlights, however, is a trip out to the ruins of Victoria Settlement, one of the four ill-fated northern outposts that were abandoned before Palmerston (Darwin) was finally established in the mid 19th century. Boat trips and tours can be arranged through the general store at Black Point, which also sells (very expensive) fuel and can organise fishing charters. Tel: (08) 8979-0455.

Also worth visiting is the Black Point cultural centre which has an interesting display on the history of the area, particularly the early contact with Macassan traders and the traditional Aboriginal uses of the land.

Top tracks and trails

Coast Track: a coastal four-wheel-drive track threads itself through the monsoon forest along the shore line of the peninsula. You've a good chance to see both banteng and crocodiles on this drive.

Paperbark swamp near Victoria Settlement.

Best picnic spots

There are picnic facilities at Black Point overlooking the water.

Camping, caravanning and accommodation options

There are two campgrounds in Garig Gunak Barlu: campground No.1 (generators are not permitted), and camp ground No.2 where generators are permitted. No. 2 is open and airy, No.1 is in a swamp that is prone to mosquitoes—and crocodiles have been known to get a little too close for comfort. Neither have power and facilities are very basic.

You can pay to stay at Cobourg Beach Huts at Black Point. and the cost includes park permits, arranged on your behalf once you have booked www.cobourgbeachhuts.com.au.

Contact information

For permits contact The Permit Officer, Cobourg Peninsula Sanctuary and Marine Park Board. PO Box 496, Palmerston, NT 0831. Tel: (08) 8999-4814; Fax: (08) 8999-4524. For more information visit www.nt.gov.au/nreta.

Gregory National Park

How to get there

The park is approximately 160km west of Katherine (226km east of Kunnunurra) via the Victoria Highway, or via the unsealed Buntine and Buchanan highways if you have a four-wheel-drive.

When to go

The temperature range is extreme and summer is best avoided. Winter days may be warm but nights can be freezing. Some roads, including the Victoria Highway, may be impassable during the west season, November to April.

- January: 22–37°C
- July: 4–19°C

This huge park covers an area of around 13,000 square kilometres, bridging tropical and semi-arid regions of the Northern Territory on the edge of the Kimberley region. Rich in both Aboriginal and European pastoral history, the park features spectacular range and gorge scenery, extensive stands of boab trees and some beautiful camping areas near good swimming holes, although always check for warning signs before you get wet—this is prime saltwater crocodile country.

Highlights include historic boabs carved with the names of explorers and stockmen who passed through the area in the late 19th and early 20th centuries; Bullita Homestead, built in 1901 with traditional timber stockyards still standing; and Limestone Gorge, a shallow gorge set amongst unusual limestone formations and boab trees.

Although you can get there in a conventional two-wheel-drive vehicle, many of the roads inside the park are four-wheel-drive only, very rough and notoriously hard on tyres. We managed to get three flat tyres in the one day, so make sure you are prepared with a couple of spares and a puncture repair kit.

Top tracks and trails

Limestone Ridge Walk: a one-hour walk from the campground through the limestone formations to a lookout with good views of the East Baines River.

Bullita Stock Route: a 93km four-wheel-drive track that will take around eight hours to complete. It's a one-way circuit following a section of the old stock route to Wyndam used by Bullita and Humbert River Stations. The crossing of the East Baines River and the jumps up south east of Spring Creek Yard can be quite difficult.

Humbert Track: a 63km four-wheel-drive track between Humbert River Station and Bullita Homestead following the valleys of Fig Tree Creek and Humbert River. Allow six hours.

Wickham/Gibbie Tracks: linking the Buntine Highway to the park via the Mount Stanford

Station the 157km four-wheel-drive track is slow going over hilly country with some difficult sections. Allow six hours for the 92km section inside the park once you have left Mount Stanford Station, which is 65km from the Buntine Highway.

Best picnic spots

Best picnic spot is in the shade at Bullita homestead, although there are also picnic facilities at Sullivan Creek.

Camping, caravanning and accommodation options

You can camp at Big Horse Creek which is just off the sealed Victoria Highway. It has a boat ramp and is very popular with anglers, which means it can often be very crowded. Less crowded is the campground at Bullita homestead on the banks of the East Baines River. Best bet though, if you have a four-wheel-drive, is Limestone Gorge, which has a beautiful swimming hole although facilities are very basic and the track is too rough for most caravans. You can also stay at the commercial campgrounds at Victoria River Roadhouse and Timber Creek.

Contact information

For more information visit www.nt.gov.au/nreta.

A Boab tree.

Kakadu National Park

How to get there

The main route through Kakadu, the Nature's Way, is fully sealed and links up with the Stuart Highway at both ends. It begins at the turn off to the Arnhem Highway, 34km south of Darwin and roughly forms two sides of a triangle, with the mining town of Jabiru at the apex (256km east), joining up with the Kakadu Highway running south to the Stuart Highway near historic Pine Creek.

When to go

The glossy travel brochures of the Top End and Kakadu always show raging waterfalls and brimming wetlands. This is what it looks like in the wet season. Most people go, however, in the dry season (May to November), when all of the roads are open. But by then, the waterfalls have stopped flowing, the wetlands have shrunk, the waterlilies have died and the wide green seas of lush grasses are dried up, blackened and burnt from the annual dry season burning off. The best time go is at the tail end of the wet or early in the dry—May and early June. While some of the four-wheel-drive tracks to the falls will be closed (if you really want to see them the best way is by scenic flight) all the sealed roads are open.

- January: 24–33°C
- July: 18–32°C

One of the most popular, and magnificent, national parks in Australia, Kakadu covers more than 20,000 square kilometres and the entire catchment of the South Alligator River. The World Heritage area encompasses five main habitats: savannah woodlands; floodplains and billabongs; monsoon forest; rocky escarpments and tidal flats and coast. Birdlife is prolific and saltwater crocodiles inhabit most waterways and there are spectacular waterfalls during the wet season.

Despite its fearsome reputation as the last frontier, Kakadu is surprisingly easy to get around, even without a four-wheel-drive, and none of the main sites involve long walks to access them.

How much time you spend in Kakadu, and what you see and do is limited only by the amount of time you have. You really need a minimum of two days, and even then, you will only be seeing the highlights.

At the very least you should spend a couple of hours watching magpie geese, egrets and countless other birds in the cool and breezy over-water shelter at Mamukala wetlands. Call in to the Bowali Visitor Centre near Jabiru to learn about the landscape and habitats in the park and time your trip to Ubirr for great sunset views over the Arnhem Land escarpment after viewing the ancient Aboriginal rock art galleries. Take a scenic flight from either Jabiru or Cooinda and don't

Jim Jim Falls. Image courtesy Tourism NT.

Kakadu wetlands at sunset. Image courtesy Tourism NT.

miss the Warradjan Aboriginal Cultural Centre, an excellent free interactive museum telling the stories of the traditional owners. The turn-off to Jim Jim Falls and Twin Falls is just before you reach Cooinda and is four-wheel-drive only and closed until early June. The best waterfall to see for those without a four-wheel-drive is Gunlom Falls, just before you reach the southern boundary of the park.

At Cooinda make sure you do the Yellow Water billabong cruise, a two-hour cruise on a breathtakingly beautiful landlocked billabong fringed by pandanus, paperbark swamps and monsoon rainforest. Take the sunset or sunrise cruise and you'll see thousands of birds and more than likely a few big crocodiles as well.

Top tracks and trails

Short walks: there are good short walks (ranging from 500m to two kilometres) at most of the major sites.

Sandstone and River bushwalk: an easy 6.5km loop near Ubirr that takes you past Catfish Creek, floodplains, billabongs, sandstone outliers and the East Alligator River.

The Barkk bushwalk: a difficult 12km walk (allow six to eight hours) through the sandstone country of Nourlangie.

Barrk Marlam walk: a challenging dry season only trail that branches off the Jim Jim Falls plunge pool track (6km return).

Nourlangie Rock: allow at least one hour to walk around Nourlangie, an ancient Aboriginal shelter with rock art galleries.

Anbangbang Billabong: during the dry you can walk around the edge of Anbangbang Billabong at the base of Nourlangie.

Best picnic spots

There are a number of picnic areas scattered throughout the park, most of them adjacent to camping areas. A personal favourite is Anbangbang Billabong, where you can lose hours watching the birdlife around you.

Camping, caravanning and accommodation options

Accommodation options in Kakadu range from four-star motel rooms in the crocodile-shaped Holiday Inn at Jaibru and at Gagudju Lodge Cooinda to commercially operated camping areas with powered sites and park camping areas with solar heated showers, toilets and washing tub facilities. There are also several free camping areas in the park, which have next to no facilities and no drinking water. Be aware that there is no booking system for campsites and all sites are allocated on a first-come, first-served basis. For more details on campsites visit www.environment.gov.au/parks/kakadu.

Contact information

For more information visit www.environment.gov.au/parks/kakadu/index.html.

How to get there

The park is approximately 475km south-east of Katherine and 182km north-west of Borroloola. The roads are unsealed but fine for conventional vehicles in dry weather.

When to go

The dry season is early May to late October. Roads are closed and impassable during the wet season. Be aware that creek levels rise quickly after rain, which may cause road closures at any time of year.

- January: 24–33°C
- July: 18–32°C

Fern-leaved grevillea.

Tucked away in a seldom-visited corner of the Gulf of Carpentaria west of Borroloola, this park is a remote and rugged place with spectacular sandstone formations, numerous rivers and wetlands.

It's a popular fishing destination; the Roper, Towns and Limmen Bight rivers all flow through the park before emptying out into the Gulf so there's are countless good fishing spots. It's prime barramundi country. There are boat ramps at Towns River, Limmen Bight Fishing Camp and Tomato Island.

Butterfly Springs is a beautiful swimming hole surrounded by paperbacks and exquisite fern-leaved grevillea ablaze with dainty orange flowers during the dry season that attract hundreds of birds to the oasis. It's also home to thousands of common crow butterflies that cover the sandstone wall to the right of the pool and arise en masse when you approach. It is the only place in the park where you can swim, all other lagoons, rivers and billabongs are home to saltwater crocodiles. Swimming is best, however, early in the dry season as it does get very stagnant toward the end of the season.

The beautiful springs are reason enough to visit this remote park, but most people come here to see the bizarre towering rock pillars at the Southern Lost City. At 1.4 billion years in the making, these rocks are some of the oldest in the world. They consist of 95 per cent

Southern Lost City.

silica and are held together by an outer crust made mainly of iron, giving them their unique red colour, especially at sunset.

This is a remote park and there are no services or fuel available between Roper Bar and Cape Crawford (338km), so make sure you bring every thing with you that you may need.

Top tracks and trails

Southern Lost City: a two-kilometre easy walking trail among the rock formations. The track winds its way through clumps of prickly spinifex and it is prime snake habitat, so wear long pants.

Western Lost City: if you have a four-wheel-drive you can collect a key from the ranger at Nathan River (if he's there—call ahead on (08) 8975-9940 to arrange a time to meet) and visit the Western Lost City. It's a rough 28km track in, followed by a short climb to a lookout with views over the O'Keefe Valley.

Best picnic spots

Butterfly Springs gets my vote as one of the best picnic spots in the Gulf.

Camping, caravanning and accommodation options

There are boat ramps and basic campgrounds at Towns River and Tomato Island. You can also camp at Butterfly Springs.

Contact information

For more information visit www.nt.gov.au/nreta/parks.

5 Litchfield National Park

How to get there

The National Park is 120km south-west of Darwin via Batchelor, north of the Adelaide River just off the Stuart Highway. Once inside the park, you can loop back to Darwin from Wangi Falls. This road is unsealed, and may be inaccessible in the wet season, but it is very pretty with several shallow creek crossings.

When to go

The dry season is early May to late October. The park is open all year, although most four-wheel-drive tracks are closed during the wet season. Some swimming areas such as Wangi Falls become unsafe after heavy rain.

- January: 24–33°C
- July: 18–32°C

Litchfield National Park is the Top End in miniature—in just one relatively small area you can find wetlands and lily-covered billabongs, thundering waterfalls, prolific birdlife, gigantic termite mounds, weird and fantastic sandstone formations, rough and ready four-wheel-driving and an abundance of that Top End rarity, crocodile-free swimming holes.

Favourite spots include Buley Rockhole, a chain of spa-like pools linked by small waterfalls and Wangi Falls, the largest of the parks waterfalls and the most popular swimming area in the park.

Almost all of the major attractions are accessible to conventional two-wheel-drive vehicles, but if you've got a four-wheel-drive head out to Tjaynera Falls (Sandy Creek Falls), a deep waterhole every bit as gorgeous as Wangi Falls but without the crowds, and Surprise Falls, another of Litchfield's hidden gems that 99 per cent of visitors to the park don't know about.

Top tracks and trails

Magnetic Termite Mounds: a boardwalk past a large group of two-metre high termite mounds, all aligned north-south to keep the inside of the mound from getting too hot by the sun.

Florence Falls: a 15m stairway leads to a plunge pool which is popular with swimmers; or you can take the 200m walk (wheelchair accessible) to a lookout platform looking down on the twin falls. There is also a shady circuit walk (one-hour return) that winds through the monsoon forest beside the creek.

Tolmer Falls: a short walk leads to a viewing platform looking out over the very steep waterfall. No swimming.

The Lost City: a 4WD track leads to an area of bizarre sandstone block and pillar formations, formed by thousands of years of wind and rain erosion. The 10km track is fairly easy going, but narrow and one-way for the most part; you'll need to watch for oncoming vehicles and be prepared to pull off the track to let them pass.

Florence Falls.

Wangi Falls.

Best picnic spots

There are a number of picnic spots in the park, but the best is the large grassy picnic area at Wangi Falls with easy access to the swimming area and a kiosk. Florence Falls is another good picnic spot.

Camping, caravanning and accommodation options

You can camp at Wangi Falls (unpowered caravan sites), Buley Rockhole and Florence Falls. There is four-wheel-drive camping, during the dry season only, at Tjaynera Falls (Sandy Creek), Surprise Creek Falls and downstream of Florence Falls.

Odyssey Tours & Safaris has a permanent safari camp at Minjungari billabong. You can join a two-day tour or opt just for dinner, bed and breakfast if you have a four-wheel-drive. Facilities include insect-proof dining where a three-course dinner is served, permanently erected tents with single beds, solar hot water for showers and composting toilets. Tel: 1800 891 190, www.odysaf.com.au.

Contact information

For more information visit www.nt.gov.au/nreta/parks.

Lost City.

Nitmiluk (Katherine Gorge) National Park

How to get there

Katherine is 316km south-east of Darwin on the Stuart Highway and the park entrance is 29km from the town centre.

When to go

Best time to visit is between May and September. During the wet season (November-April) the river may be in flood, cutting off access to the park and/or restricting the activities available.

- January: 24–33°C
- July: 18–32°C

Katherine Gorge in Nitmiluk National Park, where the Katherine River carves a deep gorge through towering red sandstone cliffs to form 13 spectacular gorges, is one of the most impressive spots in the Top End.

During the wet season the river is a raging torrent of water-borne fury, but during the dry season you can hire canoes or take one of several cruises and explore the gorges. Wear comfortable walking shoes as there is some walking involved between gorges. Cruises depart several times daily, but the best time is in the late afternoon when the walls of the gorge glow in the setting sun.

The upper gorges are accessible to canoes but portage can be hard work as you will need to carry canoes and gear over the boulders between various gorges. You can hire canoes at the Nitmiluk Visitors Centre.

Alternatively, take a helicopter or fixed wing flight over the park for a bird's eye view of the gorge. A 12-minute flight will take you as far as the sixth gorge and 25-minute flights include the whole gorge system.

There is a swimming platform near the visitors centre, and the river is supposedly free of saltwater crocodiles: the only ones they say you'll see here are the relatively harmless freshwater variety. Swim at your own risk however, as large saltwater crocs have been caught just a few kilometres upstream; there are several traps near the swimming area that apparently keep the killers at bay.

Another good place to swim is at Leliyn (Edith Falls), located on the western boundary of the park. The paperbark and pandanus fringed natural pool at the base of the falls is safe for swimming most of the year.

Top tracks and trails

Gorge walks: there are a range of walks, all of which start near the visitors centre and climb the rocky escarpment of Katherine Gorge. They range from two hours to three days and all are rated medium or difficult but all offer fantastic gorge views and many lead to swimming holes. All overnight walkers must register at

Canoeing in Katherine Gorge.

the Nitmiluk Centre on departure and return.

Baruwei Loop Walk: the easiest and shortest of the gorge walks goes to a lookout (around two hours return) with views of the gorge and 17 Mile Valley and along the escarpment.

The Jatbula Trail: a challenging four- to six-day, 66km bushwalk from Katherine Gorge to Edith Falls that takes in diverse scenery, plunging waterfalls and Aboriginal rock art.

Best picnic spots

Both Edith Falls and the Gorge have good picnic facilities including free gas barbecues.

Camping, caravanning and accommodation options

There are tent and caravan sites at the Gorge and Edith Falls (powered sites at the Gorge only); walkers and canoeists can bush camp elsewhere in the park but must register at the visitors centre at the Nitmiluk Centre.

Contact information

For more information visit www.nt.gov.au/nreta/parks.

How to get there

Ayers Rock Resort is 445km by sealed road from Alice Springs. The resort is 18km from Uluru, shuttle buses are available.

When to go

The temperature range is extreme and summer is best avoided. Winter days may be warm but nights can get very cold so take a warm jacket.

- January: 22–37°C
- July: 4–19°C

A close up view of Uluru. Image courtesy Voyages resorts.

It doesn't matter how many photos you've seen of Uluru (Ayers Rock) and the red centre, your first glimpse of Uluru will remain in your memory forever. Join the throng of awestruck tourists who gather like religious pilgrims to watch the rock turn red, then purple, then blue and finally black in the setting sun on any given evening, and it's highly unlikely you'll hear a disappointed complaint among them.

Australia's most identifiable icon is a massive red rounded monolith rising 348m above the surrounding plains and extending 6km below the earth's surface. The circumference measures more than 9km. Its sister rock formation, Kata Tjuta, (The Olgas) which means 'many heads', is made up of 36 huge, weathered domes spread over 35 square kilometres and is just as impressive.

Your first trip to Uluru should begin at the cultural centre, where a series of exhibits, paintings, videos and interpretation boards explain the relationship that the Anangu have with the land, Uluru and Kata Tjuta. Anangu Tours operate a range of guided walks and other tours led by Anangu elders where you can learn about the traditional bush skills, foods and medicines and the ancient creation law and legends of Uluru.

Uluru and Kata Tjuta are sacred to the Anangu. They do not climb Uluru, and would prefer it if you didn't. Anangu do not like to be photographed and ask that all visitors

The domes of Kata Tjuta. Image courtesy Tourism NT.

respect this wish. It is also an offence to Anangu culture to photograph or film areas of spiritual significance. These areas are clearly signposted. Do not take photographs of the cultural centre.

Top tracks and trails

Dune Walk: a 30-minute walk from the bus sunset car park takes you along a sand dune with views of both Uluru and Kata Tjuta. Keep an eye out for animal tracks.

Uluru Base Walk: a full circuit around the base of Uluru is 9.8km (three to four hours) and is an excellent alternative to climbing the rock. The walk is quiet and you are unlikely to encounter large groups of people in most areas. Walk in a clockwise direction. It takes in the shorter Mala and Mutitjulu walks along the way.

Valley of the Winds: this 8km walk at Kata Tjuta winds along a rocky trail past sheer rock faces and unusual rock formations to a magnificent lookout. It can be steep, rocky and difficult in places.

Best picnic spots

There are picnic facilities, including gas barbecues, at the cultural centre and at the sunset viewing area of Kata Tjuta.

Camping, caravanning and accommodation options

You cannot camp in the national park. Ayers Rock Resort has seven accommodation options for varying budgets ranging from Longitude 131, a luxury wilderness camp with views of Uluru from you bed, a five-star hotel, serviced apartments, budget motel-style accommodation and the Ayers Rock campground, which has powered caravan sites. Tel: 1300 134 044, www.voyages.com.au.

Contact information

For more information visit www.environment. gov.au/parks/uluru/index.htm.

8 Watarrka (Kings Canyon) National Park

How to get there

Watarrka National Park and Kings Canyon is 330km west of Alice Springs via the unsealed Mereenie Loop Road, which at the time of going to press is generally not suitable for caravans, although there are plans to seal the road in the next few years. Sealed road access is via Yulara (Ayers Rock Resort) 305km to the south-west.

When to go

The temperature range is extreme and summer is best avoided. Winter days may be warm but nights can get very cold so take a warm jacket.

- January: 22–37°C
- July: 4–19°C

The western end of the George Gill Ranges rises sharply from the surrounding flat desert plains, producing a rugged landscape of ranges, rockholes and gorges, the best known of all being Kings Canyon in Watarrka National Park. Rising up 100m to a plateau of rocky domes, Kings Canyon is home to one of the most dramatic short walks in the outback—the Rim Walk—where you can look down over the rim into the chasm formed by the sheer-sided red sandstone walls of the canyon.

The best way to really see the canyon is from above, either on the Rim Walk or on a scenic flight. Helicopter tours are available at Kings Canyon and Kings Creek Station. The 15-minute tour flies over the canyon, the domes of the Lost City and the Garden of Eden, then along Kings Creek and over to Carmichael Crag. A longer 30-minute trip includes the spectacular cliffs of the George Gill Range to Carmichael Crag before returning via the Hidden Valley.

Top tracks and trails

The Rim walk: the best time to tackle the 6km walk is either early in the morning, before the heat and flies begin to fray tempers, or late in the afternoon, when the setting sun lights up the sheer sandstone walls of the canyon to their best advantage. The first half-hour or so is a lung-busting, muscle-destroying climb up the side of the canyon, but if you can make it that far, the remainder of the two to three-hour walk is an easy stroll around the rim of the canyon where breathtaking 300m sheer cliffs cut deep into the rock. Highlights include the weathered, buttressed domes of the 'Lost City', and the 'Garden of Eden', a sheltered valley with permanent waterholes and lush vegetation.

Kathleen Springs: an easy 2.6km stroll to a waterhole at the head of Kathleen Gorge.

The Giles Track: for those wanting a longer walk, the 22km two-day walk goes over the top of the range from Kathleen Springs at the southern end of the park to Kings Canyon. No camping is allowed in the park, so you will need to use the entrance/exit point around halfway at Reedy Creek/Lilla.

Best picnic spots

There are picnic facilities at the car park at the base of the rim walk where tables, toilets and shelter are provided, and at Kathleen Springs.

Camping, caravanning and accommodation options

You cannot camp in the national park. Kings Canyon Resort, which is just 7km from the park entrance, has motel-style rooms as well as powered caravan and camping sites. Bookings are essential, call 1300 134 044.

You can also stay at Kings Creek Station, (the largest exporter of wild camels in Australia) 36km from the national park entrance. Powered and unpowered sites are available as well as safari-style cabins. Tel: (08) 8956-7474.

Contact information

For more information visit www.nt.gov.au/nreta/parks.

Looking down into Kings Canyon. Image courtesy Sam Tinson.

West MacDonnell National Park

How to get there

From Alice Springs take Larapinta Drive to get to the turn-offs for Simpsons Gap (17km west) and Standley Chasm (41km west of Alice Springs). Follow Namatjira Drive to access the rest of the park. From Kings Canyon (Watarrka National Park) access is via the four-wheel-drive Mereenie Loop Road and you will need a permit to travel though Aboriginal land. These are available from Kings Canyon Resort, CATIA office in Alice Springs and the Central Land Office in Alice Springs, ($2.20) and must be carried with you at all times.

When to go

The temperature range is extreme and summer is best avoided. Winter days may be warm but nights can get very cold so take a warm jacket.

- January: 22–37°C
- July: 4–19°C

The West MacDonnell National Park stretches for more than 160km west of Alice Springs and has at its heart the ancient West MacDonnell Ranges.

Just 18km from Alice Springs is Simpson Gap, a spectacular cleft in the red rocky range and a few kilometres further on is Standley Chasm, less than nine metres wide and towering to a height of 80m. The best time to see it is at midday, when the sun is directly overhead and lights up the walls and floor of the rocky chasm.

Other highlights include Ellery Creek Big Hole, an intoxicatingly beautiful swimming hole, Serpentine Gorge and the Ochre Pits. Drop into Glen Helen Gorge for a cold drink at the caravan park-cum-resort with views of the rust red gorge walls. Just opposite the resort is the turn-off to Ormiston Gorge, where there is a short walk to yet another beautiful sandy swimming hole. You can also swim at Redbank Gorge and Glen Helen Gorge, although all of the swimming holes are icy, no matter how hot the day.

Be aware that every year a number of visitors to the red centre suffer from heat stroke and heat exhaustion, so always wear a hat, strong shoes and sunscreen, walk in the cooler parts of the day and carry water—and drink at least one litre per hour.

Top tracks and trails

Ormiston Pound: a three-to-four-hour loop walk that does a circuit around the pound and along the Gorge via the main waterhole.

Simpsons Gap Bicycle Path: a sealed 17km cycle path that meanders between Flynns Grave on the outskirts of Alice Springs to Simpsons Gap.

The Larapinta Trail: long-distance walking track that runs for 223km along the backbone

Redbank Gorge. Image courtesy Tourism NT.

Standley Chasm. Image courtesy Tourism NT.

West MacDonnell Ranges. Image courtesy Tourism NT.

of the West MacDonnell Ranges from Alice Springs west to Mt Sonder. It is divided into 12 sections and includes all of the key attractions of the national park. Allow 20 days if you plan on walking the entire trail and register before you leave by phoning 1300 650 730.

Best picnic spots

There are good, shady picnic facilities with gas barbecues at Simpsons Gap, Standley Chasm, Ellery Creek Big Hole, Ormiston, Redbank, Glen Helen and Serpentine gorges as well as the Ochre Pits.

Camping, caravanning and accommodation options

There are basic camping facilities at Ellery Creek Big-Hole and Redbank Gorge. You can bush camp at Serpentine Chalet and 2-Mile (4WD only). Ormiston Gorge has camping and caravan facilities with showers and toilets and there is a caravan park and motel-style accommodation at Glen Helen Gorge.

Contact information

For more information visit www.nt.gov.au/nreta/parks.

In brief . . .

10
Chambers Pillar Historical Reserve

Chambers Pillar is a towering 50m-high sandstone obelisk, formed by the erosion of sandstone deposits laid down in the area 350 million years ago. At sunrise and sunset, the Pillar glows red as the sun strikes its face. The reserve is 160km south of Alice Springs via the Old South Road west of Maryvale Station. The road is unsealed and may be closed after rain and is 4WD only after the Maryvale turnoff, Watch out for deep sand drifts.

11
Cutta Cutta Caves Nature Park:

About 29km south of Katherine, the limestone Cutta Cutta Caves (one of the few cave systems to be found in northern Australia) are some 15m below the surface and have many spectacular formations. The caves are home to a variety of wildlife including the brown tree snake and rare orange horseshoe bat. Guided tours of the cave system are conducted throughout the day but during the wet season the cave may be closed due to flooding.

Chambers Pillar. Image courtesy Tourism NT.

Cutta Cutta Caves. Image courtesy Tourism NT.

Mataranka Thermal Pool. Image courtesy Tourism NT.

12
Devils Marbles Conservation Reserve

100km south of Tennant Creek, the Devils Marbles (Karlu Karlu) are a collection of gigantic, rounded granite boulders (some are four metres high and 13–33m wide). They make for some great photo opportunities. The area is an important meeting place and rich in 'Dreaming' sites for local Aboriginal people; ownership was officially handed back to the traditional owners in late 2008. There is a basic bush camping area with fireplaces and pit toilets at the southern end of the reserve. No water or firewood is provided so you should come well equipped.

13
Elsey National Park

The Mataranka Thermal Pools are the main attraction of this park. Spring water rises from underground at a temperature of 34°C and is contained in a swimming pool surrounded by a paperbark and palm forest. The pools are sometimes closed for swimming as the area around the pool is a natural breeding ground for the Little Red Flying Fox. The breeding season is traditionally in the wet season but often extends into the dry. The park is just south of Mataranka on the Stuart Highway and has both tent and unpowered caravan sites. It is very popular with caravanners so you may need to book.

Devils Marbles. Image courtesy Bill McKinnon.

Gosse Bluff. Image courtesy Tourism NT.

14
Finke Gorge National Park

This park, 138km west of Alice Springs via Hermannsburg, is home to Palm Valley, a beautiful pocket of Red Cabbage Palm. It's 4WD access only and the last 16km follows the sandy bed of the usually dry Finke River, which means it may be inaccessible after heavy rains. It can be hard going and is for experienced four-wheel-drivers only with high clearance vehicles. The campground has hot showers and there are a range of good walking trails with information about the mythology of Western Arrernte Aboriginal culture. If you don't have a 4WD you can join a commercial tours from Alice Springs.

15
Tnorala Conservation Reserve

175km west of Alice Springs, the reserve, also know as Gosse Bluff, is a huge crater some 20km across formed by a comet more than 140 million years ago, although according to Aboriginal belief, Tnorala was formed in the creation time, when a baby in a wooden baby-carrier (a *turna*) crashed to the earth when it was dropped by its mother who was dancing across the sky as part of the Milky Way. Access is via Larapinta or Namatjira Drive. A 4WD is recommended for the last 10km drive to the Reserve and a Mereenie Tour Pass is required to travel this road. Camping is not permitted.

Palm Valley. Image courtesy Tourism NT.

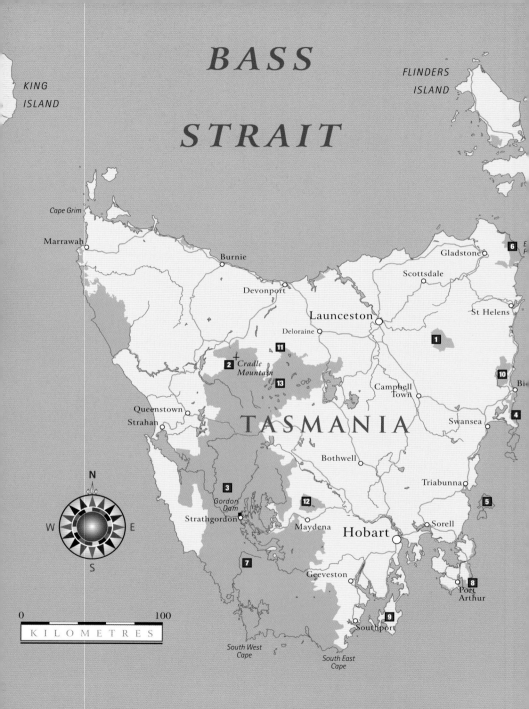

BASS

STRAIT

KING
ISLAND

FLINDERS
ISLAND

Cape Grim

Marrawah

Burnie

Devonport

Gladstone

Scottsdale

6

Launceston

St Helens

Deloraine

1

11

Cradle
Mountain

2

13

10

Bi

Queenstown

Campbell
Town

Strahan

Swansea

4

TASMANIA

Bothwell

Triabunna

3

12

5

Gordon
Dam

Strathgordon

Maydena

Hobart

Sorell

7

Geeveston

8

Port
Arthur

9

Southport

South West
Cape

South East
Cape

N

W E

S

0   100

KILOMETRES

SOUTHERN OCEAN

Tasmania

From snow-capped peaks, sun-kissed beaches, white-water rivers, convict ruins, remote rainforest and unspoiled tracks of World Heritage listed wilderness, Tasmania's National parks are both vast and varied. Their range of facilities from privately run campgrounds with hot showers and well-equipped kitchens to basic walk-in wilderness sites where you'll need to be totally self sufficient.

Entry fees apply to all national parks in Tasmania, charged on a per vehicle (covering up to eight passengers), rather than a per person basis. The entry fee does not cover camping which, depending on the park, may be an additional fee.

If you are planning on spending more than one or two days in national parks or intending to visit a number of parks throughout the state consider buying a National Parks Pass. Annual passes are available, but for most travellers the holiday, or eight-week pass, offers the best value, costing less than the price of three days entry.

You can buy a park pass at major national park visitor centres, most Tasmanian Visitor centres, all Services Tasmania shops and at selected park pass selling agents throughout the state or online at www.parks.tas.gov.au.

1 Ben Lomond National Park

How to get there

The ski fields section of the park is about 50km south-east of Launceston, via Evandale and Blessington Road. The final access to the alpine village is via the slightly scary 'Jacobs Ladder', a steep, narrow unsealed road with lots of hairpin turns. You need to give way to oncoming traffic on the way up. Snow chains and antifreeze must be carried between June and September. During the ski season, a shuttle bus operates from below Jacobs Ladder.

When to go

The weather can change rapidly at any time of the year, so always be prepared with good wet- and cold-weather gear. Snow falls on average once every four days during July and August.

- January: 9–22°C
- July: 0–8°C

You can see the craggy peaks of Ben Lomond long before you get there. The summit is the second highest point in Tasmania (1572m) and the alpine plateau is roughly 14km in length, 6km wide and more than 1500m high, surrounded on all sides by sheer escarpments and cliffs.

During winter the park is the main focus of downhill skiing in Tasmania with the state's only skiing facilities—there are six ski lifts on the downhill slopes and they operate only in

Bent Bluff.

the snow season, which usually starts in early July and closes late September. You can hire skis, snowboards and toboggans at the alpine village.

During summer the area is a popular walking destination with colourful wildflowers and a wealth of wildlife, including wombats and wallabies, pademelons, eastern quolls, potoroos, sugar gliders, possums, echidna and platypus.

Top tracks and trails

There are two cross-country ski routes which are also used as walking routes, marked by snow poles. The Carr Villa to Alpine Village walk is a 90-minute walk with some steep sections—it takes you up onto the plateau and then along the plateau to the highest point. You can continue on to Little Hell (90-minutes return) for good views across the southern part of the plateau to Stacks Bluff.

Mountain berries.

Skifields trails. Image courtesy Joe Shemish, Tourism Tasmania.

Bents Bluff: in the eastern section of the park, near Rossarden and Storys Creek, you can climb Bents Bluff, around three hours return, but it's steep and the track can be hard to find, although the views from the top over the surrounding valleys and out towards the east coast are well worth it. The Craggy Peaks resort at the mountain's base can provide walking guides. Visit www.craggypeaks.com.au.

Best picnic spots

Picnic facilities are available in the ski fields section of the park.

Camping, caravanning and accommodation options

There is a small camping area one kilometre inside the boundary of the park and another several kilometres below the summit. There are six unpowered sites that are suitable for tents or campervans with a flush toilet and drinking water. Bush camping is permitted anywhere in the park but not within 500m of any road. You must use a fuel stove.

The Creek Inn on Ben Lomond is open all year and has a licensed restaurant and six accommodation units (one is suitable for disabled). They are heavily booked during the ski season. Tel: (03) 6390-6199.

Craggy Peaks is a new golf resort in the shadow of the southern peaks near Rossarden and includes a nine-hole golf course, licensed restaurant and a range of guided walks and mountain bike trails. Visit www.craggypeaks. com.au.

Contact information

For the latest snow reports during the ski season, see www.ski.com.au/reports/benlomond. For more information on the park, contact the Parks and Wildlife Service, Tasmania. Tel: 1300 135 513 or visit www.parks.tas.gov.au.

2 Cradle Mountain-Lake St Clair

How to get there

Cradle Mountain is 144km from Launceston and 83km from Devonport. Lake St Clair is about two-and-a-half hours (180km) north-west of Hobart near the township of Derwent Bridge.

When to go

The best time to tackle the Overland Track is in summer, but even then temperatures can drop suddenly so be prepared with some winter woollies and good wet weather gear.

- January: 9–22°C
- July: 1–12°C

In the centre of the island is the rugged wilderness of Cradle Mountain-Lake St Clair National Park, part of the Tasmanian Wilderness World Heritage Area and one of the most spectacular (and popular) parks in the state. In the north, the craggy peaks of Cradle Mountain are among the most well-photographed in the country and the starting point for the famous six-day walk that takes you through the heart of some of the finest mountain terrain. Ancient rainforests, alpine heath, buttongrass plains, stands of colourful deciduous beech, icy streams, rocky mountains including Tassie's highest, Mt Ossa, and a wealth of wildlife are just some of the highlights. At the southern end of the park, carved out by glaciers over

Dove Lake and Cradle Mountain. Image courtesy Cradle Mountain Lodge.

the last two million years, Lake St Clair is the deepest lake in Australia and the headwaters of the Derwent River. There is a regular ferry service that will take you across the lake to Narcissus Bay.

Top tracks and trails

The Overland Track: the six-day, 65km Overland Track between Cradle Mountain and Lake St Clair is undoubtedly the most famous walk in Tasmania. Although much of the walk is on boardwalk in order to protect the fragile alpine environment, there are some steep and challenging sections. Between November and April you will need to book and pay an Overland Track fee of $150 per person ($120 for children and seniors). As part of this system, walkers are required to walk the track from north to south during the peak walking season.

Dove Lake Loop Track: this two-hour walk takes you under the shadow of Cradle Mountain through the tranquil Ballroom Forest and back along the western shore of the lake.

Weindorfers Forest Walk: an easy 20-minute stroll through a forest of King Billy pines, celery-top pines and myrtles that starts at Waldheim chalet.

Enchanted Walk: a lovely half-hour walk that takes you past waterfalls, pools, across moors and through rainforest before returning to the Cradle Mountain Lodge.

Lake St Clair Walk: a gentle stroll around

Enchanted Walk. Image courtesy Cradle Mountain Lodge.

Dove Lake Walk. Image courtesy Garry Moore, Tourism Tasmania.

the lake shore at Cynthia Bay. Echidnas and platypuses can often be seen around the bay.

Watersmeet trail: a one-hour walk along the crest of a glacial moraine in the Lake St Clair section of the park, with beautiful wildflowers in spring. You can continue on to Platypus Bay on the Larmairrenemer tabelti (Aboriginal cultural walk), which will take you back to Cynthia Bay via fern glades, moorlands, rainforest and towering eucalypt stags and provides interpretation of the Aboriginal heritage of the area. Allow 90 minutes for the return trip.

Best picnic spots

In the Cradle Mountain section there are picnic shelters with electric barbecues next to the visitor centre and there are picnic tables close to Waldheim. There are also picnic facilities with barbecues at Cynthia Bay.

Camping, caravanning and accommodation options

Due to the delicate nature of the environment and the large number of visitors to Cradle Mountain, camping is not permitted inside the day visitor area, although there is rustic cabin accommodation available at Waldheim inside the National Park (book at the Cradle Mountain Visitor Centre (03) 6492-1110) and a commercial campground 3km outside the park. Overland Track walkers cannot camp until they reach either Waterfall Valley Hut or the Scott-Kilvert Hut. There are basic, unattended huts at various stages along the track, which provide bunks (without mattresses), tables and either

coal-burning or gas heaters. These huts are used on a first-come, first-served basis and may be full when you arrive, so you will also need to carry a tent. Walkers are encouraged to use huts or the tent platforms provided to minimise campsite impacts—if they are fully occupied you can camp in the areas adjacent to the huts. At Lake St Clair you can camp at Cynthia Bay where there are showers and laundry facilities.

Cradle Mountain Lodge offers luxury spa cabins, licensed restaurant, a range of guided activities in and around the park and great views. It's at 4038 Cradle Mountain Road. Tel: (03) 6492-2100 or visit www.cradlemountainlodge.com.au.

Lake St Clair Wilderness resort has self-contained loft-style cabins and a licensed restaurant. Tel: (03) 6289-1137 or visit www.lakestclairwildernessholidays.com.au.

Contact information

Cradle Mountain Visitor Centre is located just inside the national park entrance. Tel: (03) 6492-1110. For information and bookings on the Overland Track go to www. overlandtrack.com.au. For ferry information call (03) 6289-1137 or email lakestclair@ trump.net.au for details of costs and running times. For general information on the park visit www.parks.tas.gov.au.

3 Franklin-Gordon Wild Rivers National Park

How to get there

The Lyell Highway (A10) connects Hobart with Queenstown, 260km to the west, and winds through the top section of Franklin-Gordon Wild Rivers National Park. There are several short walks and picnic stops along the way. You can also visit the park on a cruise boat from Strahan on the west coast (303km west of Hobart) or on a 80-minute scenic flight from Strahan in a sea plane that follows the Gordon and Franklin Rivers way beyond the reach of the cruise boats to land on a steep-sided section of the Gordon River at Warners Landing, site of the Franklin River blockade in the 1980s. After a five-minute boardwalk into the rainforest to view the very pretty Sir John Falls and some ancient Huon pines, the tiny seaplane taxis upriver to take off again, following the Gordon River back to Strahan.

When to go

Most of the west coast is exposed to cold, wet, southerly winds. Rain falls on average every second day during summer and more often in other seasons.

- January: 12–22°C
- July: 2–12°C

Tasmania's west coast is one of the world's wildest places, a sparsely inhabited region with rugged mountain ranges, ancient trees more than 2000 years old and wild rivers. The Tasmanian Wilderness World Heritage Area protects one of the last true wilderness regions on earth and encompasses a greater range of natural and cultural values than any other region on the planet.

Butting on to Southwest National Park to the south and Cradle Mountain-Lake St Clair National Park to the north, Franklin-Gordon Wild Rivers National Park is in the centre of the vast Tasmanian Wilderness World Heritage Area and features beautiful rainforest, gorges, impressive mountain peaks, deep river valleys and wild rivers.

The Franklin River became a household name in the 1980s when it became the focus

White water rafting. Image courtesy Matthew Newton, Tourism Tasmania.

of one of Australia's largest conservation battles—to save the Franklin from a proposed hydro-electric power scheme which would have flooded the river—and is one of the world's great white water rafting destinations.

Top tracks and trails

Franklin River Nature Trail: a one-kilometre, trail that winds through cool temperate rainforest to two wild rivers: the Franklin and the Surprise. Suitable for wheelchairs.

Donaghys Hill Wilderness Lookout Walk: a 30–40 minute return walk on a well-graded track that gives a spectacular wilderness panorama, taking in the Franklin River valley and domed, quartzite peak of Frenchmans Cap.

Nelson Falls Nature Trail: a pleasant 20-minute return boardwalk takes you through cool temperate rainforest to the spectacular Nelson Falls, about 4km west of Victoria Pass. **Frenchmans Cap:** one for experienced bushwalkers only, the return trip to the summit takes four to five days.

Best picnic spots

There are picnic tables and toilets on the Franklin River Nature Trail.

Camping, caravanning and accommodation options

There is a basic campsite with a pit toilet at the Collingwood River, the starting point for rafting and canoeing trips down Franklin River.

Contact information

Parks and Wildlife Service, Tasmania. Tel: 1300 135 513 or visit www.parks.tas.gov.au.

Franklin River. Image courtesy Garry Moore, Tourism Tasmania.

4 Freycinet National Park

How to get there

Coles Bay, the nearest town to the park, is 195km north-east of Hobart via the Tasman Highway (A3) and the Coles Bay Road (C302) and 37km south of Bicheno.

When to go

Most rain falls during the winter months. Roads can be icy during winter.

- January: 10–23°C
- July: 2–11°C

Jutting out from the sea, the craggy but beautiful Freycinet Peninsula on Tasmania's east coast is largely national park and consists of bare granite mountains (known as the Hazards) surrounded by sheltered bays and white sand beaches.

There are many secluded beaches in the park, with beautiful Wineglass Bay the most popular of them all. Take a drive up to the lighthouse at Cape Tourville for good sunset views and whale and dolphin watching in season, or spend a few hours on one of several longer walks in the park. Also popular is sea kayaking, snorkelling and diving in the bull kelp beds at Sleepy Bay, surfing at the Friendly Beaches, rock climbing, abseiling and mountain biking.

Beach at Edge of the Bay.

Top tracks and trails

Wineglass Bay: the one-hour climb up to the lookout over Wineglass Bay in Freycinet is one of the best short walks in Australia and the breathtaking view is worth the steep climb. What's more, while you'll see a few people on the trek, if you continue down to the beach (two hours return), you're just as likely to have it to yourself, as the walk unjustly deters most day trippers, who seem happy enough to snap a picture of this almost perfect beach and continue on their way.

Freycinet Peninsula Circuit: the 30km circuit track travels around the Hazard Mountains to Hazards Beach. The track continues south to Cooks and Bryans Beaches then crosses the peninsula over a heath-covered plateau next to Mount Freycinet (spectacular views) before heading down to Wineglass Bay. There are

The Hazards. Imge courtesy Garry Moore, Tourism Tasmania.

campsites for overnight walkers at Wineglass Bay, Hazards, Cooks and Bryans Beaches.

Best picnic spots

Honeymoon Bay and Ranger Creek both have electric barbecues, picnic tables, drinking water (boil first) and toilets.

Camping, caravanning and accommodation options

Camping at Freycinet is by the beach and each campsite has fantastic views. There are plenty of shady sites to choose from, including powered sites for campervans and caravans up to 17ft at Richardsons Beach. This is one of the most popular parks in Tasmania, and camping spots in summer (18 December until Easter) are decided by ballot drawn on 1 October and you will need to apply before 31 July.

Visit www.parks.tas.gov.au/natparks/freycinet/activities.html. There is also good camping at the Friendly Beaches close to the border of the park.

If you miss out on a camping spot there is a range of accommodation to suit all budgets in and around Coles Bay, but for a room with a view you can't beat the Edge of the Bay, it's the only resort with direct views across the Hazards. Eat at the licensed restaurant or one of the Coles Bay cafes, a 20-minute walk up the beach. 2308 Main Rd, Coles Bay. Tel: (03) 6257-0102 or visit www.edgeofthebay.com.au.

Contact information

Freycinet National Park Office, Private Bag, Bicheno, Tas 7215. Tel: (03) 6256-7000. www.parks.tas.gov.au/natparks/freycinet/index.html. Email: freycinet@parks.tas.gov.au.

 5 Maria Island

How to get there

There is a daily ferry service between Triabunna (88km north of Hobart) and the convict settlement site at Darlington on the northern tip of the island. No cars are allowed on the island.

When to go

Summer is the best time to visit when the water is warm enough to swim. Most rain falls during the winter months.

- January: 10–23°C
- July: 2–11°C

This beautiful island off the east coast of Tasmania around 90km north of Hobart is a little less than 20km long and 13km at its widest point and is essentially two smaller islands joined by a narrow sandy isthmus. Steep and mountainous in the interior, the island is ringed by stretches of white sandy beaches and limestone cliffs. It is home to a staggering array of birdlife, including the endangered forty-spotted pardalote (one of the smallest and rarest birds in Australia); short-tailed shearwaters (mutton birds); colonies of fairy penguins and the comical ground-dwelling Cape Barren goose (the

The old mill house, Darlington.

world's second rarest goose). The island is also home to large populations of possums, wallabies, pademelons, echidnas, kangaroos and wombats.

The first European settlers were whalers and sealers. The island became a penal colony in 1825 and you can wander around the extensive convict settlement ruins at Darlington. By 1832 the convict settlement was abandoned in favour of Port Arthur to the south and after a second incarnation as a convict probation station between 1842–50 it was eventually taken over by flamboyant Italian entrepreneur Diego Bernacchi who planted

igrapes, cultivated silk worms and established a cement works, none of which survived the Great Depression. By the 1930s the island was home to just a handful of farmers. It was declared a national park in 1972.

Top tracks and trails

Painted Cliffs: an easy 90-minute return walk from Darlington to some beautifully patterned sandstone cliffs. Best viewed at low tide.

The Fossil Cliffs: an easy stroll from Darlington to spectacular cliffs along the northern shores of the island which contain thousands of fossils in the limestone. Keep your eyes peeled for

Soldiers Beach.

View from summit of Bishop and Clerk. Image courtesy Bill McKinnon.

little penguin burrows in the rocks beneath the cliffs. You'll also get great views of Freycinet Peninsula and Schouten Island.

Bishop and Clerk: a strenuous four-to-five-hour return climb to the summit includes lots of rock hopping and scrambling over large boulders, but provides amazing views from the top. Not one for those scared of heights.

Maria Island Walk: a privately run fully-guided four-day walk that traverses the island from south to north and includes luxury safari tent accommodation and a stay at historic Bernacchi House. Departs Hobart on Mondays, Wednesdays and Fridays, November to April and
person, including return transport to Hobart, park entry fees, twin-share accommodation, meals and wine. For more information visit www.mariaislandwalk.com.au

Best picnic spots

There are dozens of good picnic spots around the ruins of Darlington, head to French's farm, or roll out your picnic rug on any of the beautiful beaches.

Camping, caravanning and accommodation options

There is a large open camping area close to the creek at Darlington or you can bunk down in the dorms of the Old Penitentiary. Free campsites are also available at French's Farm and Encampment Cove some three to four hours walk from Darlington.

Contact information

Maria Island National Park Office Tel: (03) 6257-1420. www.parks.tas.gov.au/natparks/maria/index.html.

The Painted Cliffs. Image courtesy George Apostolidis, Tourism Tasmania.

Mt William National Park and Bay of Fires

How to get there

St Helens is around 250km north of Hobart and the closest sizable town to the Bay of Fires area. The closest town to the Mt William section is Gladstone, 133km north-east of Launceston.

When to go

Summer is mild, winter tends to be the wetter season.

- January: 11–19°C
- July: 6–11°C

Empty beaches with large granite boulders, coastal lagoons and heathlands covered in coastal wildflowers are the main attractions of both the Bay of Fires Conservation Park and neighbouring Mt William National Park in the far north-east corner of Tasmania.

North of St Helens in the Bay of Fires Conservation Park is an area known as The Gardens, named by Lady Jane Franklin, the wife of Governor John Franklin, who spent some time in the region in the 1840s. There are sweeping views of the coastline north, good (unpatrolled) swimming beaches, lots of rock pools to explore, the ubiquitous orange lichen-covered boulders to climb over and around and paddle between.

The park stretches north to Ansons Bay, around 15km away, but to get there you either have to walk along the beaches, or take the unsealed 52km inland road. It borders Mt William National Park, which boasts exactly the same type of scenery, but with more established campgrounds and toilet facilities, although you have to pay the normal national park entry and camping fees. From the northern tip at Musselroe Bay, you can see across to the Bass Strait islands. At the southern end is the historic lighthouse at Eddystone Point, a striking pink granite tower on a point that juts out into the sea.

Both parks are a great place to go bird watching, fishing and diving as well as seeing lots of wallabies, wombats, echidnas, pademelons, kangaroos (including the Forester kangaroo, unique to Tasmania) and Tasmanian devils, at their most active at dawn and dusk, or in the case of the devils, at night.

Top tracks and trails

In Mount William walks range from easy strolls on the beach to coastal and heath walks of half a day or longer. The four-day Bay of Fires walk is a commercially run guided walk, largely along the coastline and beaches, with accommodation in a luxury lodge. Visit www.bayoffires.com.au.

Best picnic spots

The shady banksia grove picnic area of Stumpys Bay is beside a very pretty coastal lagoon and offers easy access to the beach.

Camping, caravanning and accommodation options

There are six free camping areas, most overlooking the beach, in the southern section of the Bay of Fires Conservation Park. Facilities are basic and include pit toilets but no water or firewood. There is a maximum stay of four weeks. Because it's a conservation park, rather than a national park, you can even bring your dog.

In Mt William National Park there are several sheltered camping areas at Stumpys Bay in the north of the park. There is also a campsite at the far northern end of the park, just before Musselroe Bay and at the end of the beachside road from Eddystone Point to Deep Creek in the southern end of the park. No dogs are allowed in the national park.

Contact information

Parks and Wildlife Service, Tasmania. Tel: 1300 135 513 or visit www.parks.tas.gov.au.

Stumpys Bay, Mt William National Park.

Southwest National Park

How to get there

The 70km Gordon River Road, from Maydena (85km west of Hobart) to Strathgordon, the main construction village for the development of the Middle Gordon hydro-electric power scheme, is fully sealed, although it is often steep and winding, and is subject to ice and snow, so care is needed. The Scotts Peak, which turns off the Gordon River Road at Frodsham Pass is unsealed. Maydena is your last chance to refuel.

In the southeast, the park is accessible from Cockle Creek (130km south of Hobart) —the most southerly point in Australia that you can reach by road.

In the far southwest, Melaleuca is accessible only by light plane, or boat. See the park's website www.parks.tas.gov.au for details of airlines.

When to go

Most of the south-west coast is exposed to cold, wet, southerly winds. Rain falls on average every second day during summer and more often in other seasons.

- January: 12–22°C
- July: 2–12°C

Part of the Tasmanian Wilderness World Heritage area, this 600,000ha park is the largest in Tasmania and protects some of the finest wilderness country in Australia, including untouched rivers and rainforests, jagged mountain ranges and rolling buttongrass plains.

The Gordon River and Scotts Peak roads wind through sections of the park. They were built in the late 1960s and early 1970s as part of the controversial power scheme which flooded the original Lake Pedder. The routes are lined with rainforest trees such as myrtle, sassafras and celery top pine. In season you will also see wildflowers and berries including silver wattle, leatherwood, Tasmanian waratah and snow berries. Bird life is prolific and there are numerous lookouts along both roads.

Top tracks and trails

Port Davey and South Coast tracks: the 70km Port Davey track links Scotts Peak Road and Melaleuca, while the 85km South Coast Track

Walking the South Coast Track. Image courtesy Don Fuchs, Tourism Tasmania.

traces the coastline between Melaleuca and Cockle Creek. There are no roads to Melaleuca so you must fly, sail or walk in and out. Both are extremely demanding walks and for experienced and self-sufficient walkers.

The Creepy Crawly Nature Trail: a 20-minute boardwalk through a lovely section of cool temperate rainforest near Frodshams Pass along the Scotts Peak Road. Be warned though, there are 165 steps!

Eliza Plateau: a five- to six-hour return walk with spectacular views over nearby ranges and lakes. Its starts from Condominium Creek carpark off the Scotts Peak Road and is a long steep climb up an exposed ridge and includes a scramble over large boulders to get to the summit. Watch out for mud.

Lake Judd Trail: a challenging eight-hour walk to a deep, ice-carved lake surrounded by peaks. It's also off Scotts Peak Road.

South Cape Bay: a four-hour return walk from Cockle Creek to unspoilt coastline.

Best picnic spots

Picnic in the forest at Huon campground or beside the river at Wedge River. There are also picnic facilities at Gordon Dam lookout and Serpentine Dam.

Camping, caravanning and accommodation options

There are several campsites along both the Gordon River Road and Scotts Peak Road. Teds Beach has toilets and electric barbecues. Edgar Campground has toilets and fireplaces with firewood. The Huon Campground has a shelter, composting toilets, fireplaces and firewood. There are two walkers huts at Melaleuca and in the south Cockle Creek has a large camping area around Rocky Bay.

Contact information

Parks and Wildlife Service, Tasmania. Tel: 1300 135 513 or visit www.parks.tas.gov.au.

Port Davey. Image courtesy George Apostolidis, Tourism Tasmania.

Tasmania 307

8 Tasman National Park

How to get there

From Hobart, take the A3 to Sorell and then the Arthur Highway (A9) to Port Arthur, 94km south-east from Hobart.

When to go

The Tasman Peninsula is exposed to the weather—especially Cape Pillar where places like Tornado Ridge and Hurricane Heath often live up to their descriptive names.

- January: 10–23°C
- July: 2–11°C

Scattered around various coastal sections of the Tasman Peninsula, Tasman National Park has wonderful sea views, rock formations, sea caves and hidden bays. The Tessellated Pavement, a stretch of coastline resembling giant tiles, is on the north side of Eaglehawk Neck. The Tasman Blowhole and the ruins of once huge sea caves at Tasman Arch and the Devils Kitchen are on the southern side and all are easily accessible by car. Remarkable Cave is a sea cave 6km from Port Arthur where you'll get great views to Cape Raoul from the lookout above the beach, or you can climb down to the sand to explore the cave.

Patersons Arch at the Devils Kitchen. Image courtesy Geoffrey Lea, Tourism Tasmania.

At Coal Mines Historic Site you can wander among the evocative ruins of Saltwater River Convict Station with its cramped and gloomy underground cells and great water views.

The spectacular dolerite columns and cliffs along the coastline of the Tasman National Park are popular areas for climbing and abseiling. The Tasman National Park is also a popular spot for divers who head to Cathedral Cave at Waterfall Bay, a maze of caverns, passageways and narrow swim-throughs and vast underwater giant kelp forests.

Keep a watch out for wildlife, including seals, penguins, dolphins and whales, wedge-tailed eagles, sea eagles and other sea birds.

Top tracks and trails

Canoe Bay: from the beach at Fortescue Bay a two-hour return track leads to Canoe Bay, which has the remains of a wrecked steel boat. It's a good walk if you have small children.

Tasman Coastal Trail: this three- to five-day Tasman Coastal Trail follows the coastal cliffs from Waterfall Bay through to Fortescue Beach, out to Cape Hauy and on to Cape Pillar. Highlights include some of the highest

Convict ruins at the Coal Mines Historic Site.

Dolerite Columns. Image courtesy Kim Rumbold, Tourism Tasmania.

sea cliffs in Australia; Waterfall Bay with its spectacular view across the cliff-lined bay to a waterfall which, after rain, spills straight into the sea; the squeaky white sands of Fortescue Bay; and large kelp forests and spectacular dolerite columns and cliffs at Cape Hauy. You can break the walk into shorter sections. You'll need to organise transport or a car shuffle at either end.

Cape Raoul: there are some rough uphill sections, but the views are worth it. Around five hours return.

Best picnic spots

There are picnic facilities at Fortescue Bay.

Camping, caravanning and accommodation options

There are 40 campsites, including unpowered caravan sites, at Fortescue Bay on the eastern side of the peninsula and facilities include a shower block (cold water only), toilets, barbecues and a boat launching ramp. There are also basic but beautiful campsites right on the water's edge at Lime Bay near the Coal Mines Historic Site, but you'll need to bring your own water and firewood.

Contact information

Parks and Wildlife Service, Tasmania. Tel: 1300 135 513 or visit www.parks.tas.gov.au.

The Blowhole. Image courtesy Michael Walters Photography, Tourism Tasmania.

In brief...

9
Bruny Island

Home to Tasmania's most well-known Aboriginal, Truganini, who is tragically famous for being the last of the island's full-blood Aboriginals, the island is a sleepy place with gentle countryside and wild coastlines. There are great walks, spectacular beaches, fishing, wildlife, and a rich heritage of sealers, whalers and explorers. At the southern tip of the island, South Bruny National Park features wonderful coastal scenery with cliffs and headlands, muttonbirds and penguins, seals and whales in season and long sandy beaches. Adventure Bay and Jetty Beach provide sheltered areas for swimming, while Cloudy Bay is a popular spot for experienced surfers. Cloudy Bay Corner Beach campground is 4WD-only with access via the beach. At Jetty Beach on Cape Bruny there is a larger campground with pit toilets, tank water (seasonal only), picnic shelters, and caravan access. Access to Bruny Island is via vehicular ferry from Kettering, south of Hobart.

10
Douglas Apsley National Park

Riverside walking tracks, deep river gorges, waterfalls, swimming holes and a dolerite-capped plateau are the main features of this park north of Bicheno on the east coast. Facilities are basic, but there is a small bush camping area near the Apsley Waterhole, 10 minutes walk from the car park off Rosedale Road. Other walks include the three-hour Apsley Gorge circuit and the three-day north-south bushwalk through the park.

11
Mole Creek Karst National Park

Marakoopa and King Solomons Caves are two show caves in an area with more than 300 known caves and sinkholes. Other typical karst features in this area include gorges and large underground streams and springs. The glow-worm display in Marakoopa Cave is the largest in any public access cave in Australia. The park is 40 minutes drive west of Deloraine.

Marakoopa Cave in Mole Creek, Karst National Park. Image courtesy John De la Roche, Tourism Tasmania.

Walls of Jerusalem. Image courtesy Geoff Murray, Tourism Tasmania.

12
Mt Field National Park

Tasmania's oldest national park, and one of its most popular, has a rich variety of vegetation ranging from tall swamp gum forests (some of the tallest trees in the world), immense tree ferns, rainforest, pandanus groves and alpine vegetation, sphagnum bogs and alpine tarns at the top of the mountain. Highlights include the beautiful three-tiered Russell Falls, stunning short walks, Lake Dobson, winter skiing and lots of wildlife. Camping and caravan facilities are available near the park entrance by the Tyena River. Facilities include powered sites, toilet and shower block, coin-operated washing machines and clothes driers and a communal cooking shelter with free electric barbecues and sink with hot water. The park is around an hour's drive west from Hobart via New Norfolk.

13
Walls of Jerusalem

Adjoining Cradle Mountain-Lake St Clair National Park and also part of the Tasmanian Wilderness World Heritage Area, this park is remote and not accessible via road. This is a true wilderness area with dolerite peaks and alpine vegetation exposed to the extremes of Tasmania's changeable weather. Bushwalkers who do venture into the park must be well equipped and self-sufficient—tracks are practically non-existent and ironstone deposits within the region may affect compass readings. There are no visitor facilities.

Russell Falls. Image courtesy Holger Leue, Tourism Tasmania.

Acknowledgements

The information in this guide was compiled with the assistance and information provided by state, regional and local tourism associations and various National Parks and Wildlife Services. The author would like to thank the following organisations:

Canberra Tourism
Environment ACT
Tourism New South Wales
NSW National Parks and Wildlife Service (NPWS)
Tourism Victoria
Parks Victoria
Queensland Parks and Wildlife Service
Tourism Queensland
South Australian Tourism Commission

South Australian Department for Environment and Heritage (DEH)
Tourism NT
Tourism Western Australia
Western Australia Department of Environment and Conservation and Land Management (DEC)
Tourism Tasmania
Tasmanian Parks and Wildlife Service

First published in Australia in 2009 by
New Holland Publishers (Australia) Pty Ltd
Sydney • Auckland • London • Cape Town

www.newholland.com.au

1/66 Gibbes Street Chatswood NSW 2067 Australia
218 Lake Road Northcote Auckland New Zealand
86 Edgware Road London W2 2EA United Kingdom
80 McKenzie Street Cape Town 8001 South Africa

National Library of Australia Cataloguing-in-Publication Data:

Atkinson, Lee.

Australia's best national parks / Lee Atkinson.

9781741107197 (pbk.)

Includes index.

National parks and reserves--Australia--Guidebooks.

Australia--Guidebooks.

919.404

Publisher: Fiona Schultz
Publishing manager: Lliane Clarke
Project editor: Diane Jardine
Designer: Domenika Fairy
Proofreader: Catherine Etteridge
Production manager: Olga Dementiev
Printer: SNP/ Leefung Printing Co. Ltd (China)